Greenhill Books

THE
COMPLETE
FIGHTER ACE

THE COMPLETE FIGHTER ACE

All the World's Fighter Aces
1914–2000

MIKE SPICK

GREENHILL BOOKS, LONDON
STACKPOLE BOOKS, PENNSYLVANIA

Greenhill Books

The Complete Fighter Ace:
All the World's Fighter Aces, 1914–2000
First published 1999 by Greenhill Books
Lionel Leventhal Limited, Park House, 1 Russell Gardens,
London NW11 9NN
and
Stackpole Books, 5067 Ritter Road, Mechanicsburg,
PA 17055, USA

British Library Cataloguing in Publication Data
Spick, Mike
The complete fighter ace: all the world's fighter aces, 1914–2000
1.Fighter pilots – Biography   2.Air warfare – History – 20th century
I.Title
358.4'0092

ISBN 1-85367-374-9

Library of Congress Cataloging-in-Publication Data
Spick, Mike
The complete fighter ace: all the world's fighter aces, 1914–2000
/ by Mike Spick
p.   cm.
Includes bibliographical references and index.
ISBN 1-85367-374-9
1. Fighter pilots Biography   2. Fighter plane combat History
I. Title
UG626.SG28   1999
358.4'3'0922--dc21
[B]   99-32809
CIP

Edited, designed and typeset by Roger Chesneau
Printed and bound in Great Britain by
Creative Print and Design (Wales), Ebbw Vale

CONTENTS

'Ratsy' Preddy; Robert W. Hanson; A Czech Ace: Karel 'Old Kut'
Kuttelwascher—A Finnish Ace: Nils Katajainen—A French Ace: Marcel
Albert—German and Austrian Aces: Edmund 'Paule' Rossmann; Gordon
Mc Gollob; Ludwig Becker—A Hungarian Ace: György Debrödy—An
Italian Ace: Adriano Visconti—Japanese Aces: Yasuhiko Kuroe; Saburo
Sakai—A Polish Ace: Boleslaw 'Mike' Gladych—Soviet Aces: Boris
Safonov; Alexandr Pokryshkin—Leading Aces and Their Scores*

4   Higher and Faster   175
*Battle in the Stratosphere—The MiG-15—Swept-Wing Combat—
American Aces: James 'Jabby' Jabara; Joe McConnell; Robinson
'Robbie' Risner—Russian Aces: Eugeny Pepelyaev; Sergei Kramarenko
—Aces and Their Scores*

5   Mach 2 and Missiles   197
*Homing Missiles—Limited Wars, 1953–73—India versus Pakistan—
Middle East Wars—The Six-Day War—The War of Attrition—The
October War, 1973—Israeli Aces: Giora Epstein; Asher Snir—North
Vietnam, 1965–73: Robin Olds—American Aces, Vietnam: Richard
'Steve' Ritchie; Randall 'Duke' Cunningham—North Vietnamese Aces:
Nguyen Duc Soat*

6   Dichotomy   223
*Fighters: The Next Generation—Red Star—BVR versus Close Combat—
The Ace Makers—The 'Silver Bullet' Solution—Small Wars—The First
Gulf War—The Second Gulf War—Bosnia*

    Epilogue   239
    Summary

    Bibliography   249

    Index   251

ILLUSTRATIONS

Diagrams drawn by John Richards

TABLES

PREFACE

Long before practical flying machines became a reality, they were considered as potential engines of war. The first halting steps began in 1794, when a tethered balloon was used for observation at the Battle of Fleurus. Several schemes were then devised for more offensive action, but another 55 years passed before a practical attempt was made. Then, the Austrian army launched an aerial attack on Venice, using unmanned hot air balloons with time-fuzed bombs attached. This achieved little, mainly due to an unexpected change in wind direction.

What was needed was a fully controllable powered flying machine, and for this, the military had to wait until the twentieth century. The first, less than impressive flight finally took place in the United States in December 1903, but from then on progress was rapid.

The first, and most obvious use for the new breed of machine was reconnaissance; formerly the prerogative of light cavalry. Shortly after the outbreak of the Great War, trench warfare resulted in a fixed defensive line stretching from the Belgian coast to Switzerland. With no gaps to be exploited and no flanks to be turned, the aeroplane, with its ability to fly high over enemy positions to see what was 'on the other side of the hill', was the answer. But, even as a good light cavalry squadron prided itself on the quality of the intelligence it provided, it was an equal source of pride for it to deny similar facilities to the enemy. The new-fangled flying machines found themselves in a similar situation, and aeroplanes started to carry weapons.

After a considerable amount of trial and error, mainly the latter, the machine gun emerged as the preferred weapon, while the aircraft carrying it had to be fast, in order to effect an interception. It was also found that by virtue of temperament and natural ability, some pilots were particularly suited to, and were successful at air fighting. A new breed of warrior was born – the fighter ace.

The expression was originally coined by the French press, and was defined as a pilot who had shot down, or scored victories over, at least five enemy aircraft. Assuming that they were all two-seaters, this meant that the pilot responsible had accounted for ten enemy aircrew. By the standards of the Great War, this was not a lot. Artillerymen and machine gunners in many cases accounted for far more enemy casualties, while the airborne artillery spotters, droning monotonously up and down the lines, calling out the fall of shell, were arguably responsible for making the most valuable contribution of all to the ground war. Why, then, did the fighter aces get most of the kudos? Why were fighter aces so glamorised?

The answer is simple. In wartime, nations need inspiration. What is needed are warriors who make people stand up and cheer their deeds of arms. This was never more so than on the Western Front in the Great War. The infantry-men in the front line existed like troglodytes in the mud and filth of trenches which lacked all but the most basic amenities, cowering from continual shell-fire and sniped at if they so much as peeped over the parapet by an invisible enemy. When they did try to attack, they were slaughtered in thousands by the anonymous machine gunners and artillerymen. And for what? The gain of a few shell-torn yards of terrain? Sometimes not even that. Heroic deeds there were in plenty, but in the vast and foul arena of trench warfare, these became as the doings of ants.

In mediaeval times, it was common for knights to ride out between the opposing armies prior to the battle to issue challenges to single combat. These encounters were of no real military value; to use the modern expres-sion, they were ego trips for those concerned. On the other hand, they served to hearten the troops, and when the troubadours had translated doughty deeds into song, the civilian population did likewise.

In the early days of air fighting, many combats were one-versus-one, per-formed before an audience of thousands in the trenches. Newspaper report-ers had replaced the troubadours, but retained the time-honoured tradition of never letting the facts interfere with a good story. Modern communica-tions allied to the printing press did the rest, and the general population were regaled with tales of heroic exploits in the air.

Even before the outbreak of war, pilots had a glamorous image. Aviation was publicised as a sport in which consenting adults with suicidal tenden-cies defied death, not always successfully. Actually to fight in the air in the flimsy aircraft of the period, which carried amounts of highly flammable fuel, must therefore demand super-heroes. The translation from civilian pi-lot to air warrior was easily made.

Baseball players are rated by their home runs, and soccer players by the goals that they score. Obviously a similar yardstick was needed to measure the deeds of the fighting pilots, and by default this became the number of their victories. Five victories was arbitrarily selected for the title of ace by force of circumstance. Not only were combats rare; decisive combats were rarer still. The expression came into being in the first half of 1915, as the first pilots (Frenchmen) reached a score of five. Nor is it surprising that the custom started in France. In the immediate pre-war years, France led the aviation world and the French press made sure everyone knew it!

Even in France, the ace concept never became official, but the authorities were quick to see potential morale benefits for the nation as a whole, and encouraged it. Other air forces, notably those of Belgium, Italy and the United States, followed the French lead. The British never did, arguing that to single out individuals was bad for morale and tended to undermine teamwork. What they really meant was that it smacked of ungentlemanly pot-hunting. Why make a fuss over what was after all just a sporting duty? However, this did not stop the authorities from stating scores (often inaccurately) when awarding decorations.

Germany and the Austro-Hungarian Empire also saw the potential morale benefits of the system, encouraged publicity and even produced postcards of the more successful. Neither used the expression 'ace', and demanded ten victories for the title of *Oberkanone*, which roughly translated as 'Top Gun'!

The Great War firmly established the ace tradition, which has continued until the present day with most air forces. There were of course exceptions. Italy in World War II decreed that air combat scores should not be recorded, while Japan resolutely refused to acknowledge the deeds of its fighter aces, either by medal or by promotion. Germany dropped *Oberkanone* in favour of *Experte*, an unofficial acknowledgement of exceptional prowess in air combat by one's peers, with no specific minimum score involved.

Britain continued, and still does, with its ambiguous 'stop it I like it' policy, but as the last British fighter ace was crowned in 1945, it hardly matters. By contrast, the United States, ably backed by Hollywood, has made the ace concept almost holy writ, despite the fact that at the time of writing a quarter of a century has passed since the last fighter ace was crowned!

The heyday of the fighter aces was the period 1915 to 1945. The limited wars which took place in the second half of the twentieth century have, with few exceptions, lacked sufficient opportunities for more than a handful of pilots to build a score. Very few fighter pilots have attained the 'Magic Five' in the jet and missile age.

The top-scoring fighter ace of all time, Erich Hartmann, was credited with 352 victories. As this is more than the total of aircraft in the majority of air forces, the chances are that it will never be beaten. For most of the twentieth century, the dominant factor was pilot ability. But as air combat approaches its ninth decade, technology has done much to redress the balance. The tradition of the fighter ace looks unlikely to continue, and it may well be that it was a twentieth century phenomenon. Only time will tell.

Poor record-keeping and missing documentation make absolute accuracy impossible in a work of this nature. However I have used the best sources available to me in an attempt to keep errors to a minimum. A bibliography is appended. I am indebted to many people for their kind assistance, notably my friends Chris Shores, Bruce Robertson and Brian Cocks, and also the staff at RAF Cranwell College Library.

I have avoided the use of ranks as much as possible: first, they tend to change considerably over a long war; secondly, unless the reader is familiar with rank equivalents over a wide variety of air forces, it leads to confusion; and thirdly a fighter ace is a fighter ace – it matters little whether he is a corporal or a colonel.

Mike Spick
Morton, Lincs.

PROLOGUE

The fireball from my kill was incredible. It completely lit up the sky, and I could see the airplane break up or explode into millions of pieces, burning all the way to the ground. It kept burning on the ground, too.
—Captain Steve Tate, 1st TFW

This was the first air combat victory of the Gulf War, and was the precursor of many more. To a degree a team effort, it heralded the superiority of Western technology, a superiority amply demonstrated over the next few days.

It began shortly after 3 a.m. on 17 January 1991, as a large USAF strike force headed towards targets near Baghdad. It was escorted by F-15C Eagles of the 1st Tactical Fighter Wing. Leading a four-aircraft flight, call-sign 'Quaker', was Steve Tate.

On reaching its assigned area, the flight split into pairs as briefed. 'Quaker 01' (Tate) and '02' set up a racetrack patrol line, in which one F-15 of the pair always had its radar pointed in the direction of a possible Iraqi fighter threat. 'Quaker 03' and '04' set up a different racetrack pattern, rather higher, and aligned with a different threat direction.

Many miles away, an E-3 Sentry AWACS (Airborne Warning and Control System) kept a constant watching brief over Coalition and Iraqi air activity within its radar search range. With literally hundreds of friendly aircraft in the air, flying without lights over hostile territory, the potential for confusion, leading to possible disaster, was ever-present.

It was the Sentry that gained the first contact, a bogey (unidentified aircraft) inbound towards the strike package and, by either accident or design, on course to come in astern of 'Quaker 03'. Turning north-east towards it, 'Quaker 01' gained radar contact and confirmed that it was in fact a bandit (hostile aircraft), an Iraqi Mirage F.1, heading westward at 8,000ft.

Accelerating, he locked up the bandit on his radar at a range of 12nm, continued to close, then launched an AIM-7 Sparrow. As the big missile

15

went on its way, 'Quaker 01' continued to track the bandit, illuminating it with his radar so that the Sparrow could home on the electronic emissions reflected from the target. Several seconds later it impacted, destroying the Mirage. Tate had a grandstand view, as by this time the Iraqi fighter was barely 4nm away, ahead and off to one side.

Just over 75 years had elapsed since aeroplanes were first used to fight against each other for dominance in the sky, yet in what is historically a very short period of time they had progressed from the barely capable to the barely believable. Speeds had increased twenty-fold, ceilings by a factor of six. In 1915, the situational awareness of a pilot was limited to what he could see from the cockpit, whereas an Eagle driver in the Gulf not only had on-board radar reaching out for dozens of miles; he was aided by airborne early warning which could monitor the skies out to more than 200nm around. The early machine guns were only really effective at ranges of a few tens of metres; modern missiles can not only reach out for tens of miles, they can manoeuvre in flight to follow a target which is far beyond visual distance.

The first fighter pilots flew with few instruments, and novices were quickly lost if they strayed over an unfamiliar area. The cockpit of a modern fighter is bewildering in its complexity, and allows its pilot to navigate to virtually anywhere in the world without undue problems.

In 1915, the pilot of a stricken aircraft had no choice but to ride it down to the inevitable crash. Modern ejection seats are now so automated that a quick pull on the handle sets in train an escape sequence that is close to foolproof. But modern fighters retain one thing in common with their ancestors. They still need a pilot.

Fighter Pilots

The development of the fighter down the decades has been driven by the needs of the pilot. To be successful in air combat, he has needed to fly faster and higher, to outmanoeuvre his enemy, and to hit harder than his opponent. Over time, he has been given the equipment to do all these things, although often the superiority of his aircraft has been ephemeral, measured in weeks or months rather than years. Nothing is achieved without cost, and advanced technology has been dearly bought. Combat aircraft are expensive, both to acquire and operate, and each succeeding generation becomes more so; consequently force sizes are reduced. This in turn makes each aircraft an increasingly precious asset which cannot easily be replaced.

This brings us to an interesting anomaly. Many of the top aces of the past would never have got near the cockpit of a modern fighter. A surprising number had been declared unfit for army service, decided to fight their war sitting down and found an aeroplane cockpit the most convenient way of doing this. Others could not land their aircraft right side up consistently; for example Mick Mannock and Ira Jones. Adolf Galland had a damaged eye, while Douglas Bader . . .! Yet more were slow learners, for example Bob Tuck, who, given the cost of jet training, would have been washed out at an early stage. But how much poorer would the history of air warfare have been without these men!

Sheer cost allied to the numerical paucity of modern fighters dictates that only those who can take off and land safely; who are self-disciplined and never indulge in wild stunts, and who are physically near-perfect specimens, will ever be trusted with an expensive modern killing machine. They are chosen largely for their peacetime attributes – flight safety and responsibility – rather than their warrior qualities. Taking risks and dropping aeroplanes is no part of the present-day plan.

The qualities needed in air combat seem fairly obvious – alertness, good distance vision, quick reactions, stamina (mental even more than physical) and self-control, good piloting skills, sound tactical judgement and aggressiveness tempered with caution. But, over the years, many young men with all these qualities have strapped a fighter on their backs, soared off into the blue, and never returned.

In the crucible of war, fighter aces are not made; rather they simply emerge. Many attempts have been made to predict who will be successful in air combat and who will not, but with little success. The fact is that unless the stress of battle can be realistically simulated, all such attempts are doomed to failure.

Historically, of every twenty fighter pilots, ten achieved nothing. Another nine scored the occasional victory, but only one scored five or more. Of this tiny minority, less than half reached double figures, while a law of diminishing returns applied as the score rose. Fortunately, the recent reduction in force sizes has been a two-edged sword. Although fewer fighters are available for the interception and air superiority missions, the opposition is almost certainly in the same boat!

Something more was needed. It was no longer enough to give the pilot a fighter which outperformed its opponent and hope that he would become an ace through his own endeavours. Once the science of avionics started to reach maturity, it offered a new avenue of approach. This was to make every pilot a potential ace through advanced technology.

Surprise has historically been the dominant factor in air combat, and, by definition, aces have been exceptionally difficult to take by surprise, due in part to a singular quality of alertness which at times almost amounted to a sixth sense. This problem was addressed by clever warning systems which would tell the pilot when he was under threat. They have now reached the stage where they can even advise the best action to take.

Countermeasures, another survival aid, have been brought to a fine art. On the offensive, the key is now beyond visual range (BVR) combat: detect first and shoot first, using medium-range homing missiles, preferably with passive midcourse guidance, and employing target data from a third source so as not to betray one's own presence. With at least eight missiles on board, allied to the clever avionics, every pilot has the potential to become an ace on his first mission. But once the medium-range encounter is over, and the fight becomes visual, he will still need the old skills of tactics and manoeuvre.

Fire and Movement

The first air combats were very much *ad hoc* affairs, with a variety of mainly unsuitable weapons, pistols, carbines, rifles, even blunderbusses and grapnels, used from even more unsuitable aircraft. With hindsight, it seems obvious that the machine gun should have been the weapon of choice, but it was less so at the time. This was mainly due to the lack of method. Whilst there was no lack of suggestions, proper air combat tactics had yet to emerge.

This was not surprising. The best (and simplest) definition of tactics the author has ever heard is 'the combination of fire and movement', formulated by Colonel Barry Watts USAF. The three-dimensional aerial movements required for air combat were so outside the scope of human experience that in most cases they was largely ignored. Firepower became the priority, on the unwarranted assumption that firing positions would occur because the adversary would be willing to fight on equal, or even inferior, terms.

This was to put the cart before the horse. Movement gives the ability to force battle on an opponent, to take up an advantageous position, or refuse action altogether if the circumstances are unfavourable. However effective the weaponry, it is of little use if it cannot be brought to bear.

Speed was the primary attribute of a scout, as fighters were at first known – to intercept or to escape. A few saw the future clearly. Writing in the 23

October 1914 issue of *Engineering* magazine, F. W. Lanchester showed remarkable prescience in stating:

> . . . the taking of the upper position at the start, or perhaps we may say, before the start, gives the power to outmanoeuvre an enemy, in spite even of inferior speed capacity . . . The initial difference in altitude represents a store of potential energy which may be drawn upon when the opportunity occurs . . . It will probably prove to be, and will remain, the key or pivot on which every scheme of aeronautical tactics will, in some way or another, be found to hang.

This prophecy held good for the next fifty years as 'he who has height controls the battle'. It was then incorporated into the theory of energy management formulated by Colonel John Boyd USAF, one of the founder members of the Pentagon 'Fighter Mafia' which was responsible for the F-16 light fighter concept, which set revolutionary new standards of air combat manoeuvrability from the 1970s.

Air Fighting Development

As experience was gained, suitable aircraft were evolved for the fighting mission. The next step was to form specialised fighting units. Their task was to patrol the skies in their allotted area, driving off enemy aircraft, while protecting friendly machines engaged in other tasks. The name of the game was air superiority, although it was many years before this expression was coined.

Performance, in the shape of speed, rate of climb, acceleration and ceiling, was generally judged to be more desirable than manoeuvrability, although the latter had some supporters in the devotees of close combat. Only in the supersonic era was the position gradually reversed, when it was found that the colossal top speeds and ceilings available were never used in combat.

Weaponry equally evolved over the years, from a single rifle-calibre machine gun to 30mm cannon, then on to homing missiles. These were part and parcel of new detection systems which expanded the pilot's situational awareness 'bubble' out to far beyond visual range.

At the same time, teamwork was developed beyond recognition. At first, pilots flew alone, but it was soon realised that the sky is a vast place, and that one man cannot see enough. The key was communications. Primitive hand signals, wing-rocking and coloured flares gave way to air-to-air radio and close ground control, then finally to direct information transfer by secure data link from airborne and ground control stations.

Scores of the Aces

In all walks of life, errors and inaccuracies tend to creep in. Unfortunately for us, the scores of the fighter aces are no different. Claims were almost invariably made in good faith, and their confirmations likewise. With confirmations, this could hardly be otherwise, as the data so gathered formed part of the intelligence work of the service concerned – notably on the enemy order of battle. Therefore inaccuracies were to be avoided.

In theory accuracy should be simple. Every victory demands a victim, and a check on the wrecks on the ground should give the answer. Unfortunately it does not, and for many reasons. If the victim falls into a lake or the sea, it may never be discovered. Half a century after the end of World War II, remains are still occasionally found, deep in a forest or a swamp. The artillery barrages of World War I destroyed many fallen aircraft; for example, the final resting place of French ace Georges Guynemer has never been located.

The next factor is sheer confusion. A claim made after a one-versus-one encounter, where the claimant saw his opponent hit the ground, was generally absolutely accurate; but if the victim disappeared into cloud, or the victor had to leave the scene quickly, through, for example, fuel shortage or because of the approach of a superior enemy force, an element of doubt remained.

A claim made as the result of a small-scale action is generally a little less accurate, mainly because of the need to look out for other aircraft in the immediate area. Less time is available for watching the original victim.

Multi-bogey fights, with dozens of aircraft milling about, are far more difficult. A pilot gets his sights on, fires, scores hits and sees his opponent start to go down. He must then clear his own tail as a matter of extreme urgency. Getting clear of the ruck for an instant, he looks around and sees an enemy aircraft in flames. He is pretty sure that it is his victim, but that slight element of uncertainty remains. Was he the only one to attack it? There are recorded cases of aircraft being attacked several times in quick succession before crashing, and being claimed by all (and credited to them) in good faith. Then of course, from high altitudes it is virtually impossible to see a victim actually crash.

Overclaiming is strongly linked to the confusion factor: the greater the number of aircraft in the fight, the higher the ratio of claims to actual victories. Unfortunately the discrepancies will never be resolved. Sometimes victims claimed as 'probable' or 'damaged' have later been confirmed as 'destroyed', but do not appear as such in the records. In far more cases, claims exceed known losses.

Revisionist history cannot help but be invidious. Where does one draw the line? The author has therefore chosen to take claims and confirmations as being made in good faith, using the term 'victory', which implies a defeated opponent, rather than 'kill', which implies total destruction.

Record-Keeping

The other point which causes extreme difficulty is the system of accounting used to record victories. This varied not only between nations but between wars, and even between theatres of operations with the same nation.

In the Great War, France and Germany acknowledged only those claims for which the victim could be confirmed as destroyed. A wreck on the ground within their territory was perfect; otherwise the testimony of independent witnesses, preferably on the ground, could be accepted.

When it came to the question of shared victories, French and German practice diverged. The Germans awarded the victory to the pilot who had played the major part in the combat, ignoring lesser contributors. By contrast, the French awarded a victory to each participating pilot. This gave rise to serious anomalies in the book-keeping. If three French pilots downed a German, they each were awarded a victory, but their unit was awarded just the one. In consequence, unit totals failed by significant margins to match the sum of the scores of their individual pilots.

The Germans fought defensively for the most part, staying mainly over their own territory, which made accurate accounting fairly easy. The French were often more aggressive, in part due to the need to escort frequent bombing raids, but also spent long spells on the defensive.

By contrast, the British Empire pursued a policy of gaining air superiority by carrying the fight to the enemy in a most aggressive manner, fighting not only over enemy lines but often penetrating far behind them. Most of their victories were scored over enemy territory, which ruled out confirmation by wrecks on the ground. Nor could there have been, in many cases, witnesses on the ground.

Lacking the confirmation checks available to the Germans and French, the British Empire was forced to use a less accurate accounting system, based on eyewitnesses who themselves had taken part in the battles. There were two categories, 'destroyed' and 'driven down out of control'. The latter would have been classed as 'probably destroyed' by the French and not

21

included in the individual totals. Certainly, many of the 'out of control' category victims eventually crashed; equally certainly some didn't!

There were many other anomalies. If the gunner of a two-seat fighter accounted for an enemy, both he and his pilot was awarded a victory. If the pilot scored with his fixed front guns, he was given sole credit. Observation balloons also counted as aerial victories. Whilst they were relatively easy (big targets) to hit, the cleverness was in surviving the attack in the face of intense ground fire. Finally, aircraft destroyed on the ground were included in individual totals, although this was rare.

Attitudes changed in World War II. The British, in what appeared to be a fit of belated remorse, dropped the 'out of control' category in favour of 'probably destroyed', which no longer qualified for the total score. Be that as it may, victims apparently out of control were still on occasion confirmed as destroyed even though post-war records showed that they survived! The British had no hard-and-fast system as such: announced scores depended on the method of calculation, which varied considerably.

France took the opposite route, counting 'probables' as whole victories, and including them in individual totals, Italy completely disclaimed the ace system, whilst Japan had never adopted it in the first place. Consequently, the records of Italian and Japanese aces are largely dependent on individual diaries and recollections, which are far less accurate than proper records.

Germany at first awarded decorations on the basis of numerical victories, but was later forced to adopt a points system in order to reflect the difficulties of combat on the various fronts, the destruction of a four-engine bomber taking pride of place. The Russians counted shared victories as whole units to the participating pilots; they were also more casual about confirmations – an attitude they perpetuated in Korea.

American methods varied widely according to theatre of operations and service. Not only was the USAAF involved, but the USN and USMC also. At first the United States treated shared victories as whole numbers; from 1944 they started to use fractions and decimals. This was perpetuated throughout the Korean War, but in Vietnam Phantom victories were shared, with half awarded to the aircraft commander (pilot) and the other half to his weapons system operator. This was amended half-way through the war to allow full victories to both, with the odd result that the American top-scorer of the conflict was a back-seater!

The North Vietnamese pilots perpetuated the French system of allowing shared victories as whole units. Victories were also counted against reconnaissance drones, which is just as well because the total scores of the North Vietnamese aces alone add up to considerably more than the number of American aircraft lost in air combat in the entire conflict.

Israel also used the ace system. Encircled by enemies, it was in their best interests to project their fighter pilots to the world as supermen, as a morale factor against the day when they would have to fight again. For many years their obsession with secrecy denied the names of their aces to the outside world, but it is now known that the top-scoring Israeli jet ace is Giora Epstein, with 17 victories.

The Ace Legacy

The heart of any effective fighting unit, be it a navy, an army regiment or an élite force, is its tradition, built up over many centuries, and its battle honours. Coming late into the arena, air units had no traditions nor battle honours. They had to start from scratch.

Reconnaissance aircraft and artillery-spotting lacked glamour, while bombing and 'tank-busting' did not really come into their own until World War II. By contrast, the fighter pilots could be seen in action over the lines, and it was perhaps inevitable that the lion's share of glory fell to them. Be that as it may, their traditions were quickly established.

Horrific casualty lists, with the land war apparently bogged down with no end in sight, did nothing for the morale of the civilian population. The airmen provided good news, almost the only good news to lift their spirits and stiffen resolve – something to foster the belief that the war was slowly being won.

The reality was rather different. Wars are won or lost by armies: only troops on the ground can take and occupy territory. It is arguable that reconnaissance and artillery spotting units made a far great contribution to the progress of the war than the fighter squadrons. On the other hand, the former needed aerial protection; the latter provided it.

The name of the game was air superiority; control of the air over a specified area. This was of course ephemeral: once the last fighter departed the area became neutral, while when the first hostile fighter arrived air superiority was lost until such time as it could be opposed.

If air superiority were gained to any great degree, fighters became surplus to air superiority requirements. These were then fitted with air-to-ground weapons and sent off to have at the unfortunate 'pongos'. During World War II, close air support of the ground forces became a mature art.

Bombing, both strategic and tactical, also matured during this period, but again relied on air superiority for protection, ensuring the continuation of the fighter ace tradition from World War II to the end of the Korean conflict.

As jet fighters became ever faster and were armed with homing missiles, fighter aces became fewer. A handful of Israelis attained the 'Magic Five', while in eight years of conflict over Vietnam, just two American pilots (and three back-seaters) became aces. The South Atlantic War of 1982 and the Gulf War of 1991 saw no aces as such, mainly due to lack of opportunity.

With technology rampant, much of the single-combat mystique has departed. The winner is he who has the superior technology and back-up. Yet the modern fighter pilot is no mere button-pusher, no airborne player of a sophisticated video game. He (and in some cases she) is the proud heir of the fighter pilot tradition, which still does, and always will, demand the virtues of courage, dedication, flying and weaponry skills.

1. FIRST STEPS

At the outbreak of the Great War in 1914 aeroplane design was still in its infancy. Performance varied between barely adequate and marginal. The main requirements were stability and a low landing speed, to reduce the number of accidents caused by inexperienced pilots. Underpowered, and with low wing loadings, in windy conditions aeroplanes had the handling qualities of airborne brown paper bags! Matters were not helped by the fact that in many cases lateral control was by means of wing warping, which was not only inadequate but also called for a lot of pilot muscle. Only later did ailerons become universal.

The engines of the day were short on power and unreliable. There were two basic types, the rotary engine and the inline. The rotary had a fixed crankshaft, around which the cylinders rotated. The propeller was bolted to the cylinders. While the rotary was air-cooled, and gave a high power/weight ratio, the fuel supply to the rapidly rotating cylinders could not be throttled. Consequently, the rotary engine had two speeds, flat out and stop! Engine speed, and therefore the aircraft, was controlled by a blip switch which turned the ignition on and off. The inline engine was orthodox, with a rotating crankshaft which turned the propeller. It was liquid-cooled, which made it relatively heavy for its power output, but had a smaller frontal area than the rotary. Aspirated by a carburettor, it could be throttled up and down as required, and set to run for economical cruising. On the other hand, its radiator and coolant systems were vulnerable to battle damage.

There is a modern saying, 'You never fight the war for which you are equipped and have trained; you fight the war you have got with whatever is to hand, however unsuitable.' This admirably sums up the situation at the start of the Great War: almost totally unsuitable aeroplanes were armed and turned into fighting machines.

At the outbreak of war, two radically different aircraft configurations existed. The tractor, in which the engine was mounted in the front of the fuselage ahead of the pilot, was aerodynamically the most efficient. The pusher had the engine mounted behind the pilot, which gave a superior forward view over the nose – an asset for reconnaissance and also when landing. However, the pusher still needed tail surfaces, and these had to be carried on wire-braced booms, the drag of which reduced performance. Power for power, pusher-configured aircraft were of lower performance than tractors.

Even before the war, it had been obvious that the best aircraft weapon was the machine gun. As the pilot had his hands full flying the aeroplane, it needed a second crew member to handle it. This was no great problem: reconnaissance aircraft routinely carried an observer in addition to the pilot, although the extra weight and drag reduced performance.

In a tractor, the observer was generally seated in front of the pilot, the reason being that on occasions when an observer was not wanted, the aircraft could be flown as a single-seater without disturbing the centre of gravity, and therefore stability and handling, too much. But here he was unable to fire directly ahead without hitting the propeller disc, while on both sides his field of fire was restricted by a forest of struts and wires. Astern, the pilot was in the way.

The difficulty of using a machine gun effectively under these conditions led many to conclude that it was not viable in a tractor. By contrast the pusher, with its unobstructed forward view, was well suited as a machine-gun carrier, even though the weight of the gun and its ammunition reduced an already poor performance still more.

This notwithstanding, the first air victory of the war, and of all time, was scored by a pusher, a French Voisin 3 two-seater commonly known as the 'Chicken Coop'. On 5 October 1914 pilot Josef Frantz and observer Louis Quénault of *Escadrille V.24* were patrolling high above the Belgian village of Jamoigne, when below them appeared a German Aviatik B.1. Frantz, who survived both World Wars, used his altitude advantage to dive on the German aircraft, gradually overhauling it. A stream of machine gun bullets from Quénault's Hotchkiss poured into the Aviatik, sending it down on fire. The German pilot, Wilhelm Schlichting, and his observer, Fritz von Zangen, had become the first victims of the new form of warfare, air combat.

Meanwhile, observers in tractors tried a variety of weapons – pistols, carbines, even rifles – with little success. The fact was that even men who were outstanding on the range at distances of 400 yards or more found that they did not seem to be able to hit a relatively large target like an aeroplane at a quarter of this distance, and it was soon recognised that the machine gun was the only viable air to air weapon.

Firing at a fast-moving target from an equally fast-moving, unstable, vibrating aeroplane, with a gun on a less than rigid mounting, posed particularly intractable problems. Deflection, range estimation, gravity drop, bullet trail, and target precession caused by relative speeds, in which the aim has to be behind rather than ahead of a slower-moving target on a similar heading – all had to be taken into account by a half-frozen gunner who was constantly buffeted by the slipstream. Even with a machine gun, accurate air-to-air shooting was extremely difficult.

Towards a Method

Land and sea tactics had been honed by centuries of experience, but the air, which introduced the third dimension, posed different problems. An aeroplane could be armed to shoot down an opponent, but how best to do it?

A undated Royal Flying Corps document of the period, probably from early 1915, was compiled by contemporary pilots. Entitled 'Method of Attack of Hostile Aeroplanes', it was of little use to an aspiring fighter pilot. Lieutenant Penn-Gaskell of No 5 Squadron noted several different firing positions against different types of opponent, but said not a word on how to achieve them. Major G. H. Raleigh, commanding No 4 Squadron, commented that one should always endeavour to face an adversary from about an equal height. And so on. The fact was that nobody knew how to go about the new task of air combat.

Provided both machines were willing to fight, there was no particular problem. They could fly along side by side, exchanging broadsides in the manner of sailing ships in Nelson's era. But the main purpose of reconnaissance aircraft was to provide safe and timely intelligence. For all practical purposes, this meant that they had to avoid combat wherever possible and return to their home airfield unscathed.

To prevent this, fighting aircraft had to be able to catch them and force them into action. This was easier said than done. With no means of early warning, an intruder invariably had a height advantage, which made it al-

---

However absorbed a commander may be in the elaboration of his own plans, it is sometimes necessary to take the enemy into account.
—Winston S. Churchill

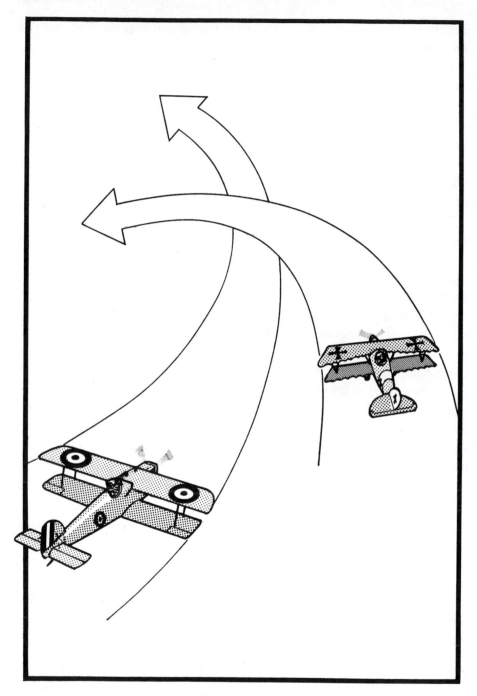

Fig. 1. The Break
To counter the standard gun attack from astern, the break,
a hard turn out of the line of fire, was used.

most impossible to catch from a standing start. Defensive patrols had to be the answer, to give at least parity in altitude from the outset.

It was not long before it was recognised that the rear cockpit of a tractor aeroplane was the best place for the armed observer, as this gave him a clear field of fire abeam and to the rear. If the machine ever needed to be flown solo, there was nothing that a sandbag in the rear cockpit could not cure. It was, however, very difficult for the pilot to fly offensively while giving the observer a clear shot. As James McCudden recalled, '. . . their way of firing at our machines was to fly along level with us and then turn away to allow their gunner to fire over their tails as they turned.' This was all very well, but having first managed to close the range, turning away immediately opened it again. It also gave the enemy observer a shooting chance.

The victory of Frantz and Quénault established two things, Lanchester's theory that an altitude advantage would be critical, and that a forward-firing machine gun was essential. What it did not do was to establish the superiority of the pusher over the tractor configuration. Frantz and Quénault had been extremely lucky: the Aviatik had appeared below at a fortuitous moment, giving them the tactical advantage. Given the pathetic performance of their machine, they could not otherwise have forced battle on the Aviatik. What was needed was a high-performance aeroplane able to catch and force battle on its opponent. The corollary was that it would equally be able to decline combat and escape when circumstances were unfavourable.

A fixed machine gun had several advantages. Its relatively rigid mounting concentrated hits in a small area; it allowed an attack from dead astern, which eliminated deflection problems and made target precession a thing of the past; and, most importantly of all, it could be fitted to a high-performance single-seater, which aided the chances of making an interception. But the problem remained: how to fire straight ahead, which was where a fleeing or surprised opponent was most likely to be?

The problem of firing through the propeller disc had been foreseen pre-war, although almost certainly in a ground strafing rather than air combat context. Attempts had been made to produce a synchronisation gear which would fire the gun only when the blades were not in line with the muzzle. It had however been thwarted by technical problems.

The pre-war French aviator Roland Garros solved the problem by fitting hardened steel deflectors to the propeller blades of his Morane Parasol. It was hardly an ideal solution, as it reduced propeller efficiency by almost 30 per cent, significantly reducing performance. Vibration from bullets hitting the deflectors caused handling problems, and the Morane, fitted with an all-moving tailplane (anticipating many jet fighters), was tricky to fly at the best of times. But deflectors did allow a machine gun to shoot through the propeller disc.

Garros was quick to take advantage. On 1 April 1915 he encountered four German Albatros two-seaters. Swooping to the attack, he fired just 72 shots, and an Albatros fell in flames whilst the rest fled. He later recalled:

> It was tragic, frightful. At the end of perhaps 25 seconds, which seemed long, of falling, the machine dashed into the ground in a great cloud of smoke . . . The observer had been shot through the head. The pilot was too horribly mutilated to be examined. The remains of the aeroplane were pierced everywhere with bullet holes.

The operational career of Roland Garros was short. Over the next fortnight he shot down two more German aircraft; sent another down 'out of control' and drove down two more to forced landings. Had he been a member of the Royal Flying Corps this would have given him six victories, making him the first fighter ace; as it was, the *Aviation Militaire* confirmed only three destroyed. On 18 April he was shot down by ground fire, and the remains of his machine was captured and examined.

The publicity given to Garros's feats turned him into some sort of aerial bogeyman in the eyes of the *Luftstreitkräfte*. That this was untrue was amply proven by later events. He escaped from captivity, returned to the Front in August 1918 and was shot down and killed on 5 October, having added one more to his score.

His mantle was assumed by two other famous pre-war flyers, Adolph Pégoud and Eugene Gilbert. Flying Moranes fitted with deflectors, Pégoud scored his fifth confirmed victory in June 1915, followed shortly after by Gilbert. Pégoud was shot down and killed in August without adding to his score; Gilbert added a sixth before force-landing in Switzerland. Like Garros, he escaped from internment and returned to the Front, but subsequently he achieved little.

The Garros legend spurred the *Luftstreitkräfte* into action. The story is too well known to bear repetition; suffice it to say that an effective synchronisation gear was developed for the Fokker Eindecker, the first really effective fighter. Just one point must be made: the widely used expression 'interrupter gear' is inaccurate, because physically preventing a machine gun from firing at the very rapid intervals needed was simply not possible. Synchronisation tied firing to propeller revolutions, which incidentally slowed the rate of fire considerably.

First Fighter

The Fokker *Eindecker* was a rotary-engined monoplane armed with one (later two or even three) belt-fed Spandau fixed, forward-firing machine guns. Its performance was unexceptional, while lateral control was by wing-warping, which restricted manoeuvrability. This notwithstanding, it soon achieved an enviable reputation.

In ten months of war the Royal Flying Corps had fought 46 engagements, most of which had been indecisive, while the *Aviation Militaire* had fought rather more, with similar results. With the arrival of the *Eindecker* in mid-1915, the tempo slowly increased.

Initially the new German fighter was distributed in penny packets among existing units, and it was left to individuals to explore its potential, which seems generally to have been done in a very cautious manner.

The first victory for the type was claimed by Kurt Wintgens on 1 July, but as his victim fell behind the French lines it was not confirmed. It was another month before the first *Eindecker* victory was confirmed, when Max Immelmann brought down a BE.2c on 1 August. This commenced the period which passed into aviation folklore as the 'Fokker Scourge', with Immelmann and Oswald Boelcke as its main exponents. For the RFC, even to see one of these machines was to be in mortal peril, and it was invested with almost supernatural powers.

End-on, the Fokker monoplane was rather more difficult to spot than a biplane, which enabled it to achieve surprise more easily. It also gave the subjective impression that it was faster than it really was, and projected a sinister appearance. At the same time, press reports ensured that Boelcke and Immelmann were rather too well-known to their opponents for comfort.

With hindsight, its formidable reputation existed more in the minds of the beholders. The facts were more prosaic. Not until 1916 was the Fokker deployed in any numbers, while even the German deadly duo only managed to score at slightly more than one a month! RFC losses in air combat were a mere 25 in November and December 1915. For the Allies, the real problem was a feeling of helplessness. The *Luftstreitkräfte* had a real fighter, and they had nothing even approaching it!

The only Allied machine remotely resembling a fighter at this time was the Vickers FB.5 Gunbus, a two-seater pusher with a Lewis gunner seated in the front of the nacelle. A handful served in France from February 1915, while on 25 July 1915 No 11 Squadron RFC arrived at the front, the first of three Gunbus-equipped units. Poor performance restricted the

31

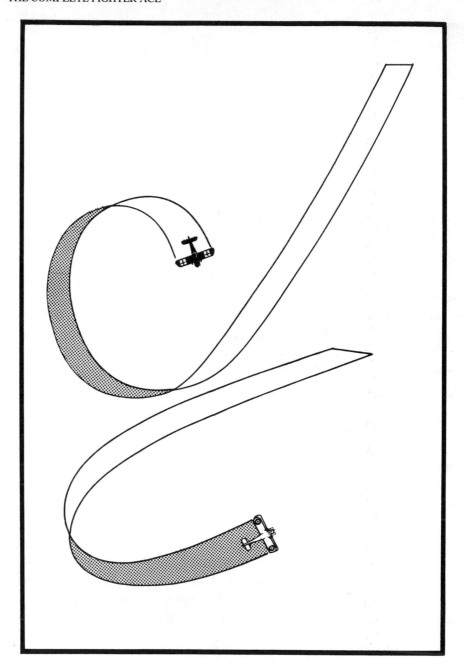

Fig. 2. The Immelmann Turn
World War I German ace Max Immelmann attacked from above and astern,
then pulled high ready to repeat the attack if necessary. In later times
the manoeuvre was adopted as a method of changing direction
during a vertical climb.

type's usefulness, and it was withdrawn from front-line service less than a year later.

Meanwhile, Oswald Boelcke adopted an analytical approach to air combat tactics – the first person to do so. His rules for air fighting, many of which hold good at the present day, the so-called *Dicta Boelcke*, followed. Immelmann, his friendly rival, contributed the turn which bears his name. Any modern attempt to describe it usually ends in a welter of controversy; suffice it to say it was a manoeuvre in the vertical plane which allowed a rapid re-attack following the first pass.

As more aircraft became available, the Fokkers began to hunt in pairs. As there were normally two of them on each airfield, this probably began fortuitously, but its several advantages were soon realised. Its opponents often flew in gaggles (formation is too strong a word), and in a multi-bogey encounter not only could one man not see enough, but a singleton enjoyed the attentions of several opponents at once. Against a single adversary, two *Eindeckers* conspired to divide his attention, making him more vulnerable. It was also a good way to introduce novices to the realities of combat. To quote but one example, Max von Mulzer was a pupil of Immelmann, and notched up ten victories before his death in September 1916 while flight-testing the Albatros D.I.

The Turn of the Tide

Lacking effective synchronisation gear, the British and French sought other means of producing a fighter. The British stayed with the pusher, accepting the inherent aerodynamic inefficiency of this configuration. The FE.2b was for all practical purposes a bigger and better Gunbus. It was very stable, and James McCudden's party piece was to leave the controls, stand on his seat, and look backwards over the top plane. Needless to say, his observer did not care for this performance, especially when one of McCudden's gloves blew into the propeller and wrecked it!

The FE.2b mounted a flexible Lewis gun to fire forward, and another on the top plane to protect the rear. To use the latter, the observer had to stand on his seat with the cockpit coaming at ankle level; an unenviable position when the pilot was taking evasive action. The other British pusher was the Airco DH.2, a rotary-engined single-seater, with a fixed forward-firing Lewis gun. Much smaller and lighter than the FE.2b, it flew faster and higher, and was much more agile.

The French solution resulted in one of the most successful aircraft series of the war. The Nieuport 11 *Bébé* was a small and agile rotary-engine tractor. Its single Lewis gun was mounted on the top plane, initially at an upward angle of about 15 degrees to fire over the propeller disc. Drum-fed, it was difficult to reload, and at first the pilot had to relinquish the controls and stand up in the cockpit. Later Nieuports were fitted with a curved slide down which the gun could be pulled to have the drum changed. This feature had another advantage: the gun could be used to fire upwards. Easy access for changing drums also allowed the mounting to be raised, taking the gun clear of the propeller disc and allowing it to be mounted level with the axis of the machine. Nieuports were used by many of the top French and British aces at some point in their careers.

The entry of the new Allied fighters coincided with the formation of the first specialist fighting squadrons. The *Bébé* entered service late in 1915, followed by the DH.2 and FE.2b in February 1916. Gradually they wrested control of the air away from the *Eindecker*, which by mid-year was in eclipse. Trials with a captured machine exposed its weaknesses, and the myth of Fokker invincibility was finally laid to rest. With it, on 18 June 1916, died Max Immelmann, shot down by McCubbin and Waller in an FE.2b of No 25 Squadron. The *Luftstreitkräfte*, unable to accept that one of its heroes could be worsted, claimed that a failure of his synchronisation gear resulted in him shooting off his own propeller, with subsequent structural failure.

Boelcke not only formulated tactics, he evaluated captured enemy aircraft against German types to discover their weak points. He also recommended that the *Luftstreitkräfte* form dedicated fighter units, as the British and French had already done. These were still many months in the future. The formation of *Kampfeinsitzerkommando*, six-aircraft detachments temporarily formed for the Verdun offensive in June 1916, were no substitute. Boelcke was fated never to lead *Kampfeinsitzerkommando Sivry*, his new unit. With his score at 19 he was grounded and sent to the Eastern Front and the Balkans on a tour of inspection.

Also in June 1916, the *Aviation Militaire* had formed a new fighter group from four successful *escadrilles*. Later numbered *Groupe de Combat (GC) 12*, this became the élite *Cigognes*. Over the next few months, many Allied aces emerged. For the French, Jean Navarre scored 12 victories before being shot down and badly wounded in June. Hard on his heels were Georges Guynemer and Charles Nungesser, while for the British, the boyish Albert Ball had commenced a career of mayhem which served as an inspiration to many aspiring fighter pilots.

The Pendulum Swings

The *Eindecker*, the unchallenged king of the air barely a year earlier, was now obsolete. New German fighters started to replace it from August. These were biplanes, the best of which was the Albatros D.I, which closely matched the latest Nieuport 17 in performance and, with two Spandaus, had greater firepower.

In August 1916, the *Luftstreitkräfte* started to form permanent fighter units, the *Jagdstaffeln* (*Jastas*), with an establishment of fourteen aircraft. This made them slightly smaller than a British squadron and comparable to a French *escadrille*. Boelcke was recalled in August to form *Jasta 2*, with hand-picked pilots.

By this time Boelcke's tactical ideas had matured. Teamwork was the keynote, but enforcing this on pilots who had hitherto hunted alone, and who all had their own pet theories, was far from easy. Not until mid-September did Boelcke unleash his *Jasta*, but when he did it soon became apparent that his methods had paid off. His death on 28 October, following a mid-air collision with one of his own men, was a dreadful blow to the morale

---

Fighter Comparisons, Summer 1916

Type	*Fokker E.III*	*Nieuport 17*	*Airco DH.2*	*RAF FE.2b*
Country	Germany	France	Britain	Britain
Span	31ft 3in	26ft 11.7in	28ft 3in	47ft 9in
Length	23ft 8in	18ft 10in	25ft 3in	32ft 3in
Height	7ft 10½in	7ft 7¾in	9ft 6½in	12ft 7½in
Loaded wt	1,324lb	1,246lb	1,441lb	3,037lb
Power	130hp Oberursal rotary	110hp Le Rhône rotary	100hp Gnome rotary	160hp Beardmore inline
Wing area	172.8 sq ft	158.8 sq ft	255 sq ft	494 sq ft
Wing ldg	7.77lb/sq ft	7.85lb/sq ft	5.65lb/sq ft	6.15lb/sq ft
Power ldg	0.097hp/lb	0.088hp/lb	0.069hp/lb	0.053hp/lb
Vmax	87.5mph	97mph	93mph	91mph
Climb	3,280ft/5min	10,000ft/9min	6,500ft/12min	6,500ft/ 18.9min
Ceiling	11,500ft	17,400ft	14,500ft	11,000ft
Endurance	1½hr	2hr	2¾hr	3½hr
Armament	2 × Spandau	1 × Lewis	1 × Lewis	2 × Lewis

N.B. In comparing aircraft performance, two of the most important parameters are wing loading and power loading. These affect speed, rate of climb, ceiling, and altitude, and to a lesser degree, turning capability. For the latter, wing loading provides lift needed to sustain the turn without losing height.

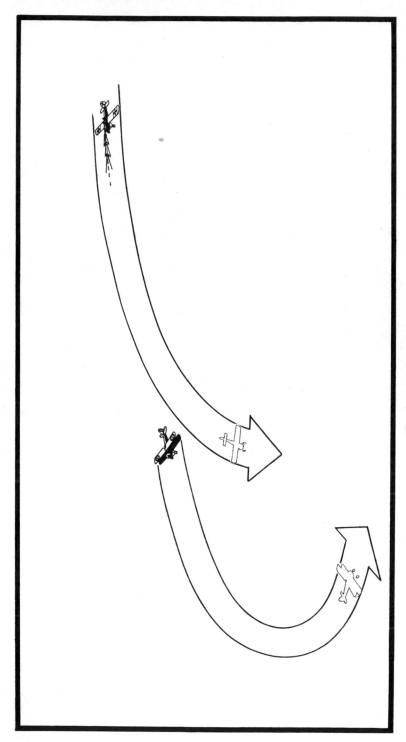

Fig. 3. Boelcke's Ruse

Boelcke often opened fire from a great distance, with little chance of hitting. An inexperienced opponent would take evasive action, which allowed Boelcke to close the range.

of the entire German Air Service. His 40 victories were made up of French and British aircraft in almost equal proportions.

Performance versus Manoeuvrability

As air fighting tactics started to move from the vulgar brawl of the dogfight to teamwork, controversy arose as to whether the most desirable characteristic of a fighter was performance or manoeuvrability. The former assisted the attainment of surprise; further, it made interception more certain, and escape equally so. The latter was an advantage in close combat as it helped the pilot to bring his sights to bear more quickly, and also defeat an attack. During the Great War, this argument was never satisfactorily resolved.

Inline engines, with their small frontal area and greater power, lent themselves to performance, whereas the rotary, with its light weight and short length, allowed all heavy weights to be closely grouped, making for greater manoeuvrability.

Performance Fighters, 1916–18

The *Aviation Militaire* adopted the SPAD VII from September 1916. Fast and very durable, it was less manoeuvrable than the Nieuport series that it

Performance Fighters

Type	SPAD VII	Albatros D.V	Fokker D.VII	RAF SE.5a	Bristol F.2B
Nation	France	Germany	Germany	Britain	Britain
Span	25ft 8in	29ft 8¼in	29ft 3½in	26ft 8in	39ft 4in
Length	20ft 3in	24ft 0½in	22ft 11½in	20ft 11in	25ft 10in
Height	7ft 0in	8ft 10¼in	9ft 2¼in	9ft 6in	9ft 9in
Loaded wt	1,632lb	2,061lb	1,936lb	2,048lb	2,590lb
Power	175hp His-pano inline	200hp Mercedes inline	185hp BMW inline	240hp His-pano inline	275hp RR Falcon inline
Wing area	200 sq.ft	229 sq.ft	236 sq.ft	247 sq.ft	406 sq.ft
Wing ldg	8.16lb/sq ft	9.00lb/sq ft	8.20lb/sq ft	8.28lb/sq ft	6.38lb/sq ft
Power ldg	0.107hp/lb	0.097hp/lb	0.096hp/lb	0.117hp/lb	0.106hp/lb
Vmax	119mph	116mph	124mph	132mph	125mph
Climb	6,500ft/ 6½min	3,280ft/ 4min	3,280ft/ 2½min	765ft/min	6,500ft/ 6½min
Ceiling	17,500ft	20,000ft	22,900ft	20,000ft	20,000ft
Endurance	2¼hr	2hr	1½hr	2½hr	3hr
Armament	1 × Vickers	2 × Spandau	2 × Spandau	1 × Vickers, 1 × Lewis	1 × Vickers, 1 × Lewis

largely replaced. It was followed into service from May 1917 by the even faster SPAD XIII, which remained in service until 1923.

The RFC, and later RAF, also flew the SPAD VII, but the SE.5, which entered service in April 1917, proved to be the most successful high-performance British fighter. In the same year, the two-seat Bristol F.2B arrived at the front. Once its pilots had learned to handle it like a single-seater, leaving the gunner to guard the tail, it proved a formidable fighter. It remained in service until 1932.

The *Luftstreitkräfte* at first deployed the Albatros series, but by the final year of the war even the D.V was outclassed. It was largely supplanted during 1918 by the superb Fokker D.VII. The SPAD XIII was by far the best French performance fighter, while the British SE.5a and F.2B more than held their own until the end of the war.

Manoeuvre Fighters

The first to appear, in September 1916, was the Sopwith Scout, or Pup as it was more commonly known. Performance was nothing special, but its incredibly low wing loading made it exceptionally manoeuvrable, to the point where, although it was vulnerable lower down, it outmatched the Albatros at 16,000ft. Incredible though it may seem, it was in fact possible to loop it straight after take-off, and continue to gain height in a series of loops.

Next in the Sopwith series was the Triplane, which was flown only by the RNAS. Based on the Pup, it had three wings of shorter span and narrower chord, allowing a reduction in wing span without loss of area. This gave a tremendous amount of lift and a sparkling rate of roll. The Triplane could handily outfly any German type then in service, and it could break off combat by climbing away. Between February and November 1917 it cut a deadly swathe through its opponents.

The best-known of the 'Tripe' (as it was called) units was the legendary Black Flight of No 10 (Naval) Squadron, led by the high-scoring Canadian Raymond Collishaw. Contrary to popular belief, aircraft of Black Flight were standard RNAS dark green. The sobriquet arose from the aircraft names – *Black Maria*, *Black Sheep*, *Black Death*, *Black Prince* etc.

Life on a Camel was certainly safer than on an SE for though you could not be sure of your man, you could be reasonably sure of getting away if hard pressed.
—Harold Balfour, No 43 Squadron

Good though the Triplane was, it was surpassed by the superlative Sopwith Camel, which reached the Front in July 1917. Credited with 1,294 victories, it was the most successful British fighter of the war. The torque of the powerful rotary engine aided a startling rate of roll in one direction, although this, coupled with instability, made the Camel a killer for the inexperienced.

The only manoeuvre fighter used by the *Luftstreitkräfte* in any numbers was the Fokker Dr.I *Dreidecker* triplane, the origins of which owed much to the Sopwith. Entering service in August 1917, the agile Dr.I was flown by many leading German aces, including Manfred von Richthofen, Werner Voss, Eduard Schleich, Kurt Wolff and many others who appreciated its manoeuvrability and rate of climb.

Which school of thought was right? Even with hindsight, this is impossible to say with any certitude given the prevailing tactical scenario. Whilst performance fighters had the advantage in the plunging attack followed by disengagement, it was not possible for them to completely stay out of multi-bogey fights. And once in them, manoeuvre fighters had the advantage.

Historically, performance dominated manoeuvrability for the next half century, but it cannot conclusively be said that this was the case in the Great War. The facts are that most of the top-scoring British and French aces used performance fighters for much of their careers, whereas the opposite is true for the German top-scorers. And Germany lost the war!

Methods of the Aces

As dedicated fighter units were formed, the nature of air fighting changed. Teamwork became the order of the day and patrols were flown in formation – one flight, two flights, or even a whole squadron. With this, multi-bogey fights became the rule rather than the exception. Plenty of pilots were, however, given a roving commission which allowed them to hunt as they thought best – solo or in small numbers.

Qualities of the Aces

It is generally stated that the prime quality of a fighter ace was marksmanship. Without the ability to shoot straight, all other qualities, such as exceptional aircraft handling, went for nothing. This author disagrees. Without a quality of exceptional judgement which allowed the ace to achieve a firing position in a highly dynamic three-dimensional conflict, marksmanship would have been of but marginal value. The key, as Robin Olds, USAF ace in World War II and with four victories in Vietnam, has stated, is

. . . what you can see, retain, anticipate, estimate in a three-dimensional move-ment of many aircraft. Can you look at an enemy aircraft and know the odds – to get him before somebody else – if he can get behind you first, and so on? It's a three-dimensional impression; you must get it in seconds. This is essential in aerial combat. The guy you don't see will kill you. You must act instantly, antici-pate the other fellow's motives, know that when you do this, he must do one of several things.

The last comment is critical. Three-dimensional manoeuvre combat is all too often regarded as an open-ended process, but this is not so. The limits are largely aerodynamic – acceleration and turning ability are both limited by aircraft energy (speed equals kinetic energy, and altitude equals positional energy) at any given moment. This determines the capability of an opponent at any given moment, which, if it can be foreseen, gives the attacker a deci-sive advantage.

In the Great War, aces tended to fall into categories. Invariably there was some overlap between them, but the following generalisations will suffice.

The most common type was the 'fangs out, hair on fire' pilot who, taking no account of the odds against him, plunged bald-headed into a fight with-out a thought except to shoot down at least one opponent. Social mores in the early part of the twentieth century, in which personal honour played a large part, aided this attitude. Charles Nungesser, who survived countless miraculous escapes, was probably the most extreme example. Ball, Guynemer and Voss were also of this breed. Only the lucky ones – and Nungesser was extremely lucky – survived the war.

A phrase that recurs frequently is 'the intoxication of battle'. There can be no doubt that this exists, even though the more mundane explanation is a surge of adrenaline. Given that we all differ physically, this may well ac-count for some of the crazy exploits of the aces.

Fighter aces are often described as fearless, but even a cursory examina-tion of the autobiographies of the period will show that this is not the case. Most admit to being terrified on occasion. Few, however, are as honest as Ernst Udet, who ended the war as the ranking surviving German ace and who at one point actually admitted to cowardice in the face of the enemy.

On his first interception, Udet, flying an *Eindecker*, encountered a twin-engine French Caudron:

He is now so close, I can make out the head of the observer. With his square goggles he looks like a giant, malevolent insect coming towards me to kill. The moment has come when I must fire. But I can't. It is as though horror has frozen the blood in my veins, paralyzed my arms, and torn all thought from my brain with the swipe of a paw. I sit there, flying on, and continue to stare, as though mesmerised, at the Caudron now to my left. Then the machine gun barks across to me. The impacts on my Fokker sound like metallic clicks. A tremor runs through my machine, a solid whack on my cheek, and my goggles are torn off. I reach up instinctively. Fragments, glass splinters from my goggles. My hand is wet with blood. I push the stick, nose down, and dive into the clouds.

Determined to blot out the stain of cowardice, Udet swore to fly and fight and salve his honour by risking his life against the enemy. The result was 62 victories over Allied aircraft.

The next type of ace was the mathematician, the calculator. His *forte* was to analyse each combat and to see how he could have done better, in order to reduce the odds against his survival. To run up a score, an ace needs first of all to survive. This is an oft-neglected factor in the ace make-up.

The calculator was sometimes a lone-wolf hunter, more often a successful patrol leader. Whereas the hot-head believed in the myth of chivalry in the air, the calculator realised that it really belonged on the ground, to a vanquished opponent. He also realised that surprise, the careful stalking of an opponent, followed by the swift and successful plunge to shoot his unsuspecting quarry in the back, was the essence of air fighting. His creed was to do the utmost damage for minimum risk.

In action, the calculator did his best to load the dice. He always sought the most favourable position using sun, cloud and altitude before launching an attack, and largely adopted dive-and-zoom tactics, disengaging immediately to seek another good position. He did not shirk a dogfight if it was forced on him, but avoided it if possible.

With thirty or more aircraft whirling around in less than a cubic mile of sky, it was impossible to keep track of events. This made it a dangerous place to be even for an experienced pilot; for the novice it was close to suicidal.

Typical calculators who were also good patrol leaders were Boelcke and Mannock, Fonck, and the elder Richthofen. The 'lone wolf' flyer was also a calculator. Temperamentally he was not a team player, and was at his happiest when carefully stalking a solitary victim. Bishop and McCudden belonged in this category.

Finally there was the balloon specialist. Observation balloons were high-value targets, and as such were defended by intense ground fire, which made them the most dangerous targets of all. Attacking a balloon did not call for clever manoeuvring or even outstanding marksmanship, just a fast sneaky approach – and a whole lot of luck. Balloon exponents included the Belgian Willi Coppens, the German Heinrich Gontermann, the American Frank Luke, the Frenchman Michel Coiffard, and the diminutive South African Anthony Beauchamp-Proctor, whose colleagues maintained that he was too small a target to be hit!

As the war progressed, the number of aces grew, at first slowly, then rapidly. In part, this was due to better aircraft and armament, but far more important was the development of fighting tactics, which enabled gifted pilots not only to score but to survive. Teamwork, with flights acting in unison, was also a factor here. The third and final factor was the growth of the various air arms, which provided ever more targets. Many high scorers achieved their greatest success in the final year of the war, primarily because they had more opportunities. If there is one thing an ace needs more than any other, it is a target-rich environment.

Physically, it was impossible to predict who would become an ace. They were of all shapes and sizes: tall and short, broad and thin, hairy and bald. There was a distinct tendency for them to be short and wiry, with pale blue or grey eyes, but there were plenty of exceptions to the rule. Nor were they necessarily very physically fit: a number of them took to flying because they were unfit, sometimes because of war wounds, to serve in the trenches. To name but a few examples, Georges Guynemer was classified as too frail for the army, as was Theo Osterkamp; Edward Mannock had a defective eye; Jean Navarre could only be classed as a delinquent; while even the great Oswald Boelcke was sometimes grounded by ill-health. There were many others.

The ability to see what was going on in the air was essential, and this had to be learned. Virtually all the aces were long-sighted. Many accounts speak of novices who, caught in a dogfight, failed to notice the presence of enemy aircraft. Often, of course, when they did it was too late. Every victory demanded a victim, and the majority of these were either two-seat reconnaissance aircraft or artillery spotters, whose attention was engaged on their main task, or inexperienced scout pilots who were easily surprised, made elementary tactical mistakes and were unable to get the best out of their aircraft.

Finally, the aces had a quality of alertness, in some cases almost amounting to a sixth sense, which made them very difficult to take by surprise.

Surprise was in fact the dominant factor in air combat: statistically, four out of every five victims failed to realise that they were under attack until their opponent had achieved a decisive advantage.

Chivalry was a word bandied about a great deal in the Great War. This implies a fair fight – hand-to-hand combat. In fact there was precious little. The method used by most leading aces was to sneak in behind their opponents and shoot them in the back. If they survived and were captured, they were then often briefly entertained by their conquerors, but that was all. Sportsmanship was another ill-used expression. Air combat was certainly not cricket, or even baseball. It was, however, a form of big game hunting, with the added excitement of the victim being able to shoot back.

The selection of aces for the biographical details section has been made on the basis of contrasting methods, temperaments, qualities and, to a lesser degree, the aircraft types flown and period of operations. Unavoidably, it is limited by the space available.

French Aces

Jean Marie Dominique Navarre The Navarre twins, of whom Jean was the dominant one, appear to have had psychological problems from an early age, one manifestation of this being an urge to vanish and live rough for a few days at certain times of the year. Jean in particular was never amenable to discipline, which caused a great deal of trouble in his service days.

A natural bent for things mechanical led him into aviation in 1913, and he emerged as an instinctive natural flyer. The outbreak of war caused his Aero Club Certificate test to be postponed; impatient to go to the front, he bluffed his way into the flying service without it. A brief spell flying Maurice Farmans operationally ended when he was expelled from his unit for a disciplinary infraction.

This proved a blessing in disguise, as his next posting was to *MS 12*, equipped with the Morane-Saulnier L. A high-winged two-seater monoplane, the Morane was notoriously sensitive fore and aft, on account of its all-moving tailplane. Navarre soon mastered it, and frequently indulged in aerobatics, a practice officially frowned on at that time.

The only armament carried was a carbine with three bullets. When, on 30 March 1915, Navarre encountered a German aircraft, his observer naturally failed to score. But just two days later, with a different observer, his luck changed. Three shots at an Aviatik wounded the pilot and holed its radiator, forcing it to land. This was only the third French aerial victory of the war.

43

With a growing reputation, both for aggression in the air and insubordination on the ground, Navarre transferred to *N 67* to fly the Nieuport *Bébé* scout, with a fixed Lewis or Hotchkiss machine gun mounted on the top plane, to sight and fire which he had to stand up in the cockpit. The *Bébé* was not the most stable of machines, which made this a perilous undertaking. Later, of course, the gun could be fired from a seated position.

Operating in the Verdun sector, Navarre's score mounted. His usual method was a hawk-like plunge, varied on occasion by coming in astern and below to close range. He painted his Nieuport red, thus anticipating the Red Baron by roughly a year. This made him instantly recognisable to friend and foe alike, while incessant patrols over the lines earned him the sobriquet 'Sentinel of Verdun' from the *poilu*. The publicity given to Navarre, the first high-scoring French ace, ensured that he was equally well-known to his opponents. Opponents seeing his red machine swoop down on them were immediately at a psychological disadvantage.

Like most other aces, Navarre showed no hatred for the enemy, and preferred if possible to bring them down alive. On one occasion he is recorded as having taken the crew of a crashed German two-seater into an *estaminet* for a drink.

On 17 June 1916 two Aviatiks of Section 17 set out on a reconnaissance but were intercepted over Verdun by three Nieuports. One was painted red – Navarre! It singled out the Aviatik crewed by Schattat and Goy, and plummeted to the attack. Goy, understandably nervous, opened fire at the exceptionally long range of 1,500ft. Navarre shot back, damaging the Aviatik's engine and controls and wounding Goy, before going down in a steep glide.

Navarre had been hit in the arm and chest by a chance shot. He landed safely, but lost a great deal of blood, and his already unstable personality was badly affected. He never returned to the Front, and his score of 12 confirmed victories and at least six unconfirmed claims, was soon surpassed. He died in a flying accident in 1919.

Charles Eugène Jules Marie Nungesser In an earlier century, Charles Nungesser would have been a pirate. An adventurer from his youth, he went to South America where he took up motor racing and learned to fly. He returned to France, joined the Hussars just in time for the war, and almost immediately started a career of mayhem by ambushing and capturing a German staff car and driving it back through the lines. His reward was the *Médaille Militaire* and a transfer to the Flying Service.

Nungesser joined *VB 106* on 8 April 1915, where he seemed to bear a charmed life. Often his elderly Voisin, which he decorated with a skull and crossbones, was badly damaged by ground fire, but somehow he always survived. But his ambition was air combat, and after several unsuccessful attempts he downed an Albatros near Nancy. This was enough to get him posted to single-seaters. In November he joined the Nieuport-equipped *N 65*, where he adopted his personal *insigne*, a white coffin, two candles and a skull and crossbones, all superimposed on a black heart!

His second victory came on 28 November, when, after expending a full drum without visible result, he manoeuvred beneath a two-seater. Pulling the Lewis gun down its slide (a recent innovation which allowed him to fire upwards), he pumped 24 bullets into its underside, sending it vertically down to crash.

Gradually Nungesser's score mounted, but then, on 29 January 1916, he crashed while testing a new biplane. His injuries were severe – two broken legs and a perforated palate, which latter ever after made his speech difficult to understand. He was back in action just two months later and his score continued to mount, but so did his injuries. A bullet scarred his lip, his jaw was broken and one knee was dislocated. Hospitalised time and again, he still returned to the Front, using crutches to get to and from his aeroplane.

Many aces, when confronted by superior numbers, made one quick strike, then broke off the action, but Nungesser stayed to fight, and even if he escaped injury his aircraft was often badly shot up. He became a byword for hairsbreadth escapes.

By August 1917 he was so exhausted that he had to be carried to and from his machine, but still he flew. Then, in September, he was fought to a draw by a Halberstadt. A spell on combat training followed, ended by further injuries in a car crash in December. His last victory came on 15 August 1918, giving him a final score of 45 confirmed. Most were scored with Nieuports of different types, but he also flew the SPAD, which although it carried his usual grim *insigne* was given the unwarlike name of *Le Verdier* (Greenfinch).

If ever the adjective 'fearless' could be applied to one man, it has to be Nungesser – or maybe he was simply indomitable. Either way he was a showman, with a habit of wearing full decorations rather than just the ribbons. The effect was however rather spoiled by a heavy limp, which made them jangle, as a fellow pilot unkindly observed, like the tinker's curse!

Nungesser was unable to adapt to peace. Flying school and barnstorming in the United States both failed him. Finally, on 8 May 1927, he and two others set off to fly the Atlantic. They were never seen again.

René Paul Fonck Photographs of René Fonck depict him as aloof and detached, with none of the intensity of Guynemer or Nungesser. His is the face of a mathematician or analyst – and this is precisely what he was, even in the air.

In the spring of 1915, Fonck was posted to *C 47* to fly twin-engined Caudron G.IVs in the reconnaissance, artillery-spotting and bombing missions. On 2 July he fired a few rifle shots at a German two-seater, with no visible result.

A whole year later the Caudrons were fitted with machine guns. Fonck's first decisive combat took place on 6 August 1916, when he and his observer damaged a Fokker and forced a Rumpler to land. Not until 17 March 1917 did a second victory follow, when, in a two-versus-five encounter, he shot down an Albatros D.III. This success secured his transfer to the *Cigognes*, who flew SPAD VIIs.

An unconfirmed victory over a two-seater on 3 May was followed two days later by the destruction of a Fokker. By now he had started to hone the methods which eventually brought him great success. Aware that surprise was the most important factor, he studied relative angles and speeds carefully. At the same time he practised his marksmanship, particularly deflection shooting. So expert did he become that often he scored with a mere handful of bullets. On the other hand, caution was his watchword. His philosophy was to cause maximum damage at minimum risk; in this he was like James McCudden and Manfred von Richthofen.

With the dashing examples of Guynemer, Nungesser and others daily before them, many *Cigogne* pilots found Fonck's approach far too clinical. 'Too much like a successful commercial traveller booking his orders,' was one comment. Two factions emerged, Fonck's supporters and the devotees of the 'go get 'em' school. So bad did the situation become that at one point Fonck was offered a transfer. He declined. Offered command of an *esca-*

It is less dangerous to attack fifteen opponents over French territory than five over German.

—René Fonck

> *. . . je place mes balles au but comme avec la main.*
>
> —René Fonck

drille within the *Cigognes*, to which he could transfer those who agreed with his methods, he refused as being unfair to the incumbent.

One other factor contributed to Fonck's unpopularity within *GC 12*. Modesty was not one of his characteristics, and he could be extremely self-righteous, quoting chapter and verse at great length to prove his case. This was hardly likely to endear him to others. Many of his confirmed victories were admittedly feats of aerial virtuosity, but others, scored when he was flying alone, were sometimes regarded as products of an over-active imagination by those who disliked what they regarded as his conceit.

Two victories on 19 January 1918 brought Fonck's score to 21. He answered those who accused him of playing safe over French territory on 5 February, when on spotting a group of eight, he penetrated some 15 miles over the German lines before turning to make a high-speed pass from the direction his opponents would least expect, picking off the leader as he went.

Multiple victories now came Fonck's way. On the afternoon of 9 May he shot down a two-seater and two fighters in the space of 45 seconds, followed by another triple victory in the evening. Then, on 14 August, he dropped three Germans in a single head-on pass in the space of ten seconds. His victims fell within 300ft of each other. Six more fell in one day on 26 September, and his 75th and final confirmed victory came on 1 November.

Fonck's record is the more remarkable in that he was never even so much as scratched. Given the number of encounters, this was absolutely amazing. To add to the legend, his unconfirmed victories amounted to 52. Had only one-fifth of these been confirmed, Fonck would have been top-scorer of the entire war.

René Fonck retired from the *Armée de l'Air* in 1939 and died in June 1953 at the age of 59.

British Empire Aces

Albert Ball Albert Ball was the first British ace to become a household name. His publicity was connived at by the authorities at a time when RFC morale was at a low ebb. Guynemer and Immelmann were well known to the public; the British badly needed a hero of their own, and young Albert Ball was there when needed.

Fig. 4. Ball's Method
Albert Ball's preferred firing position was from close underneath,
with his wing-mounted Lewis gun pulled down on its slide to
allow it to shoot upwards.

An excellent pistol shot from his youth, Ball had a natural mechanical bent, and, like his contemporary Guynemer, was at his happiest when up to his elbows in grease. Not a natural flyer, he became expert by dint of long practice.

Hating war and killing, Ball was that most dangerous type who kills not for love of the chase like Richthofen, nor in a blaze of patriotic emotion like Guynemer, nor even the clinical, calculating way of Fonck. He killed because it was his duty to do so – reluctantly but unquestioningly. He attacked against heavy odds in the same spirit, and approached combat as though it were a rugby match.

Ball was a loner. When not in the air, and not making minute adjustments to his aircraft on the ground, he spent his time playing the violin and tending his garden. He rarely flew alone; usually he was accompanied by a supply of home-made cake, which he ate when not otherwise engaged.

Like many other aces, Ball started life as a reconnaissance pilot, flying BE.2s with No 13 Squadron in France. On rare occasions he was allowed to fly the Bristol Scout attached to the squadron, which gave him a taste for more offensive action.

His aggressiveness had been noticed, and on 7 May 1916 he was posted to No 11 Squadron to fly the Nieuport *Bebé*. Delighted by its responsiveness and agility, he began to carry the fight to the enemy. His first confirmed victory was a kite balloon on 25 June, but by then he had 'driven down' five German aircraft, four of which were forced to land. Then on 1 July he shot down a Roland two-seater.

After a few weeks flying BE.2s as a 'rest', he returned to No 11 Squadron in mid-August. Five more victories followed, then all Nieuports and their pilots were concentrated in No 60 Squadron. Here it was that he developed his particular style of fighting.

His preferred method was a careful stalk, followed by rapid closing, generally in a dive, to come up and under, with the wing-mounted Lewis pulled down on its slide to fire upwards from a range of 20–30ft. Against a formation, the diving attack was used to scatter it, then he would select one victim and stay with it. In passing, it should be mentioned that staying close under an evading aeroplane long enough to get a good burst in was extremely difficult, and few ever really mastered it. It was also very dangerous: Ball had to be alert to stand from under quickly if his stricken opponent started to fall.

By 1 October his score had risen to 31 and he was sent home badly in need of a rest. As Ball commented at the time,

> To bring down a lot of Huns you have to be patient and practically live in the air. There are not many of them about and you have to be quick and seize your chance or the bird will have flown away. Sometimes you will make ten flights in a day and never get a fight.

Ten flights a day is an awful lot of flying hours. Add to this the expectation of encountering the enemy, the risk from anti-aircraft fire and the ever-present hazard of engine failure, and it can be seen that fatigue levels are very high.

In the spring of 1917 Ball became a flight commander with the newly forming No 56 Squadron, equipped with the new SE.5. Ball missed the agility of his Nieuport, and when in April No 56 Squadron went to France, he was allowed a personal Nieuport 23 for solo sorties, in recognition of his outstanding record. He had, of course, to fly the SE.5 on formation missions.

Of Ball's next twelve victories, only two were scored with the Nieuport; all the rest were with the SE.5, the better qualities of which he had learned to appreciate. He failed to return from a long and arduous mission in poor visibility on 7 May. Close examination revealed that his aircraft had not been hit. Very tired after a series of fights, he almost certainly became disoriented in cloud and lost control.

Albert Ball was credited with 44 victories. These consisted of a balloon and 21 aircraft destroyed (one of which was shared), two sent down out of control and 20 forced down to land. But at the end of the day, his value lay in the inspirational example he set rather than in his destruction of *matériel*.

James Thomas Byford McCudden Jimmy McCudden was an air mechanic in the pre-war RFC who went to France with No 3 Squadron in the first few days of war and, by dint of sheer enthusiasm, became an observer. This gave him experience of air fighting during the 'Fokker Scourge' and taught him to 'see' in the air.

Sent for pilot training in January 1916, he returned to France in July to join No 20 Squadron, flying FE.2s, which he described as extremely stable, but needing great deal of strength to throw around. Less than a month later he was transferred to No 29 Squadron to fly single-seat DH.2 scouts –very cold machines, which did not aid fighting efficiency.

Like many other aces, McCudden wrote his memoirs, which are notable for their exceptional honesty. He gave due credit to the ability of his opponents, while never seeking to gloss over his own shortcomings. Even in late

50

1916 a loop was still an unusual aerobatic. In November of that year, with his first victory under his belt, McCudden determined to try one:

> . . . I pushed the machine down till the speed got up to 90mph, took a deep breath and pulled the stick back. Halfway up the loop I changed my mind and pushed the stick forward, with the result that I transferred my load from my flying to my landing wires [positive to negative g]. The resultant upward pressure was so great that all my ammunition drums shot out of my machine over the top plane and into the revolving propeller . . .

With a broken propeller and extensive structural damage, McCudden nursed his stricken DH.2 down to a forced landing. He had learned a valuable lesson: always complete what has been begun. In the same vein, after an unsuccessful combat in January 1917 he commented:

> I honestly declare that I simply missed that Hun because I did not at that time possess that little extra determination that makes one get one's sight on a Hun and makes one's mind decide that one is going to get him . . .

Aggression, marksmanship, flying ability – all went for naught without determination.

On 23 February McCudden was posted home as a fighting instructor, flying Sopwith Pups. A brief spell with No 66 Squadron, termed a Refresher Course, followed, then he returned to the Front with No 56 Squadron on 15 August, to fly the SE.5a. It was with No 56, the nearest the British ever had to an élite unit, that he achieved his greatest fame.

As a flight commander, Jimmy McCudden proved a more than competent patrol leader, and in fact took part in the destruction of German ace Werner Voss, who put up an epic fight against odds. But his *forte* was the lone stalk of high-flying reconnaissance aircraft. To this end, he had his engine fitted with high-compression pistons for greater altitude performance, and paid exceptional attention to his guns.

It is a common misconception that a two-seater was easy meat for a scout. McCudden strongly disagreed:

> For the next five minutes I fought that DFW from 4,000 to 500ft over our lines, and at last I broke off the combat, for the Hun was too good for me and had shot me about a lot. Had I persisted he certainly would have got me, for there was not a trick he did not know . . .

McCudden made the best possible use of cloud cover, and his solitary pursuits sometimes took up to an hour. Once in position astern, he tried to align his SE with the haze on the horizon, and close to about 300ft. If he was

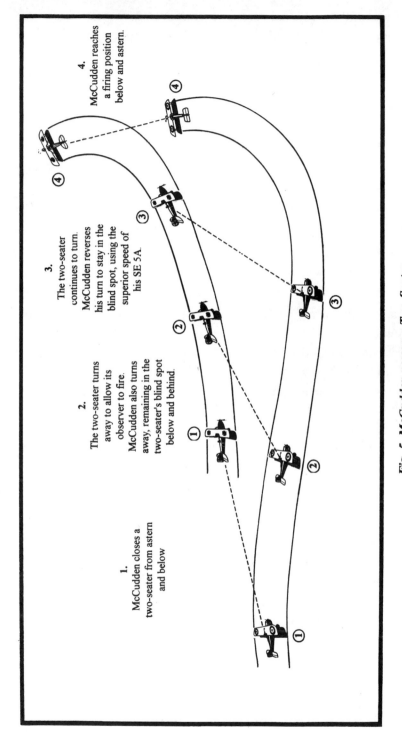

1.
McCudden closes a
two-seater from astern
and below

2.
The two-seater turns
away to allow its
observer to fire.
McCudden also turns
away, remaining in the
two-seater's blind spot
below and behind.

3.
The two-seater
continues to turn.
McCudden reverses
his turn to stay in the
blind spot, using the
superior speed of
his SE 5A.

4.
McCudden reaches
a firing position
below and astern.

Fig. 5. McCudden versus a Two-Seater

McCudden stalked two-seaters from astern and below, where the rear gun could not be brought to bear.
If the two-seater turned away to allow its gunner a clear shot, McCudden accelerated and turned outside
in what today would be called lag pursuit, to stay in the blind spot.

seen, the German two-seater would generally turn to allow the observer a clear field of fire. This was countered by opening the throttle and turning away, to stay in the blind spot beneath the tail. When the German pilot reversed his turn, McCudden hauled his nose around and opened fire, before once again seeking shelter in the enemy blind spot – move and counter-move. But Jimmy McCudden always maintained that a well handled two-seater was a match for a scout!

His 57th and last victim was a Hannoveraner CL.III, which he shot down on 16 February 1918. After a spell in England, he left for the Front in July to command No 60 Squadron. He never arrived. After engine failure on take-off, he made the elementary mistake of turning back to the airfield, stalled and crashed. In his fighting career he accounted for 45 two-seaters.

Andrew Edward McKeever When assailed by single-seaters, the usual tactic of two-seaters was to bunch together for mutual protection from the crossfire of their gunners. The Bristol F.2, commonly known as the 'Brisfit', was a horse of a different colour, but when it first arrived at the Front, in the hands of the novice No 48 Squadron, this was not recognised.

Its combat début on 5 April 1917 was a disaster. A flight of Brisfits encountered a *Kette* of five Albatroses led by Manfred von Richthofen in person. The master downed two, Karl Schaefer one and a Lt Simon a fourth. Only two Brisfits escaped, both badly shot up. Nor was this the end: over the next eleven days a further eight Brisfits went down.

The fault lay in tactics rather than in the aircraft. The Brisfit was a big fighter, far from underpowered by a Rolls-Royce Falcon of 275hp. Its wing loading was moderate, giving it a good rate of climb and a tight turning circle. The pilot had a single fixed Vickers, while the gunner had a single or twin Lewis on a Scarff ring mounting, which enabled the gun to be rapidly moved around the cockpit. Finally, the rear cockpit was exceptionally roomy, allowing the gunner free movement.

The far more experienced No 11 Squadron had handled two-seaters as scouts since 1915 – the Gunbus, then the FE.2. However, these had been pushers, which by 1917 were outclassed. This was the situation when Canadian Andrew McKeever arrived in May 1917.

McKeever, a marksman from his youth, had always wanted to be a single-seater pilot, and from the start he handled the Bristol like one. On 20 June a head-on pass against an Albatros forced it to dive away; McKeever was quickly on its tail, pouring bullets into it. More victories followed in

53

quick succession. Powell, his gunner, proved equally adept, and between them they cut a deadly swathe through the opposition. On 10 July they attacked nine German aircraft single-handed, destroying four. At this point, in contravention of orders, McKeever's Brisfit was painted white.

More multi-bogey combats occurred, during which McKeever's score increased, but which he was often lucky to survive. He returned to England on 25 January 1918 as an instructor with a confirmed score of 30. Various gunners flying with him were credited with 11 victories, of which Powell scored eight.

McKeever died in an automobile accident in December 1919.

German Aces

The highest-scoring ace of the Great War was Manfred von Richthofen, credited with 80 victories and ten 'probables'. He is not included in the biographical section for two reasons. Firstly there is nothing new to say about him. Secondly, the legend of the Red Baron has arguably exerted a pernicious influence on air warfare as a whole since his time. Air warfare is about power projection, of which air combat is only a small part.

Oswald Boelcke Boelcke has received less publicity in the English-speaking world than his friend and contemporary Max Immelmann. Primarily this is because Immelmann flew mainly against the British whereas a high proportion of Boelcke's early victims were French.

Oswald Boelcke qualified as a pilot on 15 August 1914 and spent the next ten months flying Albatros B.IIs on reconnaissance missions. After several fruitless combats, skill in positioning his aircraft to allow his observer to shoot brought his first victory, a French Morane, on 4 July 1915. This was probably only the second German air combat victory of the war. But even before this, he had started to fly the Fokker *Eindecker* single-seater.

Progress was slow. On 29 December 1915 Boelcke, with Immelmann and four other *Eindecker*s in attendance, encountered two BE.2s. The BEs, though widely regarded by the RFC as 'turkeys', put up a stout defence, and two *Eindecker*s broke off the attack. With Immelmann hotly engaged, Boelcke settled on the other:

> That was a fine fight. I had to deal with a tough fellow who defended himself stoutly. [It was in fact Sholto Douglas, later to command Nos 43 and 84 Squadrons, and future head of Fighter Command in World War II.] But I forced him on the defensive at once. Then he tried to escape me by turns, etc., and made an

effort to get at me on my weak side [probably the side at which the *Eindecker* had to turn against the engine torque]. He did not succeed, but the only success I scored was forcing his machine ever further down – we began at 2,000m, and in a short time I fought him down to less than 1,000m. Finally he could defend himself no longer, because I had mortally wounded his observer. [Here Boelcke was mistaken: Douglas's observer was incapacitated by airsickness, having vomited all over his pilot!]

At this point Boelcke ran out of ammunition and was joined by Immelmann, whose gun immediately jammed. Low on fuel after a 45-minute combat, and losing oil from his sump, Douglas spiralled to ground level and escaped to his own lines with a virtuoso display of agricultural flying!

The foregoing passage has been quoted to show two things, first that a well-handled BE.2 was not necessarily easy meat, and secondly that the *Eindecker* was far from a 'super-fighter'.

Boelcke's eighth victory came on 12 January 1916. By later standards this was slow scoring, but at the time it was a revelation. It highlighted future possibilities.

As in all else, Boelcke was cautious and analytical. He realised that advantages had to be sought, and gradually his tactical thinking crystallised. This culminated in his so-called '*Dicta Boelcke*', which specified rules for air combat and earned him the title 'The Father of Air Fighting'. Oddly enough, these rules made no reference to the Immelmann Turn, but were more concerned with gaining surprise and an advantageous position. These have survived to the present day with few changes. He also was the first to evaluate enemy aircraft, using examples captured in flying condition.

Boelcke was more than just a fighter ace or a tactician. He was a leader in every sense of the word. He formed *Jasta 2* in August 1916, and carefully trained his men in teamwork before allowing them to fly against the enemy. He died on 28 October 1916 as the result of a mid-air collision with one of his colleagues, by which time his score had reached 40. His mantle was assumed by Manfred von Richthofen ,who, while he doubled Boelcke's score, added rather less to the new-born art of air combat.

Ernst Udet The diminutive Ernst Udet learned to fly before joining the Army. A series of unrelated events saw him flying *Eindecker*s with *Kampfeinsitzerkommando Habsheim*, but, as previously related, his first combat was a disaster. Determined to prove himself, he attacked a large French formation in March 1916 and scored his first victory, a Farman F.40.

With the reorganisation of the *Luftstreitkräfte* fighter force he went to *Jasta 15*, where he came under the influence of Heinrich Gontermann (39 victories). In June 1917, with his score at six, he encountered a lone SPAD. In the manoeuvring combat that followed, Udet made out the name on his opponent's machine – *Vieux Charles*: Guynemer himself, at the height of his powers!

> I do a half loop in order to come down on him from above. He understands at once, and also starts a loop. I try a turn, and Guynemer follows me. Once out of the turn, he gets me in his sights for a moment. Metallic hail rattles through my wing plane and rings out as it strikes the struts. I try anything I can, the tightest banks, turns, sideslips, but with lightning speed he anticipates all my moves and reacts at once. Slowly I recognise his superiority. His aircraft is better, he can do more than me, but I continue to fight.

A brief shooting chance, but Udet's gun had jammed. For endless minutes they circled, then Guynemer broke away. Why, we shall never know – fuel shortage or a gun jam?

Transferred to *Jasta 37* in August, Udet started to score more rapidly. By February 1918 his score had risen to 20, then he was invited to join Richthofen's élite *Jagdgeschwader 1*. Flying the Fokker Dr.1 and the Fokker D.VII, the latter with a red fuselage and a red and white candy-striped upper wing, his score rose, despite time away from the Front with an ear infection. Apparently impressed by the Brisfit, he had a tinplate rear gunner mocked up on a D.VII, although whether this fooled anyone is hard to say.

Udet ended the war as the top-scoring surviving *Oberkanone*, with 62 confirmed victories. Of these 42 were British, the rest French. Unusually, the majority of these, 42, were single-seaters.

A famous post-war stunt flier, he later became responsible for aircraft procurement for the *Luftwaffe*. Made a scapegoat by Hermann Göring (22 victories), he shot himself in November 1941.

Theo Osterkamp Theo Osterkamp was unique in becoming an ace in both World Wars. Too sickly for the Army, he joined the *Marineflieger* as an observer. He became a pilot in April 1917, and believes that he was shot down by Albert Ball during this month. After several victories, and an inconclusive combat with Guynemer in which he was chased from 17,000ft down to 150ft, he rose to command *Marine Jasta 2*. He flew a variety of fighters – the Albatros D.III and D.V, the Fokker D.VII, and finally the Fokker D.VIII monoplane. His unit colours were yellow and black; his personal markings were yellow and black rings around the fuselage.

Based near Bruges, *Marine Jasta 2* operated at greater altitudes than were customary on the Western Front. Lacking manoeuvrability in the thin air, they concentrated on diving passes, avoiding turning combats where possible.

Osterkamp described Richthofen as not a particularly good flier, but a genius with guns, and ascribed the whole of his success to this. His own record was remarkable: 32 victories in the Great War; action against the Bolsheviks in the immediate post-war years; then six victories in the Second World War, which he survived.

American Aces

The United States officially entered the war in April 1917, but it was several months before the first US Army Air Service squadron reached the front, and not until the following year that the Americans arrived in any strength. They had, however, been well represented before this, flying with the British and French. The *Escadrille Americaine*, renamed *Lafayette* after German protests, was formed by the *Aviation Militaire* in 1916, and became the nucleus of the 103rd Aero Squadron in February 1918. In the RFC and RAF, many squadrons were international in composition, and the Americans added an exotic leavening.

Edward Vernon Rickenbacker Eddie Rickenbacker did not have the best of starts in life. The death of his father when he was thirteen curtailed his education and forced him into a succession of factory jobs. But luck was with him, and he progressed from mechanic to champion racing driver. When America finally entered the war, he enlisted and became a chauffeur to the US General Staff in Paris, where he drove for Colonel Billy Mitchell (and not General Pershing, as is so often stated). Mitchell it was who encouraged him to transfer to flying school. Here, his judgement of speed, distance and time, honed in his racing era, allowed him to earn his wings in just seventeen days – an exceptional performance. Rickenbacker joined the newly formed 94th Aero Squadron in April 1918, where his uncouth manners and arrogance made him extremely unpopular. Only slowly was he accepted.

For a while, success eluded him. His Nieuport 28 was once mistakenly attacked by a French SPAD, and on another occasion he nearly fell for a German decoy and only noticed the three diving Albatros scouts at the last

57

moment. Evading hard, he dived into cloud and got away unharmed. But these experiences were not without value: he was learning to stay alive.

His first victory came on 29 April, when he and former *Lafayette* ace James Hall (6 victories) intercepted a lone Albatros – or possibly it was a Pfalz. While Hall dived to engage, Rickenbacker stayed high and cut off its retreat. When his chance came, there was a quick plunge and a burst of fire, and the black-crossed machine went down just inside the German lines.

By now he had learned the value of the unseen approach, and to pick his targets. A dive from the sun to close range was his favoured method of attack. But this nearly cost his life on one occasion. Instants after shooting down his target, the fabric on the top plane stripped away; a weakness of the Nieuport 28. Gingerly, Rickenbacker nursed his sick bird home and landed.

His fifth victim went down on 30 May, but it was so deep into German territory that confirmation took a fortnight. Shortly afterwards, an ear infection took him out of the action. He did not return for several weeks, by which time the 94th had received the sturdy, if less manoeuvrable, SPAD XIII.

Rickenbacker was appointed to command the 94th late in September. He had matured, and his first task was to weld his by now sadly depleted, and largely inexperienced, squadron into a team. Fellow pilot Reed Chambers (7 victories) now said of him, 'When he stopped trying to win the war all by himself, he developed into the most natural leader I ever saw!' Victories now came thick and fast; 21 in eight weeks, of which two were shared and four were balloons. His final score of 26 was the highest of the war for an American pilot.

Between the wars Rickenbacker was a successful businessman, with interests in aviation and automobiles. During the Second World War he undertook many special assignments for the USAAF.

William C. Lambert Bill Lambert flew his first sortie on the Western Front on 1 April 1918, the day that the RFC became the RAF, and all his victories were scored with the new service. Assigned to No 24 Squadron, he flew the SE.5a.

Prior to arriving in France he had flown the Camel for a short while, but had not enjoyed the experience:

> To me, that was a dangerous airplane . . . But you had to give it your personal attention with your eyes and hands all the time. You had to fly it all the time due to the torque of those rotary engines . . . slap you over in the opposite direction

into a spin . . . The rumour around France at the time was that the Camel killed more of its own pilots than the Germans killed.

To him the SE 5a was excellent. A perfectionist, Lambert worked on his machine to get it to fly hands-off. One of his innovations was to reduce the wing dihedral to improve control response by making the aircraft slightly unstable.

Lambert's first victory, on 7 April, was a complete fluke. Like most novices he had not learned to 'see' properly in the air. Having lost contact with his flight, he noticed a small formation approaching, and tucked into the midst of it for safety, only to find that his 'friends' all wore black crosses:

> So I shut my eyes, kicked the stick back and forth, kicked the rudder back and forth, pulled her up and down; anything. Didn't see what happened.

On his return, Lambert was congratulated for sending down an Albatros on fire. His flight, sitting above, had seen the whole thing as they dived to the rescue.

Stories abound of pilots running out of ammunition and firing their revolvers at the enemy more in hope than expectation. Lambert went one better. He once threw an empty ammunition drum at an opponent, on another occasion it was his fire extinguisher. The latter actually hit, but did no damage.

The final few months of the war was the era of the large formation, leading to massive dogfights often with 50 or 60 aircraft involved. It was impossible to keep track of all the aircraft around, and most pilots very quickly became defensive, confining their attacks to fleeting targets of opportunity.

Some British squadron commanders, notably Sholto Douglas of No 84 Squadron, which also flew SE.5as, had by this time evolved dive-and-zoom tactics, which involved keeping each flight together to work as a team, only splitting up when it became totally unavoidable. This was not the case with No 24 Squadron, but Lambert gradually evolved his own solution, as did many others.

His closest friend in the flight was a West Indian, James Daly (7 victories). Always together on the ground, they began to fly as a pair, abreast, in trail and so forth:

> We didn't leave the flight, but we worked two to a team. Sometimes Daly would pull somebody off my tail, sometimes I'd knock somebody off his tail. And it

---

. . . from then on you thought of nothing but survival for yourself.
—Bill Lambert

---

worked out a pretty nice scheme, because we always, some way, had protection behind us.

On seeing this, the others in the flight copied it. At the time, the basic fighter formation was the three-ship vic, which made the pair a radical departure.

Lambert survived the war with a score of 22 confirmed victories, making him the second-highest scoring American pilot of the war. Of these, six were out of control and three forced to land. The remainder included a rare and formidable Siemens-Schuckert D.III destroyed, one balloon and one shared victory. He died in 1983.

A Belgian Ace

Willy Coppens de Houthulst Although the *Aviation Militaire Belge* was active throughout the war, it was numerically very small. Relatively few Belgian pilots were given the opportunity to fly fighters, with the result that only a handful of its pilots became aces. Only three were credited with double figures.

Willy Coppens began his operational career in the summer of 1916, flying reconnaissance missions. His first taste of air combat came on 1 May 1917, when his Sopwith 1½-Strutter was engaged by four German scouts. Although his aircraft was hit 32 times, he returned safely. In July he transferred to a fighter squadron, where he flew Nieuports, then Hanriot HD.1s. But for a long time success eluded him.

His first victory, a German single-seater, came in April 1918. Shortly after this he downed two observation balloons, and these became his favourite prey. His final sortie, on 14 October, saw him destroy two more balloons before he was wounded by ground fire and crashed. One leg was amputated as a result. Coppens' final score was 37, all but the first of which were balloons. This made him the greatest balloon-buster of the war. He remained in the service after the war, but moved to Switzerland in 1940 rather than live under German occupation.

Other Fronts

Nowhere was the air fighting as fierce and sustained as on the Western Front, and it was there that all tactical and most technical innovations were made. By contrast, the other fronts were side-shows.

Little air power was available for the Russian Front, the vast length of which meant that assets were thinly spread. Some indication is given by the fact that gigantic four-engine Ilya Mourometz bombers carried out 442 raids in 34 months, and claimed 40 hostile aircraft brought down by their gunners for only three bomber losses.

As on the Western Front, the Russian Imperial Air Service was at first devoid of a method. On 26 August 1914 Piotr Nesterov brought down an Austrian two-seater by ramming, thus setting a precedent that a few Russians perpetuated into the jet age. A grapnel was deployed on at least one occasion, without success. The October Revolution in 1917 brought hostilities with Germany and Austro-Hungary to an end.

Italy entered the war on the side of the Allies in May 1915, but for some considerable time the *Aeronautica del Regio Esercito* concentrated on reconnaissance and bombing at the expense of fighter aviation. This deficiency was gradually made good, and at the end of 1917 fighter strength had risen to eight *squadriglie* of Hanriot HD.1s, four of SPAD VIIs, and three of Nieuport 17s. After the Caporetto defeat, the Italians were reinforced by three French and four British squadrons, the latter with Camels.

Like Italy, the Austro-Hungarian Empire was heavily dependent on foreign-built aircraft for much of the war, and only slowly was the strength of its air service built up. The success at Caporetto late in 1917 was heavily supported by German forces. Stabilisation of the situation and rapidly growing air fleets on both sides resulted in bitter air fighting during 1918.

Compared with the West, the number of aces on the Southern Front was limited, although a handful managed to achieve very respectable scores. A factor was that operations over the inhospitable Alps gave little chance of a safe forced landing.

Piero Ruggiero Piccio 'Not the boldest, but the oldest' might have been written for Piero Piccio. A regular infantry officer who became a pre-war aviator, he made many pioneering and record-breaking flights. A 34 year old *squadriglia* commander on the outbreak of war, he soon gained a reputation as a fighter pilot in what was popularly supposed to be a young man's game. Even when promoted to *Tenente-Colonello*, he continued to fly operationally, attaching himself to the famous 91st, led by Italian top-scorer Francesco Baracca. Piccio flew Nieuports until mid-October 1917, when he converted to the SPAD XIII. He survived the war as the third-ranking Italian ace, at the ripe old age of 38.

Frank Linke-Crawford Frank Linke-Crawford is an unlikely name for an Austrian air ace, especially as he was born in Poland. Originally a dragoon on the Russian Front, he became an infantryman by default after his unit lost most of its horses. He then volunteered for flying, and after a few months at the front he transferred to *Flik 41J*, a famous fighter unit commanded by ace Godwin Brumowski, also Polish-born.

He first flew the odd-looking Brandenburg D.1 'Starstrutter', then from the summer of 1917 the Albatros D.III, and his score slowly mounted, speeding up with the increased air activity following the Caporetto offensive, until he was challenging Brumowski's score. At this point he was given command of *Flik 60J*. Of his methods, little can be said: he flew a fighter, and he fought. His usual opponents were Hanriots, Nieuports and Camels, all of which were more manoeuvrable than his mount, but he did not hold back. Often his aircraft was badly damaged, but somehow he survived – until 31 July 1918, when his score had reached 30. Flying a Phönix D.I at the head of a group of novice pilots in Albatros scouts, he fell in flames during a multi-aircraft dogfight. He was probably the victim of an Italian Hanriot.

Alexandr Alexandrovitch Kazakov

The owner of a bristling handlebar moustache, Alexandr Kazakov was a pioneer flyer with the Imperial Air Service. His first victory came on 18 March 1915 when, a grapnel with which he proposed to disable the enemy having jammed, he rammed his opponent, an Albatros, with his Morane, afterwards successfully crash-landing with a damaged undercarriage. The dearth of opportunities meant that his score mounted slowly, but, like many aces on the Western Front, he developed a technique of creeping up beneath the tail of his target. Aircraft of his unit carried a skull and crossbones on the rudder. He was credited with 17 confirmed victories, though he achieved possibly as many as 32, and his career with the Imperial Air Service came to an end with the October Revolution. He then flew with the White Russians against the Reds. He died on 3 August 1919 when he mishandled his Sopwith Camel and crashed.

Aces and Their Scores (* = approx.)

Score	Name	Remarks
RFC/RNAS/RAF		
British		
68*	Mannock, Edward 'Mick'	KIA 22.7.18
57	McCudden, James T. B.	KIFA 9.7.18
49	McElroy, George E. H.	KIA 31.7.18; 'McIrish'

44*	Ball, Albert	KIA 7.5.17
43	Hazell, Thomas F.	
42	Fullard, Philip F.	
40	Gilmour, John	
40*	Jones, J. Ira T.	
36	Woollett, Henry	
34	Jordan, William L.	
32	Bowman, Geoffrey H. 'Beery'	
31	White, J. L. M.	
28	Rochford, Leonard E. 'Tich'	
27	Constable-Maxwell, Gerald J. C.	
27	Frew, Matthew B. 'Bunty'	
27	Hoidge, Reginald T. C.	
26	Campbell, William C.	
26	Gurdon, John E.	
26	Staton, William E. 'Bull'	
26	Thompson, S. F. H.	KIA
25	Compston, Robert J. O.	
25	Leacroft, John	
25	Harvey, W. F. J.	
25	Luchford, Henry G. E.	
24	Andrews, John O.	
24	Clayson, Percy J.	
24	Shields, William E.	
24	Thomson, George E.	KIFA 1918
23	Hepburn, A.	
23	Jenkin, Louis F.	KIA
23	Rhys-Davids, Arthur P. F.	KIA 22.10.17
23	Whistler, H. A.	
22	Booker, C. D.	
22	Cochrane-Patrick, W. J. C. K.	
22	Latimer, D.	
22	Thomson, McK.	
22	Venter, C. J.	
21	Carpenter, P. C.	
21	Minifie, R. P.	
20	Bell, D. J.	
20	Cubbon, F. R.	KIA May 1917; gunner
20	Harrison, T. S.	
20	Harrison, W. L.	
20	Johnston, E. C.	
20	King, C. F.	
20	Maybery, R. A.	KIA 19.12.17
20	McDonald, I. D. R.	
20	Murlis-Green, Gilbert W.	
20	Stewart, D. A.	With DH.4
19	Beaver, W.	

19	Bell-Irving, H. B.	
19	Goode, H. K.	
19	Howell, C. E.	
19	MacLanachan, William 'McScotch'	
19	Miles, S. M.	
19	Molesworth, W. E. 'Moley'	
19	Wilkinson, Alan M.	
18	Barlow, Leonard M.	KIFA Feb. 1918
18	Cowper, A. K.	
18	Dickson, E.	
18	Enstone, A. J.	
18	Reid, Ellis V.	
18	Thayre, F. A.	KIA May 1917
18	Trollope, John L.	
18	Wood, Walter B.	
17	Burden, J. H.	
17	Cock, G. H.	
17	Jenkin, Louis F.	
17	Nounhouse, M. A.	
17	Swale, Edwin	
16	Baldwin, O. M.	
16	Hickey, C. R. R.	
16	Mellings, H. T.	
16	Middleton, T. P.	
16	Oades, S. A.	
16	Oxspring, K.	
16	Pender, S. F.	
16	Roxburgh-Smith, B. 'Dad'	
15	Carpenter, P. C.	
15	Findley, M. H.	
15	Grosvenor, R. A.	
15	Richardson, H. B.	
15	Tudhope, J. H.	
15	Tyrrell, W. A.	
14	Galbraith, M.	
14	Gibbs, G. E.	
14	Highwood, S. W.	
14	Mark, R. T.	
14	McEwen, N. F. K.	
13	Brown, C. P.	
13	Delhaye, R. A.	
13	Hedley, J. H.	Gunner only
13	Jones-Williams, A. G.	
13	Lagesse, C. H. R.	
13	Mawle, N. W. R.	
13	Olley, G. P.	
13	Reeves, A. G.	

13	Ross, C. G.
13	Scott, A. J. L.
13	Vickers, O. H. D.
12	Chappell, R. W.
12	Coler, E. S.
12	Crowe, C. M.
12	Draper, Christopher 'The Mad Major'
12	Drewitt, H. F. S.
12	Gerard, Alan
12	Huskinson, Patrick
12	Lale, H. P.
12	Mealing, M. E. 'Standback'
12	Montgomery, K. B.
12	Southey, W. A.
12	Webb, N. W. W.
12	Whittaker, J. T.
12	Wilson, P.
11	Carlin, Sidney 'Timbertoes'
11	Dodds, R. E.
11	Gates, G. B.
11	Hamersley, H. A.
11	Joseph, S. C.
11	Leaske, K. M. St C. G.
11	Lowe, C. N.
11	McCudden, A. KIA Apr. 1918
11	McKenzie, R. W.
11	McMillan, Norman
11	Morgan, A. J.
11	Pearson, W. R. G.
11	Reed, A. W.
11	Scott, M. D. C.
11	Thompson, S. F. H.
10	Baker, B. E.
10	Banks, C. C.
10	Boswell, A. J.
10	Graham, G. L.
10	Hayne, E. T.
10	Horry, T. S.
10	Hubbard, W. H.
10	Kearley, V.
10	MacGregor, D. V.
10	Makepeace, R. M.
10	Maudit, R. F. S.
10	Pinder, J. W.
10	Redler, H. B.
10	Rose, T.
10	Scott, T.

10	Scott, J.	
10	Smith, S. P.	
10	Tonks, A. T. B.	
10	Vaucour, G. M.	
10	Wells, W. L.	
10	Young, W. E.	

Australian

51	Dallas, Roderic S.	KIA 19.6.18
47	Little, Robert A.	KIA 27.5.18
32	Cobby, Arthur H.	
28	King, R. 'Bow'	
26	Pentland, A. A. N. D. 'Snowy'	
23	Kingston-McCloughry, Edgar J. K.	
13	Smith, F. R.	
12	Phillips, R. C.	
12	Taplin, L. T. E.	
12	Travers, F. D.	
10	Watson, H. G.	

Canadian

72	Bishop, William A. 'Billy'	
62	Collishaw, Raymond	Inc. 2 in Russia, 1919
54	McLaren, Donald M.	
52	Barker, William G.	
37	McCall, Frederick R.	6 with RE.8
36	Claxton, William G.	PoW 17.8.18.
34	Fall, Joe Stuart T.	
33	Atkey, Alfred C.	
31	Carter, Albert D. 'Nick'	PoW 19.5.18.
30	McKeever, Andrew E.	
27	MacEwen, Christopher M.	
27	Whealy, A. T.	
25	Quigley, Francis G.	Died 20.10.18.
23	Rosevear, Stanley W.	KIA
12	Brown, A. Roy	
12	Mulock, Redford H. 'Red'	
11	Rogers, W. W.	
11	Sharman, J. E.	
10	Baker, G. B. A.	

New Zealand

25	Caldwell, Keith L. 'Grid'	
20	Park, Keith R.	
19	Saunders, Hugh W. L. 'Dingbat'	
18	Collett, Clive F.	KIFA 23.12.17

South African

54	Beauchamp-Proctor, Anthony W. 'Proccy'	
35*	Kinkead, Samuel M.	Inc. c.5 in Russia 1919
11	Kiddie, A. C. 'Old Man'	

More than 350 aviators with the RFC, RNAS, and RAF were credited with between five and nine victories; many of these men were observer gunners.

AVIATION MILITAIRE

French

75	Fonck, René P.	
54	Guynemer, Georges M. L. J.	KIA 11.9.17
45	Nungesser, Charles E. J. M.	
41	Madon, Georges F.	
35	Boyau, Maurice	KIA 16.9.18
34	Coiffard, Michel	KIA 27.10.18
28	Bourjade, Jean P. L.	
27	Pinsard, Armand	
23	Dorme, René 'Père'	KIA 25.5.17
23	Guérin, Gabriel	KIFA 1.8.18
23	Haegelen, Claude M.	
22	Marinovitch, Pierre	
21	Hertaux, Alfred	
20	Duellin, Albert	
19	Slade, Henri J. H. de	
19	Ehrlich, Jacques	PoW 18.9.18
18	Romanet, Bernard de	
16	Chaput, Jean	
15	Turenne, Armand O. de	
15	Sardier, Gilbert	
14	Ambrogi, Marius (Marc)	Plus a Ju 52 in WW2
13	Demeuldre, Omar	
13	Garaud, Hector	
13	Noguès, Marcel	
12	Artigau, Bernard	
12	Casale, Jean H.	
12	Daladier, Gustave	
12	Sévin, Xavier de	
12	Guyou, Fernand	
12	Hugues, Marcel	
12	Jailler, Lucien	
12	Leps, Jacques	
12	Navarre, Jean M. D.	WIA 17.6.16
12	Tarascon, Paul A. P.	
11	Berthelot, Armand	
11	Bouyer, Jean	

11	Bozon-Verduraz, Benjamen
11	Hérisson, William
11	Lenoir, Maxime
11	Maunoury, Ernest
11	Montrion, René
11	Nuville, Léon
11	Ortoli, Jacques G.
10	Bizot, Maurice
10	Chainat, André
10	Gasser, Marcel
10	Herbelin, André R.
10	Lahoulle, Auguste
10	Macé, Charles
10	Pezon, Jean
10	Quette, Charles
10	Waddington, Robert P. I.

More than 100 *Aviation Militaire* pilots were credited with between five and nine victories, including a handful of Russians and Americans. It is believed that one Japanese pilot, Chigueno, and one Chinese, Tsu, flew with the *Cigognes*. Jean Darré scored six victories during the Great War, then went on to account for at least three more in the Spanish Civil War nearly 20 years later. Two others who did well in later life were Edouard Corniglon-Molinier, credited with eight victories in the Great War, who claimed another four during World War II, and Lionel de Marmier, who added three in 1940 to his Great War score of nine.

LUFTSTREITKRÄFTE
German

80	Richthofen, Manfred von	KIA 21.4.18
62	Udet, Ernst	
53	Löwenhardt, Erich	KIA 10.8.18
48	Jacobs, Josef	
48	Voss, Werner	KIA 23 9.17
45	Rumey, Fritz	KIA 6.10.18
44	Berthold, Rudolf	WIA 10.8.18
43	Bäumer, Paul	
41	Lörzer, Bruno	
40	Boelcke, Oswald	KIA 28.10.16
40	Büchner, Franz	
40	Richthofen, Lothar von	WIA 13.8.18
39	Gontermann, Heinrich	KIFA 30.10.17
39	Menckhoff, Karl	PoW 28.7.18
36	Müller, Max	KIA 9.1.18
35	Buckler, Julius	
35	Dörr, Gustav	
35	Könnecke, Otto	

35	Schleich, Eduard von	
34	Veltjens, Josef	
33	Wolff, Kurt	KIA 15.9.17
33	Bongartz, Heinrich	
32	Osterkamp, Theo	Plus 6 in WW2
32	Thuy, Emil	
31	Billik, Paul	PoW 10.8.18
31	Bolle, Karl	
31	Sachsenberg, Gotthard	
30	Allmenröder, Karl	KIA 27.6.17
30	Degelow, Karl	
30	Kroll, Heinrich	
30	Mai, Josef	
30	Neckel, Ulrich	
30	Schaefer, Karl	KIA 5.6.17
29	Frommertz, Hermann	
28	Bülow, Walter von	KIA 6.1.18
28	Blume, Walter	
28	Röth, Fritz von	
27	Bernert, Fritz	KIA 28.10.18
27	Fruhner, Otto	
27	Kirschstein, Hans	KIFA 17.7.18
27	Thom, Karl	WIA 23.12.17
27	Tutschek, Adolf von	KIA 16.3.18
27	Wüsthoff, Kurt	PoW 17.6.18
26	Auffahrt, Harald	
26	Boenigk, Oskar von	
26	Dostler, Eduard	KIA 21.8.17
26	Laumann, Arthur	
25	Beaulieu-Marconnay, O. von	KIA 18.10.18
25	Greim, Robert von	Inc. one tank
25	Hantelmann, Georg von	
25	Näther, Max	
25	Pütter, Fritz	KIA 10.8.18
24	Böhme, Erwin	KIA 29.11.17
23	Becker, Hermann	
23	Meyer, Georg	
22	Göring, Hermann	
22	Klein, Hans	
22	Pippart, Hans	
22	Preuss, Werner	
22	Schlegel, Karl	
22	Windisch, Rudolph	PoW 27.5.18
21	Adam, Hans von	KIA 15.11.17
21	Christiansen, Friedrich	Inc. submarine
21	Friedrichs, Fritz	KIA 15.7.18
21	Höhn, Fritz	

20	Altemeier, Friedrich	
20	Bethge, Hans	KIA 18.3.17
20	Eschwege, Rudolph von	KIA 21.11.17
19	Frankl, Wilhelm	KIA 8.4.17
20	Goettsch, Walter	KIA 11.4.18
20	Noltenius, Friedrich	
20	Reinhard, Wilhelm	KIFA 3.7.18
19	Fieseler, Gerhard	
19	Kissenberth, Otto	
19	Schmidt, Otto	
18	Baldamus, Hartmuth	
18	Hemer, Franz	
18	Oskar, Heinrich	
18	Wintgens, Kurt	KIA 26.9.16
17	Böning, Walter	
17	Hess, Ernst	KIA 1917
17	Ray, Franz	
17	Rolfes, Hans	
17	Schwendemann, Josef	
16	Boehning, Hans	
16	Freden, Hans von	
16	Hanstein, Ludwig	
16	Klimke, Rudolf	
16	Odebrett, Karl	
16	Weiss, Hans	KIA 2.5.18
15	Dossenbach, Albert	KIA 3.7.17
15	Donhauser, Christian	
15	Haussmann, Albert	
15	Heldmann, Aloys	
15	Immelmann, Max	KIA 18.6.16
15	Klein, Johannes	
15	Löfler, Otto	
15	Pressentin, Viktor von	KIA 31.5.18
15	Quandt, Theodor	
15	Schmidt, Julius	
15	Schneider, Kurt	KIA
14	Bormann, Ernst	
14	Francke, Rudolf	
14	Nathanael, Edmund	KIA
14	Piechurek, Franz	
14	Plauth, Franz	
14	Seitz, Wilhelm	
14	Schäpe, Emil	
14	Schlenker, Georg	
14	Straehle, Paul	
14	Wendelmuth, Rudolf	
13	Bohnenkamp, Karl	

13	Buddecke, Joachim	KIA 10.3.18
13	Büttner, Siegfried	
13	Geigl, Heinrich	
13	Heibert, Robert	
13	Jörke, Reinhold	
13	Janzen, Johann	PoW 9.6.18
13	Mesch, Christel	
13	Rosenfeld, Otto	
13	Schoenfelder, Kurt	
13	Wedel, Erich Rüdiger von	
12	Buder, Erich	
12	Collin, Dieter	
12	Cammann, Theodor	
12	Ehmann, Gottfried	
12	Esswein, Otto	
12	Festner, Sebastian	KIA 25.4.17
12	Höhndorf, Walter	KIFA 8.9.17
12	Kuhn, Max	
12	Mueller, Hans	
12	Manschott, Friedrich	
12	Schlieff, Franz	WIA Apr. 1918
12	Wenzl, Richard	WIA 11.8.18
11	Arntzen, Heinrich	
11	Busse, Joachim von	
11	Barnekow, Raven von	WIA 23.8.18
11	Döring, Kurt von	
11	Dannhuber, Xavier	
11	Drekmann, Heinz	
11	Gabriel, Willi	
11	Kirmaier, Stephan	KIA Nov. 1916
11	Keudell, Hans von	
11	Lindenberger, Alfred	
11	Loerzer, Fritz	WIA 6.7.17
11	Pfeiffer, Hermann	
11	Schaefer, Hugo	
11	Theiller, Renatus	
10	Aue, Paul	
10	Averes, Dietrich	
10	Berr, Hans	KIA 6.4.17
10	Brandt, Franz	
10	Classen, Fritz	
10	Dehmisch, Martin	
10	Frickart, Wilhelm	
10	Grassmann, Justus	
10	Mulzer, Max	KIFA 26.9.16
10	Matthaei, Rudolf	
10	Nagler, Alfons	

10	Neuenhofen, Wilhelm	
10	Schuez, Hans	
10	Steinhauser, Werner	KIA 20.6.18
10	Turck, Paul	
10	Thomas, Erich	
10	Ultsch, Bernhard	
10	Wenzel, Paul	
10	Wolff, Hans-Joachim	KIA 16.5.18

In addition, roughly 200 *Luftstreitkräfte* aviators were credited with scores of between five and nine.

AMERICAN ACES
Many Americans served with British and French units. Some transferred to the US Air Service when this entered the war, while others remained with their original units.

26	Rickenbacker, Edward V.	USAS
22	Lambert, W. C. 'Bill'	RAF
18	Hale, F. L.	RAF
18	Iaccaci, August T.	RAF
18	Luke, Frank.	USAS, KIA 28.9.18
17	Gillet, Frederick. D.	RAF
17	Lufbery, G. Raoul.	AM, USAS, KIA 19.5.18
16	Kuhlberg, Howard	RAF
16	Rose, Oren J.	RAF
15	Springs, Elliot W.	RAF, USAS
15	Warman, Clive T.	RFC, WIA 19.8.17
14	Unger, Kenneth R.	RAF
13	Putnam, David E.	AM, USAS, KIA 12.9.18
13	Vaughn, George A.	RAF, USAS
12	Baylies, Frank L.	AM, KIA 17.6.18
12	Bennett, Louis B.	RAF KIA 24.8.18
12	Kindley, Field E.	RAF/USAS
12	Landis, Reed G.	RAF/USAS
11	Iaccaci, Paul T.	RAF
10	Lord, Frederick	RAF
10	Richardson, L. L.	RFC
10	Swaab, Jacques M.	USAS

At least 86 American aviators of all services were credited with between five and nine victories during the war.

AVIATION MILITAIRE BELGE
Belgian

37	Coppens, Willi	WIA 14.10.18

| 11 | Meulemeester, Andrew de | |
| 10 | Thieffry, Edmond | PoW 23.2.18 |

Just two Belgian aviators are credited with between five and nine victories.

THE AUSTRO-HUNGARIAN EMPIRE
Luftfahrttruppen

40	Godwin Brumowski	
32	Arigi, Julius	
30	Linke-Crawford, Frank	KIA 31.7.18
29	Fiala, Benno	
19	Kiss, Josef	KIA 25.5.18
16	Gräser, Franz	
15	Fejes, Stefan	
15	Bönsch, Eugen	
14	Gruber, Kurt	
14	Strohschneider, Ernst	
12	Stojsavlejevic, Raoul	
10	Rudorfer, Franz	
10	Heyrowski, Adolf	
10	Navratil, Friedrich	
10	Meier, Josef von	

Fifteen Austro-Hungarian aviators are believed to have scored between five and nine victories.

AERONAUTICA DEL REGIO ESERCITO
Italian

34	Baracca, Francesco	KIA 19.6.18
26	Scaroni, Silvio	WIA 12.7.18
24	Piccio, Pier R.	
21	Baracchini, Flavio T.	KIA 1918
20	Calabria, Fulco Ruffo di	
17	Cerutti, Marziale	
17	Ranza, Ferruccio	
12	Olivari, Luigi	KIFA 13.10.17
11	Ancillotto, Giovani	
11	Reali, Antonio	

Thirty-three Italian aviators are credited with between five and nine victories.

THE IMPERIAL AIR SERVICE
Russian

| 17 | Kazakov, Alexandr A. | KIFA 13.8.19 |

15	Argue'ev, Paul V.	Mainly with Av. Mil.
13	Seversky, Alexandr P.	
12	Smirnoff, Ivan W.	
11	Safonov, Mikhail	
11	Sergievsky, Boris	
11	Tomson, Eduard M.	KIA 1917

Eleven Russian aviators are believed to have scored between five and nine victories.

2. COUNTDOWN TO WORLD WAR II

On 11 November 1918 the guns on the Western Front finally fell silent. *Luftstreitkräfte* aircraft were taken back to Germany and largely destroyed before the Allies could lay impious hands on them, while British, French and American aircraft flew unmolested over previously German-held territory. But the Allied victory eventually proved hollow. The German Army believed that it had not been defeated on the battlefield; it had been betrayed by revolution at home. Its terrible sacrifices had been in vain.

This was a myth; the German nation had been soundly beaten militarily. Its population was half-starved, due to the blockade imposed by the Royal Navy, and it was merely a question of time before the Front collapsed due to lack of resources. But the fact that the German Army had not been hunted home to Potsdam, and that German towns and villages had not been laid waste, as had happened in France and Belgium, reinforced the myth. As it was, the capitulation caused resentment and humiliation, exacerbated by the terms of the Treaty of Versailles in 1919, which sowed the seeds of a future, and much greater, conflict.

A second myth was that of the Fokker D.VII. The Treaty of Versailles contained an interdiction against it. Why the D.VII was thus singled out remains a mystery, but the impression given was that the aircraft was some sort of 'super-fighter', an expression of German technical superiority. While this was patently not the case, it reinforced the myth that the German armed forces were not defeated.

The third myth that arose from the Great War was that of the Red Baron, who, if legend is to be believed, was the greatest (and certainly the most publicised) fighter pilot of all time. As this myth has been perpetuated into the modern age, what are the facts?

Manfred von Richthofen was not actually a Baron, but a rather lesser *Freiherr*, a title which has no exact English equivalent. Given massive publicity by the German propaganda machine, he added to it with his autobiography *Der Rote Kampfflieger*, written before his death in action. From an early stage, he flew a series of all-red machines. He ascribes this to a whim, but this is unlikely.

There are several possible reasons. An all-red machine made him easy to identify in the heat of battle, by friends and foes alike. Doubtless he was aware of the legend of the 'Sentinel of Verdun', Jean Navarre's red Nieuport, and knew of the awe that this had inspired among his countrymen. Perhaps he sought a similar morale advantage over his opponents.

His habit of awarding himself a silver cup for each victory (until the supply of silver ran out), marks him as an egotist, which may equally account for his flamboyant choice of colour. A further factor which enhanced his legend was the crazy colour schemes adopted by his units, first *Jasta 11* and then *Jagdgeschwader 1*, which led to his outfit being dubbed the 'Flying Circus' by his British opponents.

Manfred von Richthofen has often been criticised for his love of hunting; as a boy he once shot tame ducks on the family pond. This has been interpreted as a love of killing. But, in all fairness, a fighter pilot is a trained killer. Should we really expect a man to be expert in killing his fellow men, and still retain tender feelings towards lesser creatures? This calls to mind a remark by a USAF Aggressor Squadron member, who had better remain nameless: 'Kill something every day, no matter how small and insignificant, just to maintain proficiency!'

Richthofen was an unexceptional pilot; he once stated that his first twenty victories were scored at a time when he still found handling his aircraft difficult. The secret of his success was marksmanship. Like Boelcke, he believed in teamwork; he never hunted alone, and actively discouraged those under his command from doing so. Only rarely did he overfly the Allied lines; on the day of his death he not only did this, but had become target-fixated and detached from his unit. His men were devoted to him, but it seems probable that this was born of admiration and respect rather than affection.

The question remains, why has his reputation endured? There are many contributing factors. Firstly, it is unarguable that he was the ranking ace of the Great War. His only real rival of the conflict was Frenchman René Fonck. If even a small percentage of Fonck's 'probables' actually went down, his score would exceed that of Richthofen. Fonck flew fighters, and his aircraft was only ever hit by a single bullet, unlike that of Richthofen, who on more than one occasion was lucky to survive. But Fonck's cold and abrasive personality, which made him unpopular even within the *Cigognes*, failed to catch the public imagination as did that of Guynemer or Nungesser. By contrast, Richthofen was fêted as a hero in his own country. The fact that he did not survive the war helped. Dead heroes are quickly deified, whereas live ones are still around to exhibit human traits – halitosis, slow to call for a round of drinks etc. It is arguable that Boelcke contributed more, but he died too early and was overshadowed by the deeds of those still living.

More puzzling still, Richthofen became an icon of the Western fighter community. He was of course well-known to his British opponents by reputation, and made more so by the garish colour schemes worn by his Circus. The British sporting ethos of giving credit to an opponent (especially when he has been beaten) came into play. For the record, large paintings of Boelcke and Richthofen hung for years in the library at the RAF College Cranwell! What else can one expect from the nation which invented cricket?

This notwithstanding, the main impetus came from the United States. Less war-weary than the British and French, America was still a young nation. Weaned on stories of their pioneering history – Kit Carson, Davy Crockett *et al* – the Americans were more ready to accept legend. A Prussian nobleman who flew an all-red fighter to become the top-scoring ace of the Great War was the very stuff of legend. Denizens of a huge country, with vast distances to be covered, they were also fascinated by aviation – little wonder, then, that the Red Baron legend is stronger in the US than in any other country, to the extent that the classified studies of air combat in Vietnam were coded 'Red Baron'.

There is a reverse side to the coin. It is arguable that the greatest contribution to the Great War was made by artillery-spotters and reconnaissance aircraft. These, however, lacked glamour, and comparatively little has been written about them. The sole function of fighters was to clear the skies of enemy aircraft, to allow these, and the equally mundane bombing aircraft, to perform their tasks unmolested.

To a degree, the result has been pernicious. Wars are won by surface forces, and the function of air power is to assist them in their tasks. Reconnaissance, bombing and close air support are of direct assistance, making the function of fighters tertiary – supporting the assistants.

Yet how many young men join an air force to fly transports, bombers or even attack aircraft? Fighter pilots became an élite, and the more gifted naturally gravitated to fighter squadrons, regardless of the true needs of a homogenous force.

The fighter pilots of the Great War attracted publicity, and Richthofen more than his share. This was perpetuated at post-war flying displays, in which fighter pilots were portrayed as daredevils and all others as lowly bus drivers or pencil necks. Lesser mortals had to make the best of things. Three decades ago, the writer spotted a piece of doggerel on a notice board at Wing HQ, RAF Alconbury. The actual wording was rude, but briefly it stated that if you were a fighter-bomber pilot, all others were obliged to make osculatory obeisance to an unmentionable part of one's anatomy! This is the pernicious legacy of the Red Baron.

The Great War was over, but in the east fighting continued, with the resurgent Poland, the Baltic states, the Ukraine, and the Bolsheviks in Russia all trying to carve out a future for themselves. Air power played a part, but it was small-scale, using the tactics, aircraft and, to a degree, the same pilots as were employed in the Great War.

The cream of their young manhood dead, the Western European nations started to rebuild their shattered economies. For most, this involved drastic reductions to their armed forces. In Germany the *Luftstreitkräfte* was disbanded, while the 185 squadrons of the RAF were reduced to a rump of 28 by 1921, 21 of which were stationed overseas. France, contrary as always, retained no fewer than 126 *escadrilles*, most of which were based at home.

It should have been a time of consolidation, of turning the lessons of war into doctrine for the future. But the accountants, then as now, had got into everyone's affairs, seeking short-term (and short-sighted) savings. Many lessons, so dearly bought in blood and treasure, were forgotten.

One area in which advances were made was the provision of parachutes for the RAF. The idea was hardly new: second-ranking German ace Ernst Udet survived a parachute descent. They were not infallible – third-ranking German ace Erich Löwenhardt died when his parachute failed to open after a mid-air collision – but they gave a fighting chance of survival. Even the Austro-Hungarians had been issued with them, Frigyes Hefty successfully baling out of his burning Albatros D.III on 22 August 1918. During the war the RAF had been denied them, although they were issued to balloon observers. Only in peacetime did they become standard issue to British pilots.

Tactics had also been developed. The standard fighting formation had been the V-shaped vic of three or five aircraft, stacked up from the leader, which gave all pilots a good view of the leader's signals. It was also good for holding formation in poor visibility. The main problem with the vic was

> *Cairns, as soon as he saw the machines, turned sharply left to get away from them as they dived to the attack. Skeddon and Birch went with him and Begbie and Giles, by crossing over positions, managed to turn fairly quickly too.*
> —Ira Jones (40 victories)

station-keeping during a radical change of course. The inside man had to throttle right back, while the outside man was forced to pour on the coals to avoid straggling. With a three-ship vic this was manageable, but with larger formations the difference in radius of turn between the inside and the outside man was too great.

The answer was for them to cross over, changing flanks on the formation. This probably began some time in late 1917. Future ace Ira Jones recorded its use on the very first patrol flown by the newly arrived No 74 Squadron, on 12 April 1918, making it certain that it was taught during training.

On this occasion Jones's was the sixth aircraft in the formation, a tail-end Charlie wide to the right. Left floundering by the hard left break, he was attacked by Bavarian ace Edouard Schleich in an all-black Fokker Triplane. Reefing into a vertical bank, Jones was able to keep his SE.5a turning just sufficiently tightly to avoid Schleich's bullets. Waiting until the Bavarian pulled up to attempt what in modern times would be called a high yoyo, Jones spun his SE through 1½ turns and ran for the lines, his faster machine opening the range to give him the advantage.

The cross-over turn was further developed by the RAF, to the point where the leader turned as hard as possible and his wingmen all changed positions, aircraft on the inside of the turn pulling up and over their counterparts as featured in the RAF Training Manual of 1922. This, however, called for much practice, and when fighter doctrine changed to formations made up of multiple vics of three it became less useful and fell into abeyance.

The advance that really should have been formalised, but for many reasons was not, was the use of the pair. Boelcke introduced hunting in pairs in 1916, although this was for support rather than a formal tactical system of mutual protection. With the increase in formation sizes, added to the fact that the standard vic generally consisted of an odd number, the formal pair was impractical. When a large multi-bogey combat developed, a certain amount of coincidental support was usually available. This made it difficult for any one pilot to make a sustained attack without becoming vulnerable in his turn. On the other hand, many pilots accepted the risk and pressed home their attacks.

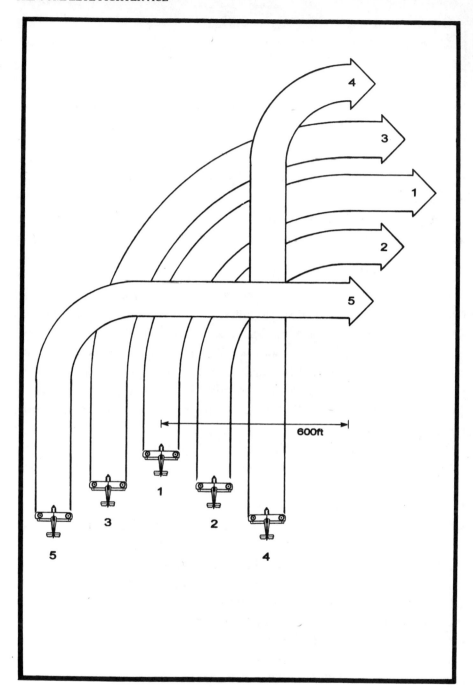

Fig. 6. Partial Cross-Turn
To enable formations to turn tightly, the inside and outside men crossed over,
changing places in the formation. As described by Ira Jones, No 74 Squadron RAF.

It was this that made the pair, consisting of shooter/cover, desirable, and many pilots experimented with it. Bill Lambert was just one of these, and as his account, given in the preceding chapter, shows, the pair, with each guarding the other's tail, proved to have great merit. But formalising it as a tactical system would have meant abandoning the tried and trusted vic.

Technical Advances

Over the two decades following the end of the Great War, aviation technology improved beyond all recognition. There were two main reasons. The first, and lesser reason, was national prestige. The *Daily Mail* prize for the first non-stop crossing of the Atlantic, the Gordon Bennett Cup for landplane speed and the Schneider Trophy for seaplanes, the latter linked to the absolute world speed record – all brought glory to the winning country. The second, and more important, reason was, as always with military development, the nature of the threat, real or perceived.

Aero-engine development had always been a contest among three factors, power, weight and drag. As previously noted, the air-cooled rotary engine was, power for power, considerably lighter than the water-cooled inline, but the latter was less draggy and its output could be closely controlled. Towards the end of the war, steps had been taken to make the power output of the rotary more controllable. This was achieved by ignition settings which sparked cylinders every so often rather than every time. It was hardly a satisfactory solution, but it was better than nothing.

The main problem with the rotary was the way the cylinders whirled around the fixed crankshaft, making lubrication, fuel feed and ignition matters of extreme difficulty. The solution was obvious: make the crankshaft rotate and the cylinders remain static, as with the inline, and fuel feed and ignition became easy, while lubrication was no more difficult. This resulted in the radial engine – air-cooled and light for its power output, albeit still with a large and draggy frontal area.

The quest for increased performance saw power output increase by more than 50 per cent between 1925 and 1935, while weight per horsepower fell by 20 per cent and fuel consumption was reduced by roughly the same amount. One failing had been that power output fell away with altitude; this was offset by supercharging, compressing the air as it entered the engine. Fuels were also improved: in Germany fuel injection started to replace carburation, while variable-pitch propellers gave improved efficiency.

The other avenue of approach to greater performance was aerodynamic. As with many other things, this involved a trade-off of weight against drag. A retractable undercarriage involved a considerable weight penalty, but the drag reduction was worth it. By the same token, cantilever-construction mono-planes and enclosed cockpits also showed advantages. Streamlining came into vogue.

Strategic thinking also changed. In many quarters air power was no longer regarded as an adjunct to surface forces: the bomber was seen as a war-winning weapon in its own right. All it needed was the ability to penetrate to its target with a low probability of interception, assured by high speed at moderately high altitude. Consequently aerodynamic and propulsion ad-vances of the period initially benefited bombers rather than fighters.

Even in the mid-1930s, fighters in service were still mainly biplanes, barely able to catch the new monoplane bombers even when well positioned to do so. Under normal operational circumstances, they had little chance of suc-ceeding. A whole new breed of fighter was needed – the bomber de-stroyer. This needed an overwhelming performance advantage to stand a chance of intercepting the new breed of bomber, the firepower to destroy it quickly, and most importantly of all, some means of finding it. It was a tall order.

One thing was certain: without some effective means of ground detection and control, the bomber could not be located. Rudimentary systems, con-sisting of a network of observers linked to a fighter control centre by landlines, were easy to set up, although efficiency was another matter. High-frequency radio provided air-to-air and air-to-ground communication, although recep-tion was terrible, leading to the old chestnut 'Send reinforcements, we're going to advance' being heard as 'Send three and fourpence, we're going to a dance!' But the adoption of simple code-words was a step in the right direction. If ground control knew the approximate speeds, altitudes and courses of the bombers, they could at least send the fighters in the right direction with a sporting chance of interception.

The need for defence against bombers demanded performance above all; manoeuvrability had become secondary. In any case, aircraft had reached the point where hard manoeuvring caused the pilot to black out as the blood drained from his brain. At the time it was not known whether this could cause permanent damage; consequently hard manoeuvring was viewed with caution. It was also questioned whether a pilot could be effective under these conditions. Thus the dogfight was pronounced dead by the pundits.

The main visible change was the gradual switch from biplane to monoplane. The latter was rather faster, accelerated better and had a higher ceiling than the lower wing-loaded and generally more manoeuvrable biplane. Only in rate of climb was there little difference at first. As to the demise of the dogfight, this had been greatly exaggerated, as was demonstrated during a series of limited wars in the 1930s.

The Spanish Civil War, 1936–39

Whilst it is not generally recognised, the outcome of the Spanish Civil War was critical for the future of Europe. It was won by the Nationalists, a fascist dictatorship under Franco, with the aid of Mussolini's Italy and Hitler's Germany. The Republicans, a grouping dominated by communists, were assisted by Stalin's Soviet Union. Had they won, Spain would almost certainly have become a Soviet satellite.

The consequences for Europe would have been incalculable. In 1939 Hitler and Stalin formed an unholy alliance to carve up Poland between them. With a potentially hostile Spain at her back, would France still have joined Britain in declaring war on Germany? Would Britain then have gone it alone? It is unlikely. Hitler would then have had a clear run in the East, and, with his full military potential available, might just have forced a Soviet surrender. Then what? The mind boggles!

In the event, Franco gave nominal military assistance to Germany on the Russian Front, but made no move to recover Gibraltar, even when Britain was most heavily beset. Nor did he allow German troops access to Spanish territory. Had he done so, it could have proved disastrous. What had at first seemed bad for the Allies turned out surprisingly well.

The air war was for the most part tactical – supporting the ground forces, reconnaissance and gaining air superiority. Both sides started with a handful of Nieuport-Delage NiD.52 biplanes, which offered only small advantages over Great War machines.

Until August 1936, air fighting was on a small scale, but from that month reinforcements started to pour in. Italian Fiat CR.32 biplane fighters were flown extensively by Nationalists until the end of the war, as well as by the Italian 'volunteer' pilots of the *Aviacione Legionaria*. Simultaneously, a handful of Heinkel He 51 biplanes arrived for Nationalist use, although it was not long before German pilots of the *Legion Condor* started to fly them operationally.

The Russians first arrived in October, bringing Polikarpov I-15 biplane and I-16 monoplane fighters. This was bad news for the Nationalists: the I-

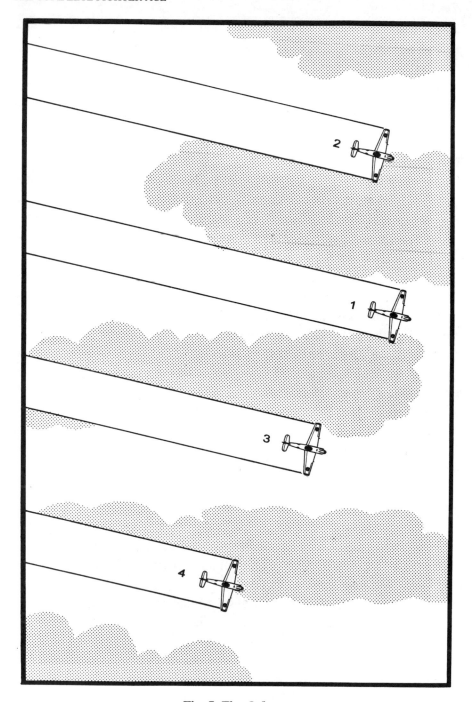

Fig. 7. The Schwarm
This was the best fighter formation of the gun era, consisting of two pairs
or elements giving mutual cross-cover. Also known as the finger-four.

> *One Rata swooped out of the broken clouds above. I saw her just in time, banked hard, and pulled up my nose to meet her. We both fired a short burst simultaneously; she dove down over my head and was gone before I could turn on her tail . . .*
>
> —José Lario, 5 victories

16 was at that time the most advanced fighter in service anywhere in the world. With cantilevered wings, a retractable main gear, an enclosed cockpit and armour protection for the pilot, the Rata, as the Nationalists called it, was the first of the new fighter generation.

The He 51 was outclassed by the new Russian fighters, and was quickly relegated to the close air support role. The CR.32 could only hold its own by virtue of superior agility and clever flying. It had just one other advantage: the Polikarpov fighters were armed with rifle-calibre machine guns, whereas the Fiat usually mounted two 12.7mm heavy machine guns. The Fiats were also in trouble against the Russian-flown Tupolev SB-2 twin-engined monoplane bombers, which could outrun them in level flight. They could only intercept if exceptionally well-placed at the start of the engagement.

The spring of 1937 saw the combat début of one of the most famous fighters of all time, the Messerschmitt Bf 109. The early B and C models, powered by Jumo 210 engines and mounting three or four rifle-calibre machine guns, were not as potent as the later cannon-armed, Daimler-Benz-powered E, F, and G variants, but they were effective against the opposition they faced.

Up to this point, fighter tactics had not varied from those of the Great War: gain an altitude advantage, and attack out of the sun. The vic was still the basic fighting formation, and once combat was joined a whirling dogfight often ensued, with pilots desperately trying to get on each other's tails.

To be fair, the Fiat drivers usually had little choice. Both Polikarpov fighters were faster, the I-16 significantly so. Unable to dive away from the fight, their salvation lay in tight turning, and they had little margin to spare against the I-15. It was little wonder, then, that Italian pilots in the world conflict to come put manoeuvrability before all else.

By a strange quirk of fate, it was an initial shortage of Bf 109s that led to a fundamental change in fighter tactics. The standard *Legion Condor Kette* of three aircraft often became unworkable, with the result that Bf 109 pilots were forced to fly in pairs. At first they flew in echelon, with the wingman

85

sucked back on the leader. They tried trail, with the wingman guarding his leader's tail. But best of all was flying abreast, where each had a good view around the other. Radio communication allowed wider spacing between aircraft; trial and error showed a spacing of about 600ft to be the optimum, mainly because it approximated to the turning radius of the Bf 109 at normal combat speeds. A maximum rate turn through 90 degrees put the 109s in trail; an attacker who followed a 109 around the turn became the meat in the sandwich.

All this took time, but in April 1938 a new German commander arrived on the scene. This was Werner Mölders, and to him is generally ascribed the credit for turning the pair into an outstanding combat system. Under his guidance the pair, or *Rotte*, was doubled up to form the four-ship *Schwarm*. One of his refinements was to pull the wingman back from his leader a fraction, then pull the second *Rotte* back even more, into the classic 'finger four formation. He then staggered the second *Rotte* vertically, positioning it higher and down-sun, thus giving cover on the most dangerous side.

The typical *Schwarm* frontage of about 1,800ft made station-keeping during radical changes of course difficult. Mölders' answer was the cross-turn, with the outside man pulling high, and vertical adjustments made after rolling out on the new heading. He has often been credited with inventing it, but, as we have seen, it had been in use since at least 1918. Twenty years later the difficulties were considerably eased by the wide spacing between aircraft. In combat, the freedom of action and the mutual cover and teamwork involved made the *Legion Condor* fighter *Staffeln* a force to be reckoned with.

The Bf 109 had the highest wing loading of all major fighter types during the war, and despite the use of leading-edge slots it was, speed for speed, out-turned by both Russian types. On the other hand, it had the best performance, and this was optimised by using dive-and-zoom tactics. With an initial altitude advantage, the 109s plummeted down on an opponent, fired, then used their excess speed to regain a high perch, from where they could repeat the dose. This was not always possible, especially during bomber escort missions when they were forced to take their chance in manoeuvre combat. Teamwork and the *Schwarm* formation compensated for these shortcomings to a degree.

Soviet/Republican I-16 pilots had exactly the same problems against the nimble Fiat CR.32s, which they also countered with dive-and-zoom tactics.

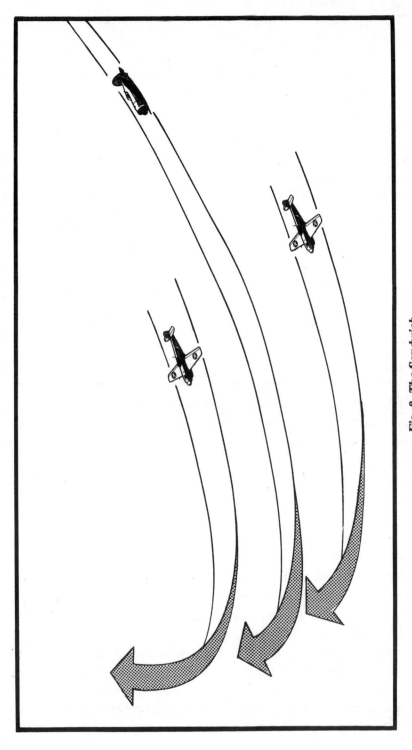

Fig. 8. The Sandwich

The pair as a basic fighting formation, coupled with the wide spacing allowed by air-to-air radio, gave rise to this defensive move. An attacker from astern quickly found the wingman on his tail.

Spanish Civil War Fighters

Type	Fiat CR.32	Messerschmitt Bf 109B	Polikarpov I-15	Polikarpov I-16 Type 10
Country	Italy/Nat	Germany/Nat	USSR/Rep	USSR/Rep
Span	31ft 2in	32ft 4¼in	32ft 0in	29ft 6½in
Length	24ft 3½in	28ft 4in	20ft 0in	20ft 0¾in
Height	8ft 7½in	8ft 2½in	9ft 3in	8ft 5in
Loaded wt	4,222lb	4,850lb	3,120lb	3,783lb
Power	1 × Fiat A30 RA inline rated at 600hp	1 × Jumo 210D inline rated at 635hp	1 × Shvetsov M25 radial rated at 715hp	1 × Shvetsov M25V radial rated at 750hp
Wing area	238 sq ft	174 sq ft	236 sq ft	161 sq ft
Wing ldg	17.74lb/sq ft	27.87lb/sq ft	13.22lb/sq ft	24.50lb/sq ft
Power ldg	0.142hp/lb	0.131hp/lb	0.229hp/lb	0.198hp/lb
Vmax	220mph	292mph	218mph	282mph
Climb	19,685ft/ 14.42min	19,685ft/ 9.8min	n/a	16,400ft/ 6.5min
Ceiling	25,264ft	26,575ft	24,673ft	26,245ft
Range	485 miles	c.400 miles	451 miles	497 miles
Armament	2 × 12.7mm Breda-SAFAT	3 × 7.9mm MG 17	2 × 7.62mm PV-1	4 × 7.62mm ShKAS

Having observed the *Legion Condor* 109s at work, they started to use the pair (*pary*) and the four (*zveno*), although as they lacked radio communications aircraft spacings were rather closer than those used by the Germans. So well did this work that in 1938 a recommendation was made that the system be adopted by the entire Soviet fighter force. But many of the Spanish veterans vanished in Stalin's murderous purges, and it was never implemented.

Spanish Civil War Aces

The number of Spanish Civil War aces is uncertain. Twenty Germans and the same number of Nationalist Spaniards scored five or more victories. Of the others, Italians were not encouraged to keep scores, and consequently there is no consistency about their unofficial records. The Soviets were, as always, secretive, and political reliability may have played a part. The records of Republican Spaniards and of the international contingent that flew with them were, as is often the case with the losers, incomplete. However, it would appear that the three-year war produced between 80 and 90 aces. The top scorer, by a wide margin, was Spanish.

Nationalist aces

40	Morato y Castaño, Joaquin Garcia	KIFA 4.4.39
25	Benjumea, Julio Salvador Diaz	PoW 30.10.38
21$^{1}/_{3}$	Sagaztizobal, Manuel Vazquez	KIA 23.1.39
17	Lopez, Aristides Garcia	KIA Russian Front
16$^{1}/_{3}$	Larrazabal, Angel Salas	Plus 7 in Russia, WWII
13	Garcia, Miguel Guerrero	
12	Pardo, Miguel Garcia	KIFA 28.3.39
11	Nespral, Joaquin Velasco Fernandez	
11	Alexandri, Carlos Bayo	Plus 2 in Russia, WWII
10	Grunne, Rodolphe de Hemricourt de	

De Grunne was a Belgian who later flew with No 32 Squadron RAF in 1940, accounting for a Bf 109 and another damaged, and a shared Do 17. Shot down and badly burned, he returned to No 609 Squadron in 1941, but was shot down and killed by a Bf 109 in April.

Republican aces (the following scores are approximate)

21	Rubio, Leopoldo Morquilla	
11	La Calle, Andres Garcia	
10	Fernandez, José M. B.	
10	Bravo, Emilio Ramirez	
10	Martinez, Miguel Zambudio	
10	Claver, Manuel Zarauza	KIFA Russia

An early feature of the Republican air arm was its international flavour, with volunteer pilots from many countries. But when in 1937 the going rate for mercenaries was cut by two-thirds, many became disenchanted and returned home. The top-scoring foreign ace was Frenchman Abel Guides with 11 victories. Other international pilots were Americans Frank Tinker (8) and Albert 'Ajax' Baumler (4), who later joined the Flying Tigers in China, where he scored another five victories against the Japanese; the Yugoslav Bozno Petrovic (7), KIA 1937; and the Czech Jan Ferak (7).

German aces

14	Mölders, Werner	101 in WWII; KIFA 22.11.41
12	Schellmann, Wolfgang	13 in WWII; MIA 22.6.41
11	Harder, Haro	6 in WWII; KIA 12.8.40
10	Boddem, Peter	KIFA 20.3.39

Many *Legion Condor* fliers went on to greater things. Among them were Herbert Ihlefeld (7 in Spain, 123 in WWII); Walter Oesau (8 in Spain, 117 in WWII; KIA 11.5.44); Reinhard Seiler (9 in Spain, 100 in WWII); Gunther Lützow (5 in Spain, 103 in WWII; MIA 24.4.45); Rudolf Resch (1 in Spain, 93 in WWII; KIA 11.7.43); Wolfgang Ewald (1 in Spain, 77 in WWII; PoW 14.7.43); Hubertus von Bonin (4 in Spain, 73 in WWII; KIA 15.12.43); Wilhelm Balthasar (7 in Spain, 40 in WWII; KIA 3.7.41); and Rolf Pingel (4 in Spain, 22 in WWII; PoW 10.7.41).

Italian aces

15	Bonzano, Mario	Plus 2 in WWII
15	Mantelli, Adriano	
10–12	Ricci, Corrado	Plus 2 in WWII
10	Nobili, Guido	

Corrado Ricci, later Chief of Staff of the *Regia Aeronautica*, was uniquely honoured. A piazza off the Imperial Way, Rome, was named after him.

Soviet aces

16	Serov, Anatoliy K.	KIFA May 39
15	Rychagov, Pavel K.	Purged by Stalin 1941
14	Yeremenko, Ivan T.	
13	Bobrov, Vladimir I.	Plus 30 in WWII
12	Lakeiev, Ivan A.	Plus 1 in Khalkin Gol
12	Denisov, S. P.	

As the Spanish Civil War dragged on, Stalin increasingly came to view it as a lost cause. By October 1938, most Russian personnel had been withdrawn, leaving only a handful of advisers. Many died in Stalin's infamous purges of the next few years, possibly because they were associated with failure.

Yakob Shmushkievich, the Soviet air commander in Spain under the *nom de guerre* 'General Douglas', took control of air operations against the Japanese at Khalkin Gol in 1939; was promoted to head the Soviet Air Force; was sacked in April 1940 after the disastrous Winter War against Finland; and was executed by the NKVD on 28 October 1941. Shmushkievich was replaced as Head of the Air Force by Pavel Rychagov 'Pablo Palencar', who also fell from favour and was executed barely two months before the German attack in June 1941. Nor was it just these two: thousands of officers were purged during this period, and with them, the most valuable air combat lessons were lost.

The Spanish Ace of Aces: Garcia Morato

Morato was a very experienced pre-war pilot and aerobatic champion with 1,860 hours in his logbook. One of the secrets of his success was almost certainly the total mastery he had over his aircraft. At first he flew the NiD.52, in which he opened his account with a Vickers Vildebeeste on 12 August 1936. His next three victories, two NiD.52s and a Potez 540, were scored with a Heinkel He 51, after which he mainly flew the Fiat CR.32. Amazingly, all his subsequent 36 victories were not only with this type but with the same aircraft, although he also flew the Bf 109B and He 112 operationally. Only once was he shot down, and then by a stray bullet from a 'friendly' Fiat which caused minor engine damage.

After having flown with the Italians for a spell, he formed an all-Spanish three-ship flight, the famous *Patrulla Azul* (Blue Patrol), on 24 December 1936, initially with Salvador and de Castro. Pardo joined in January 1937, while Benjumea (25) and Larrazabal (16$\frac{1}{3}$ victories), became its most distinguished members later.

Morato was a devotee of the dogfight, in which he joined enthusiastically after the opening attack, making the most of the superb manoeuvrability of his CR.32. Nor was he hidebound by rules. On 25 June 1938, flying a solo reconnaissance sortie, he encountered an estimated 50 Republican machines:

> . . . the speed at which I acted allowed me to profit by the tactical disadvantage of lower altitude for, choosing a favourable moment, I attacked the bombers from below, so that they screened my aircraft from the higher flying fighters. Before they or the bomber pilots were aware of an enemy in their midst two aircraft were falling in flames. The remaining machines, thinking they were being attacked by a large number of aircraft, scattered all over the sky, and by the time that the Ratas reacted it was too late. The invisible enemy, of which they had seen neither the arrival nor departure, had already gone.

Daring, coupled with marksmanship and impeccable timing, had paid off for Morato. During the war he flew 511 sorties and engaged in 56 combats for his 40 victories. This gives a strike rate of one victory every 1.4 combats – good by any standards. His death, like that of so many aces, was the result of unnecessary stunting barely a week after the end of the war.

The Sino-Japanese Conflict

Twentieth century Japan had much in common with ancient Rome. It had few natural resources, a god-emperor, a militaristic tradition and government, and colonial interests (in Korea and Manchuria). This was an explosive combination which made military expansion inevitable.

A blatantly trumped-up incident in Manchuria in 1931 gave the Japanese a pretext for a war of conquest. At first air power was minimal, but in the Shanghai area on 5 February 1932 Chinese and Japanese aircraft first met in combat. One Chinese fighter was damaged. A second action on 22 February saw American Robert Short shot down in his Boeing 218 biplane by three Nakajima A1Ns (licence-built Gloster Gamecocks). Three days later 18 Japanese fighters tackled five Chinese and claimed three of them. An armistice on 8 May ended the conflict.

Chinese skies remained quiet for the next five years, but on 7 July 1937 an undeclared war flared up, again on a dubious pretext, which lasted for the next eight years. Chinese Curtiss Hawk biplane fighters claimed six Mitsubishi G3M bombers over Shanghai on 14 August. Imperial Japanese Navy A3N biplane carrier fighters proved ineffective, so Mitsubishi A5M monoplanes were rushed to the scene. In a few months they virtually swept the skies clean of Chinese aircraft.

The fledgeling Japanese air arms had a policy of producing highly manoeuvrable fighters to win the dogfight, and all else was secondary to this aim. It has been suggested that Japanese fighters lacked structural strength, but this was untrue: they were stressed for hard combat manoeuvring. Their vulnerability lay in the fact that protection was lacking. Armour for the pilot and the engine, self-sealing for fuel tanks and the provision of radios simply added weight, which in turn reduced manoeuvrability. What need for them if the fighters themselves were too agile to be hit? Another consideration was range/endurance; extra weight reduced this. This thinking presupposed that Japanese pilots, who were very highly trained, would never be surprised. Six years passed before this fallacy was exposed, during which time many Japanese fighter pilots died unnecessarily.

Early in 1938 Russian-built fighters flown by 'volunteer' Russian pilots entered the fray on the side of the Chinese. The resultant fighting led what followed to be dubbed the 'adding machine' war. On 10 April a dozen Nakajima A4N fighters led by Tamiya Teranishi took on about 30 I-15s over Koitoh, claiming 24 destroyed. In a series of six combats, the Japanese claimed 81 victories for just four losses. Just three weeks later, 80 Chinese fighters were intercepted over Hankow by 30 Japanese, who claimed 51 victories for two admitted losses. Claims like these should be treated with a certain amount of caution.

This was overlapped, between May and September 1939, by the Khalkin Gol, or Nomonghan, incident. A border clash caused direct hostilities between Japan and the Soviet Union, during which air combat claims reached ridiculous heights. Japan claimed 1,260 victories, the Russians 660. Both figures were probably inflated by multiple accounting arising from shared victories. Admitted losses were 168 Japanese and 207 Russian. Some idea of Japanese accuracy can be given by their loss breakdown – 96 Type 95 fighters, 18 Type 97 light bombers, six Type 97 heavy bombers, 13 Type 97 reconnaissance aircraft, and 83 other aircraft – a total of 216 and over 28 per cent greater. Another 94 aircraft had suffered varying degrees of damage. In

Fighters of Khalkin Gol

Type	Polikarpov I-153	Polikarpov I-16 Type 17	Nakajima Type 97 (Ki 27)
Span	32ft 0in	29ft 6½in	37ft 1¼in
Length	20ft 0in	16ft 6¼in	24ft 8½in
Height	9ft 3in	8ft 5in	10ft 8in
Loaded wt	4,100lb	3,990lb	3,946lb
Power	1 × Shvetsov M 63R radial rated at 1,100hp	1 × Shvetsov M 25V radial rated at 750hp	1 × Nakajima Ha-1 radial rated at 780hp
Wing area	236 sq ft	161 sq ft	200 sq ft
Wing ldg	17.37lb/sq ft	24.78lb/sq ft	19.73lb/sq ft
Power ldg	0.268hp/lb	0.188hp/lb	0.198hp/lb
Vmax	276mph	264mph	292mph
Climb	n/a	16,400ft/6½min	6,560ft/2.1min
Ceiling	35,107ft	25,920ft	c.27,000ft
Range	559 miles	497 miles	390 miles
Armament	4 × 7.62mm ShKAS	2 × 20mm ShVAK, 2 × 7.62mm ShKAS	2 × 7.7mm Type 89

many ways the terrain was ideal, comprising miles and miles of flat steppe. Many aircraft disabled in combat were thus able to land safely and were later recoverable. The obvious inference is that total losses were approximately equal for both sides.

During the course of the fighting the Soviet Air Force made two innovations. The first was the Polikarpov I-153, which was basically an up-engined I-15 with retractable main gears, which made it, with the Fiat CR.42, the fastest biplane ever to enter service. Soviet I-153 pilots often waited with gear down until they were almost engaged, thus giving the appearance of the I-15, before retracting the gear, opening the throttle, and breaking into their opponents.

The other was the Polikarpov I-16 Type 17, which featured a more powerful engine, 9mm armour protection for the pilot and two 20mm ShVAK cannon, the best aircraft gun in the world of its time. Just one or two hits from the fast-firing ShVAK were enough to assure the destruction of unprotected Japanese fighters. And whereas the Japanese preferred to 'mix it' in the dogfight, the Soviet pilots, notably the I-16 drivers, used dive-and-zoom tactics as pioneered in Spain.

One thing is however certain: the experience of the Japanese pilots led them to clamour for self-sealing tanks and greater hitting power, and also hit-and-run tactics. But the real lessons of the conflict were obscured from the Japanese High Command by the apparent kill/loss ratio. What appeared to work should not be changed, and Japanese fighter pilots soldiered on with their high-powered but vulnerable aeroplanes. The air war continued, but following the entry of Japan into World War II air combat over China became largely a sideshow.

Aces of the Sino-Japanese War

Japanese

14	Iwamoto, Tetsuzo	Plus c.80 in WWII
13¹⁄₃	Kuroiwa, Toshio	
13	Handa, Watari	
13	Koga, Kiyoto	KIFA 15.9.38
12	Tanaka, Kuniyoshi	Plus 5 in WWII
11	Akamatsu, Sadaaki	Plus 16 in WWII
11	Suho, Motonari	Plus 5 in WWII
10	Matsumura, Mamoto	Plus 3 in WWII

The foregoing were all IJN flyers. The leading Army flyer, Tateo Kato, claimed nine. He was shot down over the Bay of Bengal by an RAF Blenheim on 22 May 1942, his final score 18.

Chinese

12	Li, Kwei Tan
11	Liu, Tsui Kan
11	Lo, Chu

Few details are available of Chinese aces; those listed claimed their victories between 1937 and 1945. The first Chinese ace was Yuan Pao Kang, who claimed eight victories between August 1937 and December 1938. At least eight others scored five or more.

Russian

11	Kozachenko, Piotr	Plus more in WWII; KIA Apr. 1945
8	Suprun, Stepan	Plus 6–7 in WWII; KIA 4.7.41

Japanese (at Khalkin Gol)

58	Shinohara, Hiromichi	KIA 27.8.39.
28	Tarui, Mitsuyoshi	Plus 10 in WWII; KIA 1944
27	Shimada, Kenjii	KIA 15.9.39.
25	Hanada, Tomio	KIFA 7.10.39.
25	Saito, Shogo	
23	Kato, Shoji	KIFA 1941
22	Togo, Saburo	
22	Ohtsaka, Zenzaburo	
22	Asano, Hitoshi	

21	Hosono, Isamu	Plus 6 in WWII
21	Saito, Chiyojii	Plus 7 in WWII
20	Furugori, Goro	Plus 5 in WWII
20	Iwahashi, Jozo	Plus 2 in WWII
20	Yoshiyama, Bunji	KIA

Another 36 Japanese fighter pilots are credited with becoming aces in the Khalkin Gol incident, but even those listed total more than the admitted Soviet losses.

Russian (at Khalkin Gol)
Unlike the Japanese, whose claims certainly appear to be wildly inflated, few Russians became aces at Khalkin Gol. While this seems to indicate a Japanese victory, it could also be that with Stalin's mad purges in full swing, and a political commissar with each unit, few wished to draw attention to themselves.

| 12 | Kravchenko, Grigoriy | Plus 3 in China; KIA 22.2.43. |
| 6 | Vorozheikin, Arseniy | Plus 46 in WWII |

The Winter War

By November 1939, World War II was under way. Poland had been overrun by Germany from the west and the Soviet Union from the east, while Britain and France faced the Third Reich state from behind the Maginot Line. Despite his pact with Hitler, Stalin distrusted the Nazi leader. Concerned about the vulnerability of Leningrad (currently St Petersburg), he tried to negotiate the cession of Finnish territory. Negotiation having failed, Stalin resorted to muscular politics and sent in the Red Army.

It was a David-versus-Goliath contest, which could only have one outcome. The Soviets reckoned it would last no longer than twelve days, but in the event it was 105 before Finland finally capitulated to overwhelming force. In part this was due to over-confidence on the part of the Soviet High Command, which totally underrated its opponents. In the air, Soviet bomber formations usually flew unescorted, which eased matters for the defenders.

The Finnish fighter force was initially equipped with the Dutch-built Fokker D.XXI. A monoplane with a fixed undercarriage, this was powered by a Bristol Mercury radial engine rated at 840hp, which gave it a top speed of 286mph and a time of 1.45 minutes to 3,281ft. Wing loading was high for the time at 27.64lb/sq ft, while its armament of four 7.7mm Browning machine guns was adequate against unarmoured Russian bombers. Although supplemented late in the conflict by Gloster Gladiator biplanes, some flown by Swedish volunteers, and a handful Fiat G.50s, the D XXI bore the brunt of the air fighting. The Soviet air force fielded I-15s, with I-16s in the later stages of the war.

There were no Soviet aces in the conflict; three pilots were credited with four victories each. Of these, Aleksandr Semyonov and Anatoliy Sokolov, added to their scores later in the war. The top scorer in the Winter War was D XXI pilot Jorma Sarvanto with 12 victories, while another nine Finnish pilots claimed between five and nine. All Sarvanto's victims were bombers – Tupolev SB-2s and Ilyushin DB-3s. On 6 January 1941 he encountered seven of the latter:

> Have I been seen? I carefully edge closer to the formation, selecting the port wingman of the three-plane V as my victim. Four hundred yards . . . three hundred yards . . . safety catch off.
>
> Damn! They have spotted me. A hail of machine gun bullets stabs at my Fokker as she bounces around in the bombers' slipstreams. I sense rather than feel the bullets ripping through my wings. Fifty yards, twenty yards, and I loose a burst from my guns at the DB-3 looming in my sight. My bullets ripple along the Russian bomber's fuselage; it staggers and swings out of formation. A kill!

Braving a storm of return fire, Sarvanto worked his way across the bomber formation, this time firing at the engines, sending down another five. Six victories in less than five minutes! It has however to be admitted that Sarvanto was lucky; his D.XXI was, in his own words, 'riddled with more holes than a Gruyere cheese!' He claimed another four victories in World War II.

Finland joined the fray against the Soviet Union after the German invasion in June 1941 not because the Finns were pro-Hitler but because they wanted to recover the ceded territory from the Soviet Union. The blue swastika carried by Finnish aircraft originated as a good luck emblem, had been formally adopted in 1918, and had no Nazi, or even German, connections.

3. WORLD WAR II

Unlike the Great War, the Second World War was truly a global conflict. Combatant aircraft ranged from Newfoundland eastward to the Urals, from the North Cape and Iceland southwards to Dakar and Madagascar, from Hawaii westwards to Ceylon and from Mongolia southwards to Australia. Britain's participation brought in combatants from the Dominions – Canadians, South Africans, Rhodesians, Indians, Australians, New Zealanders and others, and even former colonials from the United States.

The war was also notable for shifting alliances. France and Britain were allies against Germany until the capitulation in June 1940. While the Free French kept faith, the Vichy government fought against Britain, and later America, until 1943. Then, with the total occupation of their country by the Third Reich, the formerly hostile French forces returned to the Allied camp. Many French flyers baulked at serving with the British for a variety of reasons, including language problems, and headed for Russia, where they served with distinction.

The Soviet Union started out allied to Germany, only to be treacherously attacked in June 1941. Stalin obviously had not read *Mein Kampf*. Although glad to accept aid from the West, the USSR fought what was essentially a private war of survival against Germany and its allies, which included Finland, whose position was made clear in the preceding chapter. Soviet history does not refer to the Second World War: to the Russians the conflict is the Great Patriotic War. Most of Germany's other allies – Romania, Bulgaria, Croatia, Slovakia etc. – turned their coats at a late stage when they realised which way the wind was blowing. Only Hungary remained steadfast to the bitter end.

Mussolini's Italy proved an embarrassing ally to Germany. Initially neutral, *Il Duce* declared war on 10 June 1940, and attacked southern France, Corsica and Tunisia. This left the Italians confronting the British in North and East Africa, leading to a series of defeats. The invasion of Greece in

October 1940 fared no better, as Britain rushed in reinforcements. In both Greece and North Africa, Hitler was forced to intervene, resulting in a drain on his forces. With Mussolini's downfall in 1943 the *Regia Aeronautica* was divided against itself. Part formed the Co-Belligerent Air Force supporting the Allies, while the *Republica Sociale Italiana* (RSI) continued the war on the side of the Third Reich.

Spain's neutrality proved critical for the Allies. The Spanish provided a contingent against the Soviet Union, regarded as hostile since the Civil War, but took no action to recover Gibraltar, which would have closed the Mediterranean to the British fleet. Portugal, though also neutral, allowed the Allies to use airfields in the Azores under a treaty of alliance with Britain dated 1386!

The underlying causes of World War II were primarily economic. Hitler had revitalised a shaky German economy with a massive programme of rearmament, and a defeated German people with an equally massive injection of patriotism. The former could be paid for by pillaging defeated nations; victory would restore national self-respect. The cause was Hitler's demand for *Lebensraum*. What was not foreseen was that Britain and France would intervene. Italy was a different matter. Mussolini saw himself as heir to the Caesars, and fed his dream of a New Roman Empire by adventurism in Africa and the Balkans.

Japanese conquests in Manchuria and China were detrimental to British and American interests in that area. When in June 1941, with the reluctant compliance of the Vichy French, Japan occupied French Indo-China, Britain and the United States reacted by freezing Japanese assets and placing an embargo on oil supplies. War became inevitable.

Japanese strategy was simple. She was already in possession of several groups of islands in the Pacific, and her fleet was slightly larger than that of the combined British, American and Dutch naval forces in the area. More importantly, Japan had a ten-to-three advantage in aircraft carriers. Holding a central position, and with superiority in naval and land-based air power, she struck in several directions at once.

The surprise attack on Pearl Harbor in December 1941 nearly paralysed the American Pacific fleet, although it missed the US Navy's carriers, which were at sea. This was followed by simultaneous landings in the Philippines and Malaya, to neutralise Allied bases at Manila and Singapore. Further advances were implemented over the next few months, the Japanese establishing a defensive perimeter of Pacific islands, capturing the oilfields in the

East Indies, threatening Australia and swarming up through Thailand and Burma to the very gates of India. It was the Japanese hope that the US would be daunted by the magnitude of the task of expelling them, and would eventually accept a *fait accompli*, while the British had their hands full closer to home. It was a vain hope.

War in Western Europe, 1939–43

Germany invaded Poland on 1 September 1939. The Polish Air Force was small and ill-equipped, and in a matter of days it was swept from the skies by greater numbers, superior tactics and better aircraft. The top scorer in the conflict was the German Hannes Gentzen with seven victories. He was killed over France on 26 May 1940, having added another 11 to his total. He was closely followed by the Pole Stanislaw Skalski with six. This was a truly remarkable performance for a pilot flying the slow and lightly-armed PZL P-11c, even though none of his victims were fighters. Skalski escaped from Poland, joined the RAF and survived the war with 21 victories.

Britain and France immediately declared war on Germany, but were unable to take effective action. For months, both sides sat tight behind their respective borders, with occasional bitter clashes in the air. British attempts to strangle the German war machine by interdicting its supply of Swedish iron ore ended in April 1940, when Germany occupied Denmark and Norway.

On 10 May 1940 German troops violated Dutch and Belgian neutrality and, spearheaded by the *Luftwaffe*, stormed into France. The Dutch and Belgian air forces were quickly overrun and destroyed on the ground. The *Luftwaffe* held the initiative, forcing the hard-pressed British and French fighters to dance to their tune. The Allies were outclassed. *Luftwaffe* fighter tactics and formations, honed in the Spanish Civil War, were superior. The French had made little tactical progress since 1918, while the British had trained for an altogether different task – to repel mass attacks by unescorted bombers. Moreover, the RAF Hurricanes and *Armée de l'Air* Morane Saulnier MS.406s, Curtiss Hawk 75s and Dewoitine D.520s were in many ways inferior to the latest Messerschmitt Bf 109Es.

On the ground there was no static front; the *Luftwaffe* blasted holes through which the fast-moving *Panzers* poured. In this period was born the adage 'the ultimate in air superiority is a tank in the middle of the runway!' British and French squadrons were constantly at risk of being overrun on the ground. They were pushed ever westwards, with poor or non-existent communications, and confusion reigned and fighting effectiveness fell. On 25 June France capitulated.

The top scorer in France was *Luftwaffe* ace Werner Mölders with 25 to add to his 14 in Spain, although he was shot down and taken prisoner on 5 June. He was closely followed by Wilhelm Balthasar with 23, all of which were scored after 10 May. Balthasar had previously scored seven in Spain. Neither survived the war: Mölders was killed in a flying accident in November 1941, his total 115, and Balthasar was shot down by Spitfires on 3 July 1941, his final score 31.

The top scorer for the RAF in France was New Zealander 'Cobber' Kain with 16 victories. He was killed in a flying accident in France on 6 June 1940. Close behind Kain was 'Fanny' Orton with 15 victories. Shot down and badly burnt in France, Orton returned to the fray, added two more to his score, but was shot down and killed on 17 September 1941. Of the leading RAF aces in France, only Frank Carey (13 victories) survived the war. His final total of 25 included seven Japanese.

French scores of this period often include shared victories, so absolute totals are a little suspect. For example, Edmond Marin la Meslée was credited with 16 victories, of which 12 were shared. Camille Plubeau and Michel Dorance are both credited with 14. One of the more unusual characters was Pierre Le Gloan. He claimed three shared victories flying the MS.406; he converted to the D.520 in time to take on the Italians in June 1940, against whom he claimed another seven victories, some of which were shared. Posted to Syria in 1941, he claimed four RAF Hurricanes and a Gladiator. Flying a P-39 Airacobra with the Allies in 1943, Le Gloan was killed in a landing accident in September.

Bloody but unbowed, the RAF now faced the *Luftwaffe* across the narrow sea. They were heavily outnumbered, but the fighting was at last on their terms. Their bases were secure from the *Panzers*, while a finely honed detection and fighter control system based on radar deprived the enemy of the advantage of surprise. Finally the best RAF fighter, the Spitfire, was available in quantity.

The events of the summer of 1940 marked a turning point. The all-conquering *Luftwaffe* failed to gain air superiority, without which invasion was impossible. It was defeated by a combination of excellent detection and control, determined pilots and good aircraft.

The *Experten* outscored their RAF opponents during the Battle of Britain. Between July 1940 and the end of the year Adolf Galland claimed 45 victories to add to his 13 in France. Close behind was Helmut Wick, who scored his 42nd victory over England on 28 November, moments before he himself was shot down and killed. Hans-Karl Mayer added 33 to his French score before he was killed in action on 17 November, while Werner Mölders, who was wounded on 28 July and out of action for several weeks, trailed with 31. Wilhelm Balthasar, the top scorer during the *Blitzkrieg* period in France, found victories over England more difficult. He added just nine more before being wounded and put out of the battle on 4 September.

During the period 1 July and 31 October 1940 the RAF top-scorer was Spitfire pilot Eric 'Sawn-Off' Lock, with 21. He was posted missing while strafing near Calais on 3 August 1941, his final score 26. Second was Hurricane pilot James 'Ginger' Lacey with 18 to add to his five in France. He survived the war with a total of 28, including one Japanese. Equal third with 17 were Archie McKellar, who was killed in action on 1 November, and Czech Josef Frantisek, who died in a landing accident on 8 October. Another 15 RAF pilots reached double figures.

The discrepancy in scores is not hard to understand. The *Jadgflieger* usually had numerical superiority, altitude and positional advantages, in addition to a superior tactical system. Also the British fighters were instructed to concentrate on the bombers, ignoring the German fighters if possible. But, with all these advantages, the *Jagdflieger* signally failed adequately to protect their own bombers, which paid a very heavy price.

The daylight assault on Britain quietly fizzled out and was replaced by the night Blitz. At first the defenders were all but helpless, but the introduction of a radar-equipped night fighter of adequate performance gradually turned the tide. By May 1941 German bomber losses were rising steeply. However, at this point most *Luftwaffe* units moved east for the invasion of the Soviet Union.

When in 1941 it became obvious that the *Luftwaffe* was not about to renew its daylight onslaught on Britain, the RAF took the offensive, cautiously at first, then at an ever-increasing tempo. During 1940 they had experimented with wings of between two and five squadrons, in order to counter the German *Gruppen*. This arrangement was now formalised with wings of three squadrons each commanded by a proven fighter leader. Attempts were made to evolve a tactical system to match that of the *Jagdflieger*, though many months passed before this succeeded.

The main RAF operation was the Circus, typically eight wings amounting to nearly 300 fighters, with a handful of bombers in the middle as bait to draw up the *Jagdflieger*. The outnumbered German fighters either nibbled at the edges of this huge swarm, or tried fast plunges through it from a high perch. Either way, they had rather the best of things, with a victory/loss ratio which often exceeded 3:1. The perennial bogey of overclaiming, which was exacerbated by the confusion factor caused by the vast number of RAF fighters milling around in a small area of sky, largely concealed this from the British, which served to keep their morale high. Believing that one is winning is far better than knowing that one is losing!

A massive Circus approaching at high level could be seen from miles away by radar, and the *Jagdflieger* were able to take off and gain altitude, then jockey for position before attacking. This was just one advantage. Another was that whereas a high proportion of German pilots were veterans, an equally high proportion of RAF pilots were novices. With the massive expansion of Fighter Command, allied to the fact that the RAF tended to rest its veterans, this was inevitable. But it created a target-rich environment for the *Experten*.

In war, nothing stands still for long. What was one day a superb fighter might be outclassed three months later. During 1941 the RAF started to phase out the Hurricane and introduce the far more potent cannon-armed Spitfire V. The *Jagdflieger* switched to the Messerschmitt Bf 109F and before long the G model. Then in September, the Focke-Wulf FW 190A made its combat début. Designed as a rough and tough cavalry horse, it completely outclassed the Spitfire V, although it was not available in sufficient numbers to make a significant difference until the spring of 1942. The Spitfire IX, which was basically a Mk V with a more powerful engine, was rushed into service to counter it in July 1942.

August 1942 saw two major events. The first was the combat début of USAAF heavy bombers. Initially these stayed within the range of their Spitfire escorts, only later roving further afield unescorted. This, plus the arrival of effective medium bombers, spelt the death knell of the Circus. It was preferable to mount really damaging raids with fighter escort, rather than to pursue what were essentially fighter-versus-fighter encounters.

The second event was the Allied amphibious raid on Dieppe. This was a trial run for the invasion of 1944, and one of its lessons was that an air umbrella over the beach-head was liable to leak. Despite overwhelming numbers, the RAF lost 88 fighters in return for 48 German aircraft, of which only 20 were fighters. But, this apart, the air war was gradually moving the Allied way.

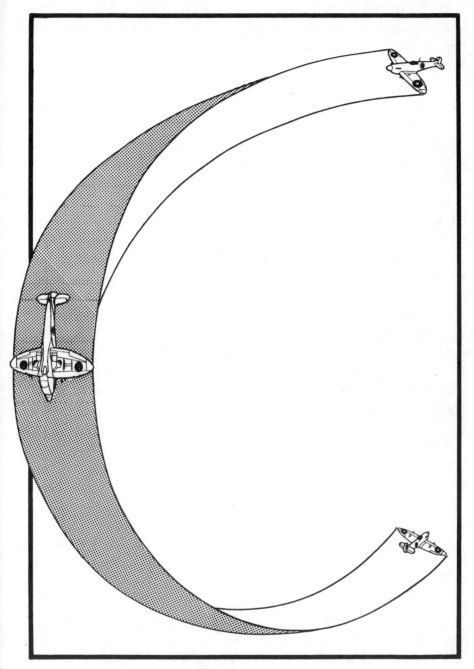

Fig. 9. The Split-S
*In this standard means of evasion the fighter rolled on to its back and pulled
through. Rolling while vertical could bring it out in any desired direction.
The RAF called this the half-roll; the Luftwaffe name was Abschwung.*

During this period the *Experten* again outscored their RAF opponents by a wide margin. Adolf Galland added 35 to his score by 8 November 1941, before being taken off operations. In the same time-span, 'Pips' Priller claimed 38 victories, and another 38 by 13 April 1943. But the price was high. Gustav Sprick (31 victories total) was killed on 28 June 1941; so was Balthasar (40) on 3 July of that year. Fast-scoring Walter Adolph claimed 28 victories in just 79 sorties, but went down on 18 September 1941. Another novice, Galland''s younger brother 'Wutz', claimed 55 victories between 27 July 1941 and his death in action in August 1943. But these were the exceptions: the Western Front did not lend itself to the survival of tyros.

RAF Circuses were a far cry from the defensive operations of 1940. The hit-and-run tactics of the *Jagdflieger* generally gave only fleeting opportunities for shooting, while the huge numbers of RAF fighters employed tended to get in each other's way. New Zealander Al Deere had notched up 13 victories in 1940, but in the second half of 1941 he was only able to claim five damaged.

Of the better-known names, 'Sailor' Malan claimed 13 and three shared victories by 24 July, while Douglas Bader managed eight and another three shared before 9 August, when he was shot down by Max Mayer of *II./JG 26*. It is usually stated that Bader went down following a mid-air collision with a 109 which cut his entire tail off. This can be refuted fairly easily. In flight, the tailplane provides a download which balances the aircraft. Remove this and the aircraft topples end over end. From Bader's own account, we may be sure this didn't happen.

Of the lesser-known aces, Jamie Rankin claimed 15 victories (including Spanish veteran and 18-victory *Experte* Robert Menge), plus six shared, between June and October 1941. Don Kingaby claimed 13 of his eventual total of 21 between February 1941 and March 1943. In the course of two tours between March 1941 and October 1942, Free French pilot Jean-François Demozay shot down 18 *Luftwaffe* aircraft, all except one of them fighters. He flew mainly with No 91 Squadron, operating generally alone and, usually at low level.

The fact that the Spitfire V was outclassed by the superb FW 190A compounded the problems for the RAF. Only one Spitfire V pilot, the Belgian Ivan du Monceau, managed to shoot down five FW 190As, and that took him nine months. One notable novice who started to carve out a reputation at this time was 'Johnnie' Johnson. Flying with the Tangmere Wing under Bader's leadership, he claimed six 109s between 26 June and 21 September

1941. One more victory, an FW 190A, was gained over Dieppe in August 1942. Then as Kenley Wing Leader, flying the Spitfire IX, he accounted for another 14 *Luftwaffe* fighters, 12 of them the formidable FW 190A, plus five shared, between 3 April and 5 September 1943.

The Mediterranean and North Africa, 1940–43

This theatre of operations covers a wide span – Malta, Greece, Syria, East Africa, Egypt and Libya, Tunisia and, finally, Sicily and Italy. The forces involved were British, German, American, Italian, Vichy French, and Greek. By contrast with the Western Front, fighting was small-scale, but bitter for all that. Radar was available, but it played a much smaller part. Information on enemy movements was gathered largely by the radio monitoring services on both sides. Neither, with the exception of Malta, was strategic bombing a significant factor.

The entry of Italy into the war on 10 June 1940, although specifically aimed against France and her colonies in North Africa, automatically meant confrontation with the RAF, in East Africa, on the Egyptian/Libyan border, over Malta and, the following year, on the Greek/Albanian border. The defence of Malta had certain similarities with the Western Front; all other areas involved operations to support ground forces.

For the British, the RAF in the theatre was a poor relation. The fighters available were those not required for the Western Front – Gladiator biplanes, Curtiss P-40 Tomahawks and Kittyhawks,Hurricanes when they could be spared and, only later, Spitfires.

At first this was no great problem. The *Regia Aeronautica* fielded Fiat CR.32s of Spanish Civil War vintage, and the rather better Fiat CR.42 *Falco* biplanes. The Fiat G.50 *Freccia* monoplane entered service at the end of 1940, the far better Macchi MC.200 *Saetta* in July 1941. Not until the superb Daimler-Benz-powered Macchi MC.202 *Folgore* entered service in December 1941 did the Italians have a really modern fighter at their disposal.

The *Regia Aeronautica* had learnt little or nothing from the Spanish Civil War. They flew in tight vics of three, believed in manoeuvrability rather than performance, and put too much faith in aerobatics. This did not, however, prevent a few pilots from doing very well. In East Africa, Mario Visentini claimed 16 victories, plus four shared, before he was killed in a flying accident on 13 February 1941. His main rivals in theatre were South Africans Ken Driver with nine and Jack Frost with eight and one shared.

105

Both flew Hurricanes. Driver was eventually shot down by *Experte* Ludwig Franzisket on 14 June 1941 and made prisoner, having added one to his score. Frost was shot down and killed by Bf 109s on 16 June 1942, his total 14 and two shared, plus 23 destroyed on the ground.

The Italian top-scorer of the war was Adriano Visconti, credited with 26 victories, seven of which were scored after the armistice with the *Aeronautica Nazionale Repubblicana*. He claimed one over the Western Desert, four over Malta and another 14 over Tunisia and Sicily. He was murdered by partisans on 29 April 1945. Next in order came Teresio Martinoli with 23, ten scored over Malta and one while flying with the Co-Belligerent Air Force. He died in a flying accident in August 1944. Spanish veteran Franco Lucchini added 21 to his five victories over Spain. Flying the Macchi MC.202, he claimed at least 16 victories and several shares over Libya, but was shot down and killed over Sicily on 5 July 1943. Leonardo Ferrulli was lost over Sicily on the same day as Lucchini, his final score 22, including one in Spain. The surviving Italian top-scorer was Franco Bordoni-Bisleri, with 19 victories with CR.42s and MC.202s. Twelve were over Libya and the final seven were American bombers. The top-scoring Fiat G.50 pilot was Furio Lauri, who had claimed 11 by the end of 1941. His final score was approximately 18. The top scorers for the ANR were Ugo Drago and Mario Bellagambi – both of whom flew Bf 109Gs – with 11 apiece. Drago had five previous victories, Bellagambi two.

Most RAF fighter pilots in the Mediterranean theatre flew extensively against both Germans and Italians. Top scorer South African 'Pat' Pattle has been unofficially credited with about 50 victories. The area of uncertainty lies in the loss of squadron records for April 1941, during which time he appears to have accounted for no fewer than 25 enemy aircraft, most of them German, before being shot down and killed by a Bf 110 over Eleusis Bay. In total, 26 victims were Italian; 15 were downed with Gladiator bi-planes, the rest with Hurricanes. Other pilots who did well against the Italians include Australian 'Ape' Cullen with 15, six of them with Gladiators, before he was shot down by Fiat G.50s and killed on 4 March 1941. Hurri-cane pilot 'Imshi' Mason claimed 13 Italian victims out of his total of 15 victories. The other two were a Bf 109E, and uniquely, an Iranian Hawker Nisr. He was shot down by *Experte* Otto Schulz on 15 February 1942. 'Cherry' Vale claimed 12 Italians in his total of 30. Of his 15 *Luftwaffe* victims, seven were scored during the defence of Crete; the final three were Vichy French off the coast of Syria on 11/12 June 1941. He survived the war. Malta top-scorer 'Screwball' Beurling included nine Italians in his tally of 26 over the island. He also survived the war, with a total of 31 victories.

German intervention in the Mediterranean theatre arose from Italian military disasters. East Africa was indefensible anyway, while British forces in Greece posed a threat to the German right flank for the proposed invasion of the Soviet Union. But the loss of Libya might have taken Italy out of the war, opening up Allied supply routes to and from the Far East. The critical spot was Malta, the unsinkable aircraft carrier and naval base, which dominated Italian supply routes to North Africa.

Germany reinforced the Italians in the spring of 1941. This resulted in the occupation of Greece, taking in Yugoslavia *en route*, the partial neutralisation of Malta and a switch to the offensive in the Western Desert. Had the airborne forces used to capture Crete that spring been launched against Malta, the whole course of the war might have been different. But this was not to be. Malta was not invaded. The island endured a horrific aerial siege and bombardment, but survived as a perpetual thorn in the Axis side.

Desert operations were largely influenced by the status of Malta. When the island was swamped by overwhelming air power, supplies reached North Africa and the Axis took the offensive. As soon as the pressure eased, Allied air and naval assets built up on the island, supply routes were interdicted and the Axis forces were driven back. Outside forces were also at work. Events in the Soviet Union determined what could be spared at any one time. The harassed *Luftwaffe* was used as a fire brigade, sent to fly on the Eastern Front one month and rushed back to Sicily or Libya the next. Air power see-sawed from one to the other.

The air defence of Malta was a fight at odds. Short of aircraft, fuel, ammunition, and spares, the RAF still had a surplus of pilots. This was mainly because it took one pilot to bring one fighter to the island, but fighters proved less durable than pilots, who flew infrequently but were heavily outnumbered when they did. Perhaps the ultimate case of being outnumbered arose in the summer of 1942. American ace Reade Tilley recalled:

Every morning the Germans sent over a reconnaissance machine, escorted by two 109s. If we could spare the Spitfires (and we often couldn't) we would send up a pair to intercept. The job of the 109s was to protect the recce machine, so they couldn't be really aggressive. That meant we could tease them a little.

On this particular day, I was flying with Tiger Booth. We sneaked in astern of the Germans, but suddenly realised that four more were coming in behind us! And four more, and four more after that! The sky was full of 109s; must have been near a hundred of them rascals. We spent all our time evading. How we got back in one piece was a miracle.

I checked with Macky Steinhoff [postwar *Luftwaffe* chief, with 176 victories in World War II) after the war. Turns out one of their aces, Günther *Freiherr* von Maltzahn [13 victories over Malta, 68 total; *Kommodore JG 53*] was missing over the sea, and the whole *Geschwader* had turned out to look for him. And we blundered right into the lot of 'em!

The first high-scoring ace over Malta was Bf 109E pilot Joachim Müncheberg, who arrived in Sicily at the head of *7./JG 26* in February 1941, credited with 23 victories over Germany, France and Britain. With the advantages of altitude and position, and using dive-and-zoom tactics, his *Staffel* cut a deadly swathe through the defending Hurricanes. By late May it had claimed 41 victories, of which Müncheberg had accounted for 18. At this point *7./JG 26* departed for North Africa, then Western Europe. They did not return until December, by which time Malta had recovered.

Jagdflieger top-scorer over Malta was Gerhard Michalski with 26 (of a final total of 73). Close behind was Siegfried Freytag with 25 out of 102. Six other *Experten* recorded double figures. For once, the RAF top-scorer matched that of the *Luftwaffe*: 'Screwball' Beurling was also credited with 26. Eight more Spitfire pilots reached double figures. The top-scoring Hurricane pilot was Fred Robertson with 10 out of 11 between November 1940 and 23 March 1941. The leading night fighter pilot over Malta was Moose Fumerton, who flew Beaufighters, with nine (out of 14).

Whereas air operations over Malta were primarily defensive, in the desert they were mainly tactical. One effect of this was that the altitude performance of the Bf 109 was largely negated; most fighting took place at medium and low level, which was to the benefit of the Hurricane, Tomahawk and Kittyhawk. For tactical operations British fighters frequently had bombs hung on them, the weight and drag of which reduced performance and manoeuvrability, making them vulnerable when intercepted.

Coincident with the Battle of El Alamein, an Anglo-American force landed at the western end of North Africa (Operation 'Torch'). Vichy French resistance was quickly overcome, leaving the Axis forces between the hammer and the anvil. The end was just a matter of time.

Jochen Marseille arrived in the desert with a score of seven, which had cost him four aircraft to achieve, and a history of insubordination. His début was unimpressive: on 23 April 1941 he became the seventh victim of a small and elderly (35-year-old) Hurricane pilot, Free Frenchman James Denis, who survived the war with a score of eight victories and one shared.

Marseille survived the subsequent crash-landing and went on to record a total of 158 victories, a record against Western-flown aircraft. In the desert it consisted of 101 P-40s, 30 Hurricanes, 16 Spitfires, and four twin-engine bombers. At the height of his powers he expended an average of just 15 cannon shells and bullets per victory. He died on 30 September 1942 when his parachute failed to open after baling out of his burning Bf 109G after engine failure.

Werner Schroer, with 61 victories in North Africa out of a total of 114 and a tactical imitator of Marseille, had an even faster strike rate. He survived the war. Other high-scoring *Experten* in the theatre were 'Fifi' Stahlschmidt with 59, killed on 7 September 1942; Gustav Rödel, 52 out of 98; Gerhard Homüth, 46 out of 63, missing over Orel on 3 August 1943; Otto Schulz, 42 out of 51, killed on 17 June 1942; Kurt Bühligen, 40 out of 112; and Günther Steinhausen, also with 40, killed on 6 September 1942. Other major *Experten* who went down over North Africa were Müncheberg, who collided with his 135th and final victim over Tunisia on 23 March 1943; Wolfgang Tonne (122 total), killed on active service over Tunis on 20 April 1943; and Wilhelm Crinius (114), taken prisoner in Tunisia on 13 January 1943.

While the British fighters in North Africa were generally better than those of the Italians, for the most part they were inferior to those of the Germans. This, combined with a numerical advantage, an inferior tactical system and the fact that many British and Commonwealth single-seaters were used as bomb trucks, explains in part why the *Experten* handily outscored the West. Another reason was the level of combat experience: a high proportion of the *Jagdflieger* posted to Africa were veterans, whereas many of their opponents were novices. The Spitfire V was offset to a degree by the FW 190A, and only when the Spitfire IX finally arrived, were the Allies able to fight on something approaching level terms. The USAAF in Algeria and Tunisia flew Spitfire Vs, P-38 Lightnings, P-39 Airacobras and P-40E Warhawks, none of which were a match for the FW 190A or Bf 109G in close combat. A few pilots managed to beat the odds. Hamish Dodds claimed 14 destroyed between 1 December 1941 and 17 June 1942. Six of these were Bf 109s and four were MC.202s. This was a remarkable feat in the Hurricane II. Texan Lance Wade scored 20 and two shared, twelve of them while flying Hurricanes and eight in Spitfires. Two more victories over Italy brought his total to 22 before he was killed in a flying accident in November 1943.

Australian 'Killer' Caldwell was the top-scoring Tomahawk pilot with 16, eight of which were 109s. He went on to claim four more victories in the Kittyhawk, then in 1943 he was sent home to fly Spitfires against the Japanese, adding a further eight to bring his total to 27, plus three shared. Three *Experten* were among his victims: Wolfgang Lippert (54 victories) was taken prisoner, Erbo von Kageneck was killed, but 'Fifi' Stahlschmidt crash-landed and lived to fight again.

Billy Drake, a veteran of France, arrived in North Africa credited with four victories, one of which was a Vichy French M-167 off Sierra Leone. Between June and December 1942 he flew Kittyhawks and was credited with 13 victories; he was the top scorer on the type, while his war total of 18 may well have been higher. Canadian Eddie Edwards claimed 12 of his eventual 15 victories, one of whom was leading *Experte* Otto Schulz, with the Kittyhawk. The highest-scoring Spitfire pilot in North Africa was Neville Duke. He arrived in the desert with two victories on the Western Front. Flying Tomahawks and Kittyhawks, he added a further four and three shared between 21 November 1941 and 14 February 1942, although he was shot down twice, once by *Experte* Otto Schulz. After a rest, he flew Spitfires over Tunisia and increased his score to 20 by 16 April 1943. Further victories over Italy brought his final total to 26 and two shared. After the war he became a noted test pilot and, briefly, the holder of the World Air Speed Record.

At least 16 other RAF pilots scored five or more victories by day during the Italian campaign, mainly in the early months. But, as the war progressed, opportunities became increasingly scarce. The RAF's top-scorer by day over Italy was New Zealander 'Rosie' Mackie, who claimed nine victories between 4 July 1943 and 2 February 1944. He had previously scored six over Tunisia, then, flying Tempests over Northern Europe in the final months of the war, he brought his total to 20.

USAAF fighter pilots outscored their RAF counterparts over Italy. Opportunity was the key: bombing raids drew Axis fighters like a magnet, and escort duty was a fairly sure way to see some action. Furthermore, the long range of the American fighters enabled them to make deep penetrations, looking for trouble on their own account.

The top scorer for the Fifteenth Air Force was Mustang pilot John Voll, who claimed 21 victories between June and November 1944. In second place was Herschel Green with 18, scored with Warhawks, Thunderbolts and Mustangs. On 30 January 1944 he accounted for four Ju 52s, a Do 217 and a Bf

109G. James Varnell claimed 17 entirely with the Thunderbolt, but he was killed in a flying accident in April 1945. A dozen others reached double figures.

At the other extreme is the case of Mustang driver William Coloney, who flew a complete tour of operations in Italy from mid-1944. Although he ranged as far afield as Romania, Bavaria, and southern France, he never once saw an enemy aircraft in the air! His experience was far from unique – he was one of hundreds.

Battle over the Reich, 1943-45

Daylight raids by unescorted RAF bombers in the first months of the war had proved disastrous, but in 1942 the USAAF's doctrine of daylight precision bombing was a holy cow; they had to try. It was considered that the unprecedentedly heavily armed B-17 Flying Fortress, which bristled with 0.50-calibre machine guns, would, flying in tight formation, be able to beat off fighter attacks.

Insofar as the traditional fighter attack from astern went, this thinking was partially correct. The *Jagdflieger* soon found that they were far too vulnerable to massed cross-fire, and switched their attack to head-on. Given the brief firing time this allowed, it was difficult to destroy a B-17 in one pass but relatively easy to knock it out of formation, where it could be dealt with later.

It soon became obvious to the USAAF that only escort fighters could redress the balance. But what? The Spitfire was demonstrably too short-legged; the Thunderbolt was not a lot better, although a large drop tank allowed it to reach the German border, and still later to reach into Germany. The bombers could be escorted just so far – after that they were on their own.

The crunch came with the Schweinfurt/Regensberg raid of 17 August 1943. The defenders held off until the escorts turned back; then threw everything in. Bomber attrition reached an unacceptable 16 per cent, which was compounded by a similar proportion stranded in North Africa, too badly damaged to return. A repeat raid on 14 October saw bomber attrition reach 20 per cent, while another 47 per cent suffered moderate to severe damage. This was the death-knell for unescorted deep penetration.

The twin-engine Lightning was longer-ranged than the Thunderbolt. It became available during October 1943 but was no match for the *Luftwaffe* single-engine fighters. The problem was finally solved by fitting the P-51

Mustang with a Rolls-Royce engine and a large fuel tank in the fuselage. Available in numbers from the spring of 1944, the Mustang combined the range to roam the length and breadth of the Third Reich with an agility and a performance to match the German defenders.

Like the *Luftwaffe* in 1940, the American fighters found that staying close to the bombers was not the best way to defend them. It was preferable to roam out ahead and on the flanks, to break up the *Jagdwaffe* formations before they could launch an attack.

With the advent of the Mustang, the *Jagdwaffe* were caught on the horns of a dilemma. To deal with the US heavy bombers, they had developed very heavily armed and armoured fighters, able to take punishment and to dish it out. This had been done at the expense of performance and manoeuvrability, making the bomber-destroyers extremely vulnerable to orthodox fighters. Therefore a combination was tried – high performance fighters to fend off the escorts and heavy fighters to deal with the bombers. In practice this proved unworkable: the escorts frequently got among the heavy fighters, with devastating consequences.

The top scorers against the US 'heavies' were Walter Dahl and Georg-Peter Eder, with 36 each, out of totals of 128 and 78 respectively. Herbert Rollwage, frequently quoted as amassing 44 'heavies', appears to have been the victim of a 'typo': recent research indicates just 14 out of 71. At least six *Experten* scored 20 or more, including Anton Hackl, 32 of 192; Egon Mayer, 24 of 102, and the first to score 100 entirely on the Western Front); Heinz Baer, with 21 out of 220;, and Hugo Frey, 21 of 32, who fell to bomber gunners on 6 March 1944.

Many *Experten* fell to American escort fighters during this period – Hans Philipp (206) fell to Thunderbolts on 8 October 1943, Wilhelm Lemke (131) on 4 December, Horst-Günther von Fassong (136) on 1 January 1944, Egon Mayer (102) on 2 March and Kurt Ubben (110) on 27 April. Mustangs accounted for 'Fürst' Wilcke (162) on 23 March and Josef Zwernemannn (126) on 8 April, while Lightnings cornered Walter Oesau (123) over the Eifel on 5 May 1944. 'Tutti' Müller (140) fell on 29 May.

For the USAAF, nine pilots scored 20 or more in this period. Leading the field were Thunderbolt pilots 'Gabby' Gabreski and Bob Johnson with 28 apiece. Gabreski ended up in prison camp after touching the ground while strafing on 20 July 1944. In Korea he added six MiG-15s to his tally. Johnson, who flew just 91 sorties, was badly shot up by *Experte* Egon Mayer on 22 June 1944 and barely managed to limp home. In third place was 'Ratsy'

Preddy (25), who was shot down and killed by 'friendly' ground fire over the Ardennes on 25 December 1944.

Desperate times demand desperate measures, and in an effort to stem the endless flow of American heavy bombers the *Jagdwaffe* rushed two radically new fighters into service. The Messerschmitt Me 163 was a rocket-powered point-defence interceptor which achieved little. Its volatile fuels frequently resulted in explosions and it killed more of its own pilots than those of the enemy. So far as is known, there were no German rocket aces. Far better was the twin-jet Messerschmitt Me 262. Its overwhelming speed allowed it to penetrate the American fighter screen with ease, but once there an overtaking speed of more than 300mph gave little time to aim and fire at the bombers. But however good its performance, it was not enough. The Me 262 was ground down by overwhelming numbers.

Approximately 25 pilots became jet aces with the Me 262, of whom six reached double figures. The leading jet ace was Heinz Baer with 16, a figure not exceeded until the Korean War. Next was Franz Schall with 14, followed by Hermann Buchner, Georg-Peter Eder and Erich Rudorfer with 12 apiece.

The Western Front, 1943–45

Allied fighter operations on the Western Front in the second half of the war showed a distinct change in policy. Initially they had been little more than an attempt to obtain the moral ascendancy. By the end of 1943, however, with the invasion of Normandy in the offing, the ever higher trend had largely been reversed. The immediate task for air power was to soften up the Germans' defences and interdict their lines of communication and supply prior to the invasion. Once the invasion had begun and the opposing armies were locked in battle, close air support took priority.

With the enormous increase in Allied air strength, a high proportion of fighter squadrons were converted to the fighter-bomber role, while medium bomber units flew at altitudes where a reasonable combination of high accuracy and modest attrition were expected. From the verge of the stratosphere, the battle for air superiority descended to lower levels.

The *Jagdgeschwader* on the Western Front had never been more than a holding force; even when reinforced from the East, they were completely swamped. Four *Experten*, Weber (136 victories), Zweigart (69), Huppertz (68) and Simsch (54), were lost in the first three days of the invasion. And still the drain continued: Wurmheller (102) went down on 22 June, Fönnekold

(136) followed on 31 August, 'Bully' Lang (173), who had never before been hit in combat, was shot down by Mustang pilot Darrell Kramer on 3 September, while Klaus Mietusch (68) fell to the guns of William Beyer a fortnight later. To make matters worse, the replacements who reached the front were poorly trained and inexperienced. Not even the superb Focke-Wulf FW 190D, which entered service in the autumn of 1944, could redress the balance. It was in any case overmatched in most departments by the new Spitfire XIV and Tempest V.

During this period, established pilots found it difficult to add to their scores, and few new aces were crowned. For the *Jagdflieger* survival was paramount, while the Allies jostled each other for targets. American Mustang pilot John C. Meyer claimed 14 of his eventual total of 23 (plus two shared) between 11 September 1944 and 1 January 1945, but he was exceptional. Six RAF pilots reached double figures. Canadians Don Laubman and Bill Klersey led with 14 and 13 respectively while flying Spitfire IXs. American 'Foob' Fairbanks scored 11 of 12 with the Tempest and 'Johnnie' Johnson added another ten to his already impressive score between 16 June and 28 September 1944.

The Night Air War

Prior to the outbreak of war, night fighters were the poor relations, mainly because night raiding was regarded as posing far less of a threat than daylight operations. For the night bomber, the combination of navigation over unfamiliar blacked-out terrain, target identification and accurate bombing posed almost intractable problems. For the night fighter the problems were even worse. In clear daylight conditions, a fighter pilot could be expected to spot a bomber within a radius of about seven miles, giving a front quadrant search area of about 77 square miles. On a clear moonlit night this reduced to little more than half a mile, shrinking the front quadrant search area to barely half a square mile! On moonless nights, visual distance reduced to 300ft or less.

At the outbreak of war neither the RAF or the *Luftwaffe* had developed a dedicated night fighter and for the early years both services were forced to use day fighters and even modified light bombers. The greatest difficulty was bringing the fighter to a position where the bomber could be acquired visually. Searchlights offered a partial solution, but often the bomber passed out of range of the beam before the fighter could get near.

Victories by 'cat's-eye' fighters were rare, and interceptions were largely fortuitous. Only one pilot regularly beat the odds. Richard Stevens claimed

14 and one shared victory between 15 January and 23 October 1941. His near-suicidal speciality was to fly his Hurricane to where the anti-aircraft fire was thickest, there to search visually. He was lost on an intruder mission over Holland on 15/16 December of that year.

Bombers could of course be tracked from the ground with a reasonable degree of accuracy, and the information passed to a fighter, but this presumed that the fighter knew exactly where it was, which was not often. The answer lay in airborne radar.

Early airborne radars had an effective range of two to four miles. The problem now became how to control a night fighter to where it could gain radar contact. The solution was to track both bomber and fighter from the ground while steering the latter into the classic astern interception position.

All but a few night fighters carried a specialist radar operator. However, gaining contact was one thing, conducting a successful interception something else. It called for teamwork of the highest order, with pilot and operator understanding each other's needs. The top-scoring RAF pilot on defensive operations was John Cunningham with 20 victories between 19/20 November 1940 and 23/24 February 1944, 17 with operator Jimmy Rawnsley.

Like their counterparts by day, the *Nachtjagdflieger* handily outscored their Allied opponents on defensive operations. Again, this was a matter of opportunity. RAF Bomber Command frequently launched raids of several hundred bombers in a single night, thus creating a target-rich environment. Top of the heap was Heinz-Wolfgang Schnaufer with 121 victories, 100 of them gained with radar operator Fritz Rumpelhardt, with whom he developed an almost telepathic understanding. Helmut Lent claimed 102 victories by night, 80 with operator Walter Kubisch, plus eight by day. He was killed in a landing accident on 5 October 1944. Third was Heinrich zu Sayn-Wittgenstein with 83 victories, who fell to a Mosquito on 21 January 1944. At least 63 other *Nachtjagdflieger* claimed 25 or more.

The night air war developed into an electronics battle – countermeasures against radar and counter-countermeasures against the countermeasures. In July 1943 the RAF used 'Window' for the first time, effectively blinding all German radars. As an expedient, 'cat's-eye' fighters were used over the target area, where fires on the ground combined with searchlights to silhouette the bombers from below. This was called *Wilde Sau*.

Wilde Sau pilots initially flew Bf 109Gs and FW 190As 'borrowed' from day fighter units, a fact that led to a certain amount of friction with the host units. But when the summer of 1943 came to an end, adverse weather caused a spate of crashes. They were phased out during the following year. *Wilde Sau* top-scorer was Kurt Welter with 27 out of about 50 victories. Welter went on to claim five night victories with the Me 262, to become the only jet night ace of the war. Friedrich-Karl 'Nasen' Müller – not to be confused with day fighter *Experte* Friedrich-Karl 'Tutti' Müller – claimed 23 *Wilde Sau* victories in his total of 30 at night.

Defensive 'cat's-eye' operations were likened to seeking flies in a dark room. In pre-radar days, there was however one reliable way of finding them. Intruders lurking near the bomber airfields would be assured of a rich harvest – and the airfields could be easily located when the runway flarepaths were switched on.

Between August 1940 and November 1941 *Jagdflieger* intruders claimed 141 victories, although RAF records show rather less. Wilhelm Beier claimed 14 (of 36) victories, Hans Hahn and Alfons Köster 11 each (12 and 29) and Heinz Sommer 10 (of 19). Of these, only Beier survived the war.

The top-scoring RAF intruder pilot was Karel Kuttelwascher. A Czech, he flew with the *Armée de l'Air* in France where he shared two victories, then, with the fall of France, joined the RAF. Flying Hurricanes, he claimed 18 victories between 8 April 1941 and 2 July 1942, 15 of them at night. An area where radar-equipped intruders did very well was Sicily in 1943. A few Beaufighter pilots reached double figures, while Mosquito crew 'Ian' Allan and H. Davidson claimed 13 German and Italian bombers in just 18 nights over Sicily in July 1943. Five of these came in one night. Allan's final score was 14.

One mission for which neither the *Luftwaffe* nor the USAAF had any equivalent was bomber support. As the *Nachtjagflieger* cut a deadly swathe through the RAF bombers, a counter was needed. It duly emerged in the shape of a device which could home on German night fighter radar emissions and was first used on 17/18 August 1943 when a small force of Beaufighters accompanied the bombers. It was intercepted by four Bf 110s of *IV./NJG 1*. Three were shot down, two of them *Experten*: Georg Kraft (15 victories) was killed and Heinz Vinke (final score 54) survived after 18 hours in the sea. Their victor was Bob Braham, who ended the war with a total of 29, 20 of them at night. Nor was he finished with the *Experten*: 53-victory ace August Geiger fell to his guns less than six weeks later.

The British lead in electronic warfare proved decisive. Bomber support Mosquitos roamed the Third Reich, hunting down the *Nachtjagdflieger*, who were forced to take extraordinary measures to survive. The RAF bomber support top-scorer was Branse Burbridge, who with operator Bill Skelton claimed 16 victories over Europe between 14/15 June 1944 and 2/3 January 1945 to add to five on home defence. Their total score of 21, which included *Experte* Wilhelm Herget (72 victories), made Burbridge and Skelton the leading RAF night fighter crew of the war.

Bravely though the *Nachtjagdflieger* fought, they paid a terrible price. No less than 40 per cent of those who claimed 25 or more night victories failed to survive the war.

The Russian Front, 1941-45

Germany attacked the Soviet Union on 22 June 1941 and immediately appeared to have gained a smashing victory. However, air combat on the Russian Front was a paradox from start to finish. The destruction wrought on the Soviet Air Force on the first day of the war – 1,811 aircraft claimed destroyed by Germany; 1,200 losses admitted by the USSR – worked in its favour in the long term. As by far the greatest number of Russian fighters were destroyed on the ground, the pilots survived. This was critical: one of the lessons of World War II was that air forces ran out of fully trained pilots long before they ran out of aircraft. With the vast industrial capacity of the Soviet Union at full bore, pilots were quickly re-equipped with newer and better aircraft.

The rapid German advance into Russia constantly widened the front, with the result that by 1943 there was only one German fighter for every five miles! Not that they were ever spread this thinly: there was concentration in critical areas but vast gaps in others. The success of the advance also caused logistics problems, since, as lines of communication lengthened, supply became ever more difficult and serviceability and efficiency declined.

While the *Experten* set new scoring records which will never be beaten, easy victories made them careless. When Eastern Front *Experten* were transferred to the West, few achieved anything of note, and many fell to British and American fighters quite quickly, including seven who had scored a hundred or more in the East. Of those who fell in the East, 19 had scored a hundred or more victories in the theatre. Fourth-ranking *Experte* Otto Kittel had amassed 267 in the East before he was shot down and killed by an Il-2 attack aircraft on 14 February 1945. Six others passed 150, including Anton Hafner (184 of 204) and Max Stotz (173 of 189). But for every *Experte* who notched up a big score, hundreds of novice pilots were swallowed up in the carnage to no avail.

117

In the later stages of the war, when the Soviets had got their act together, their aces proved a match for anything the *Jagdflieger* could offer. Although initially the Soviet Air Force was completely outclassed, a combination of improved tactics, experienced leaders, better fighters and weight of numbers eventually redressed the balance.

Tactical improvements included the adoption of the pair and four as standard, while Soviet fighters started to fly at full throttle in the battle area. This provided greater energy-manoeuvrability at the start of an encounter; reduced the time taken to intercept and, by increasing the distance/time needed by the *Jagdflieger* to intercept them, reduced the chance of a surprise bounce. Whilst it curtailed combat radius and endurance, in the tactical battles on the Eastern Front neither was a primary consideration. It did nothing for engine wear, but Soviet fighters were built to have a life of just 80 flying hours. Few lasted this long.

Russian fighter pilots in 1941 proved only too ready to ram an opponent when all else failed. Following the example of Nesterov in 1914, about 200 instances of ramming were recorded in 1941. It was not suicidal; often the attacker baled out and survived. Indeed, Boris Kobzan accounted for four *Luftwaffe* aircraft in this manner, which is probably a record. Ramming was, however, only encouraged with the near-obsolete Polikarpov I-16; more modern fighters were too precious in the early stages.

The RAF had two fighter pilots who flew with two artificial legs, the immortal Douglas Bader and the lesser-known Colin Hodgkinson. Their Soviet equivalents were Alexei Marase'ev and Zakhor Sarokin. Sarokin returned to the front after losing both legs in a crash, and brought his score to 18.

Marase'ev's story was an epic of endurance. Shot down in April 1942 by Bf 109s, his fighter hit some trees and broke up. Miraculously still alive, but with both legs broken, he was then approached by a bear, which he shot with his service pistol. Far behind German lines, he limped eastwards through the snow, using an improvised crutch. After a week Alexei was reduced to crawling. He survived by eating berries, raw hedgehog and ants. After nineteen days he fell in with partisans, who arranged for him to be flown out. Even then his troubles were not over. Gangrene had set in, and both feet were amputated. Fitted with artificial feet, he flew again, and returned to the front in June 1943, where he brought his tally to 19. He survived the war to become an instructor at the Soviet Air Force Academy.

At the outset, the main Soviet fighter was the I-16 Type 24. Outperformed by the Bf 109F, it was, however, more agile, and with two 20mm ShVAK cannon – which had more than double the rate of fire, a muzzle velocity 50 per cent greater and a heavier projectile than the German 20mm MG FF – it could still prove a formidable opponent. A standard ploy was to wait until the Messerschmitts were committed to attack, then turn rapidly through 180 degrees for a head-on pass. This was not to the advantage of the *Jagdflieger*, although the fact that many I-16s carried a painted circle on the windshield in lieu of a proper gunsight, made them less effective than might otherwise have been the case. The top scorer on the I-16 was Mikhail Vasiliev with 22 victories; he was shot down and killed on 5 May 1942.

As the war progressed, more modern Soviet fighters entered service. Some were imported – Hurricanes, Spitfires, Curtiss P-40s etc. A few pilots did well with the Bell P-39 Airacobra, a fighter that had not shone in the West. Of indigenous products, the best were the Lavochkin La-5, La-5FN and La-7, and the Yakovlev Yak-3 and Yak-9. Although undergunned by Western standards, they matched the Bf 109G and FW 190A.

Air combat on the Eastern Front was almost entirely tactical in nature and generally fought at medium or low altitudes. To a degree this negated the performance advantages of the Bf 109. The Germans had a few mobile radar sets, the Russians none, but radar played little part in early warning. Observation posts in or near the front line provided tactical information. In the clear air and dry steppes of Russia in summer, fighters taking off kicked up large clouds of dust. In some cases Soviet air units, notably the French-manned Normandie-Niemen Regiment, were based so close to the front that they could see the dust clouds on the horizon and know that it was time to take off!

The first eighteen months of the war were a happy time for the *Experten*. Werner Mölders reached his century on 15 July 1941, the first pilot ever to do so. He was followed by Günther Lützow on 24 October and Walter Oesau on 26 October. It became a contest. Gordon Gollob reached 150 victories on 29 August 1942, Hermann Graf passed 200 on 2 October and Walter Nowotny attained 250 on 14 October 1943, by which time the tide of battle had turned and the Germans had begun their long retreat. Gerd Barkhorn reached 300 late in 1944, while Erich Hartmann ended the war with a tally of 352. Just one of the lower scorers deserves special mention. Günther Scheel made his combat début in the spring of 1943, claimed 71 victories in just 70 sorties, and was killed on 16 July when he collided with a Yak-9 near Orel. A few established *Experten* went through spells where they exceeded Scheel's strike rate, but none even approached it over a similar period. In all, fifteen *Experten* claimed 200 or more victories. Of these only two, Erich Rudorffer (222, 136 in the East) and Heinz Baer (220, 79 in the East), ran up high scores in the West.

What of their opponents? The official Soviet ace of aces was Ivan Kozhedub, who was credited with 62 victories, although there have been persistent rumours that one pilot amassed about 80 victories but was then purged for political unreliability! Kozhedub claimed his first victory on 6 July 1943 after being shot down on an early sortie. His tally, amassed in 520 sorties, consisted of one Me 262 jet, 22 FW 190s (of which two were FW 190Ds over Berlin on 17 April 1945), 19 Bf 109s, 18 Ju 87s and two He 111s. He flew Lavochkin La-5s and La-7s, and rose to high command post-war. In all, over 200 Soviet aces were credited with 20 or more victories, although in some cases many were shared. Women also flew with the Soviet Air Force. Their top scorer was Lilya Litvak with 13 victories gained in 66 combats, mainly over Stalingrad. She was shot down and killed over Orel on 1 August 1943. The second-ranking woman fighter pilot was Katya Budanova, with 11.

The Normandie-Niemen Regiment

France and Russia have always felt a special relationship due to their peasants' revolutions, even though these were over one hundred years apart and bore few similarities. The Normandie *Groupe* was formed in late in 1942 with French pilots and Russian Yak-1 fighters, and joined combat on the Eastern Front in March 1943. In 1944 it was expanded to a full regiment, equipped with Yak-9s. The top scorer (and top-scoring French pilot of the war) was Marcel Albert with 22 victories to add to a shared claim in France with a D.520.

In the closing stages of the war, Polish and Czech regiments flew with the Soviet Air Force, but no details are available.

German Allies

Romania joined the German attack on the Soviet Union at the outset; shortly afterwards Hungary and Finland entered the conflict, the latter to recover territory lost during the Winter War. Later still, Italy, Spain, Slovakia and Croatia provided contingents.

Gradually the allies dwindled. The Italians withdrew after the loss of Stalingrad, having produced no great aces. Croatia and Slovakia left the Eastern Front in mid-1943. Three Croatians claimed more than 30 victories;

the top two Slovakians claimed 32 and 29. The Romanians pulled out in 1944, their top three aces claiming 60, 50 and 40 points. In the same year went the Spanish, only two of whom reached double figures; Angel Salas Larrazabal added seven to his Civil War score of 17. Nine Hungarians reached double figures, but best of all were the Finns.

Finland started what they called the Continuation War with a motley mix of fighters – French Morane-Saulnier MS.406s; Italian Fiat G.50s and American Brewster Buffaloes. The last, flown by the RAF in the Far East and by the Americans in the Pacific, was rightly regarded as a 'turkey', but in Finnish hands against the Soviet Union it proved far from the case: four pilots scored more than 20 on type, while Hans Wind amassed no fewer than 42 victories with it. The top scorer with the MS.406 was Urho Lehtovara with 14, while Oiva Tuominen claimed 23 with the G.50. Later in the war the Finns re-equipped with the Bf 109G, with which Eino Juutilainen added 57 to bring his score to 92, plus two in the Winter War.

The Far East

When Japan entered the war in December 1941, her air power was very much an unknown quantity in the West. This should not have been the case: Japan had been at war with China for some considerable time, and Japanese air arms and equipment had been available for all to see during this period. Part of the problem was that China was not regarded as a first-rate air power, which led to the West largely discounting Japanese effectiveness. There were exceptions. Claire Chennault, commanding the American Volunteer Group popularly known as the 'Flying Tigers in Burma until mid-1942 evolved tactics to negate the superb manoeuvrability of the Japanese fighters. His Curtiss P-40s used dive-and-zoom tactics and rarely if ever stayed to dogfight. The top AVG ace was Robert Neale with 16; at least seven other Tigers reached double figures, although three were killed in action.

The two main Japanese fighters of the period were the Mitsubishi Zero of the Imperial Navy and the Nakajima Ki-43 Hayabusa of the Army Air Force. Both had been designed to suit the doctrine of the time: a fighter was an aircraft that fought other aircraft, that outperformed and outmanoeuvred its opponent. To do these things, it was given the lightest possible wing loading and the greatest possible power/weight ratio. In this, the Japanese made a virtue out of a necessity. Their greatest weakness was, like the Italians, the lack of a really high-powered engine, and shaving weight to the bone was the only way to achieve the desired performance.

In effect, Japanese fighters of the early war period were light sports air-craft with big engines. Because they caught fire easily, or broke up when heavily hit, some commentators have portrayed them as flimsily built. How-ever, as noted in the previous chapter, this was not the case; they were stressed for high-g manoeuvres, and could match any Allied type in this department. What made them vulnerable was a lack of self-sealing fuel tanks and armour protection. As part of the quest for light weight, even radios were omitted in the early days, while armament was generally on the light side, which re-duced combat effectiveness. The theory was that minimising weight max-imised manoeuvrability, and such agile machines would rarely be hit! This of course presupposed that well-trained Japanese pilots would never suffer a surprise bounce. This was a dangerous and quite unwarranted assumption.

Another area in which the Japanese differed from everyone else was in the widespread use of the loop in combat. As far back as 1917, pilots were warned against it. Looping enabled a pursuer to close the range quickly, while the lack of speed while going over the top reduced his deflection prob-lems. To the Japanese, a loop was merely a maximum-rate turn in the verti-cal rather than the horizontal plane. Both had the same end – to get on the tail of an opponent. At low to moderate speeds, no Allied fighter could fol-low the Zero or the Hayabusa in a turn, regardless of whether it was hori-zontal or vertical. Properly timed, the loop could prove remarkably effec-tive, even against the Spitfire.

Most Japanese pilots were of the Samurai warrior caste, to whom defeat was unthinkable; for this reason parachutes were rarely carried, as this im-plied a willingness to accept surrender and captivity. In action, they used the *shotai*, a three-ship formation in a steep echelon or offset line astern. Three *shotai* made up a nine-aircraft *chutai*.

At first the Japanese flyers, many with combat experience over China, carried all before them. The surprise achieved at Pearl Harbor caught most USAAF aircraft on the ground; only a few got airborne, although P-40 pilot 'Wheaties' Welch claimed four out of the Japanese hordes. He survived the war with a total of 16, but was killed in 1954 while testing the supersonic F-100.

In the early months of the war against Japan, Allied pilots endured a tor-rid time against the Zero, which gained a legendary reputation. It could out-turn even the Spitfire V, which made tackling it with the Buffalo, Hurricane, Mohawk, Tomahawk, Airacobra or Wildcat very much an adventure. A few, however, achieved creditable results. Two pilots claimed six victories apiece with the much inferior Buffalo. Australian Alf Clare included five Hayabusas in his tally, and New Zealander Geoffrey Fisken accounted for three Zeros in his, over Singapore. RAF Hurricane pilot Frank Carey accounted for eight over Burma. Fisken ended the war with a tally of 11, Carey with 25.

Initially the Zero gained an enviable reputation, but what was it really worth? It performed poorly at high altitude, and for the period it was not terribly fast, either on the level or in the dive. A few American accounts exist of Zeros staying with P-40s in terminal-velocity dives, but trials with captured aircraft failed to confirm this. Its rate of climb was achieved at a low speed but a steep angle, which made it appear better than it was. As indicated air speed increased, the ailerons progressively stiffened, to become almost immovable above 290mph, which made rate of roll negligible. This made the Allied counter obvious – keep air speed high! Once this was realised, the US Navy in particular took the measure of the Zero. Two examples cast doubt on the reputation of the Zero as a world-beating fighter.

On 22 July 1942 a twin-engine Lockheed Hudson of the RAAF was intercepted off Buna. While the Australian aircraft was exceptionally well-handled, it took six Zeros, three of which were flown by aces Saburo Sakai (64 victories), Junichi Sasai (27) and Hiroyoshi Nishizawa (87), ten minutes to bring it down. The second incident took place over Guadalcanal on 8 August 1942. Having lost his wingmen, Yonekawa and Hatori, Zero ace Saburo Sakai looked for them:

> I gaped. A single Wildcat pursued three Zero fighters, firing in short bursts at the frantic Japanese planes. All four planes were in a wild dogfight, flying tight left spirals. The Zeros should have been able to take the lone Grumman without any trouble, but every time a Zero caught the Wildcat before its guns the enemy plane flipped away wildly and came out again on the tail of a Zero. I had never seen such flying before.

Sakai hurtled to the rescue:

> In desperation I snapped out a burst. At once the Grumman snapped away in a roll to the right, clawed around in a tight turn, and ended up in a climb straight at my plane. Never had I seen an enemy plane move so quickly or so gracefully before; and every second his guns were moving closer to the belly of my fighter. I snap-rolled in an effort to throw him off. He would not be shaken. He was using my own favourite tactics, coming up from under.

After a great deal of difficulty, Sakai finally managed to outfly his opponent and shot him about so badly that he was forced to bale out. The performance of the American flyer was made even more remarkable by one thing: his aircraft was not a Wildcat at all – it was a Dauntless dive-bomber of the US Marine Corps. If confirmation were needed of the truism that pilot quality is more important than aircraft quality, this combat provided it.

Nor was this an isolated instance. At the Battle of the Coral Sea three months earlier, Dauntless pilot Swede Vejtasa claimed three Zeros shot down. Following this, he was assigned to a Wildcat squadron, and at the Battle of Santa Cruz in October he claimed seven Japanese aircraft in a single sortie, two dive-bombers and five torpedo-bombers. He later added one more to bring his war total to 11.

Although the Wildcat was outclassed by the Zero, the US Navy flyers held their own by a combination of sheer teamwork and the ruggedness of their aircraft. Prior to the outbreak of war against Japan, RAF veterans had visited the United States and passed on their experience. From the outset, USN fighter pilots used the pair and four in action. It was nearly two years before the Japanese began to follow suit, and by this time it made little difference. In addition, the USN was the only air arm to practice high-angle deflection shooting as standard.

With long flights over the trackless ocean the norm, endurance was far more important than for continental land-based fighters. The enemy might rate 20 or 30 per cent lethality; the sea rated 100 per cent. Whereas in Europe the British and Germans flew at combat cruise, and the Russians used full throttle, American and Japanese carrier aircraft settled for economy, throttled right back, with lean mixture and propeller set in coarse pitch. Consequently their cruising speed was slow, typically 120mph. They were therefore vulnerable to the surprise bounce, while acceleration to fighting speed took some considerable time. This made the surprise bounce potentially far more lethal, and in part accounted for the many multiple victories claimed in the Pacific.

As is so often the case, an apparent victory contained the seeds of eventual defeat. The battleship might of the US Pacific Fleet was shattered at Pearl Harbor, but the American aircraft carriers were elsewhere. Their survival was critical for the months to come, but this was not immediately apparent. For the next six months, the Japanese ran riot across the Pacific and Indian Oceans, and through Malaya and Burma on land.

An attempt to seize Port Moresby, on the southern shore of Papua/New Guinea, from which the Australian mainland could be threatened, led to the first carrier battle in history, the Coral Sea, in May 1942. The action was marked by faulty reconnaissance and high aircraft losses on both sides. The

Japanese light carrier *Shoho* was sunk and the fleet carrier *Shokaku* badly damaged, against the American loss of *Lexington*. However, the Port Moresby invasion fleet was turned back.

After this setback, the Japanese turned their attention to the small but strategically important island of Midway, more than 1,100 miles north-west of Pearl Harbor. The invasion of Midway was certain to bring the US Pacific Fleet to battle, where it could be overwhelmed in a major surface action.

The attack plan was elaborate, full of diversions, traps and stratagems designed to lure the Americans to within gun range of the Japanese battleships. Seldom has a battle plan been so reliant on enemy co-operation! So clever was it that it totally ignored the basic principle of concentration of force.

Although heavily outnumbered, the US Navy had one major advantage. Having cracked the Japanese naval codes, it knew what to expect, and when the attack came in, its three fleet carriers, including the hastily repaired *Yorktown*, escorted by cruisers and destroyers, lay in ambush to the north of the island. The initial Japanese strike force consisted of four fleet carriers. It was guarded by two battleships, three cruisers and eleven destroyers, which between them could put up a formidable array of anti-aircraft fire.

The most important function in carrier warfare is accurate and timely reconnaissance. To detect first is to strike first, which is often critical. This means that fighters must constantly patrol to neutralise enemy reconnaissance machines. Others must be at readiness for immediate launch if an attack is detected. Defending the carrier is a priority, but fighters must also be spared to escort strike forces. Given the limited space aboard an aircraft carrier, there are never enough fighters.

The four Japanese carriers normally deployed 84 Zero fighters, 84 dive-bombers and 93 torpedo or level bombers between them. For Midway, 19 extra Zeros were crammed in; these were actually the fighters assigned to the carrier *Hiyo*, which was not ready. These were opposed by 79 Wildcats, 112 dive-bombers and 42 torpedo-bombers. In addition, Midway housed about 80 aircraft, 28 of which were fighters.

Expecting the American carriers to still be at Pearl Harbor, the Japanese launched a powerful strike against Midway. Warned by radar, 21 Buffaloes and seven Wildcats of the US Marine Corps scrambled to intercept, but were cut to pieces by the 36-strong Zero escort. Only five survived in flyable condition, although future ace Marion Carl (18½ victories total) opened his score with two. But when the raiders reached the island, the cupboard was bare. Everything that could fly was armed, airborne and outbound towards the Japanese fleet.

The American carriers also launched strikes, but unexpected course changes by the Japanese fleet meant that some units failed to make contact; others arrived piecemeal. The defending Zeros wrought havoc with the early arrivals, which were largely unescorted. American losses on the first five waves averaged 65 per cent, while Torpedo 8 lost all 15 Devastators. And all without scoring a single hit!

Their sacrifice was not in vain. Successive attacks had drawn the Japanese fighters down to low level, when 54 Dauntless dive-bombers arrived high overhead. Unopposed, they reduced three of the four Japanese carriers to blazing wrecks within minutes. After an exemplary initial defence, the Zeros had failed to protect their charges.

On a smaller scale, the same fate befell the Japanese riposte. Two strikes flown from *Hiryu*, the sole survivor, lost 71 per cent and 57 per cent respectively, although they did succeed in inflicting mortal damage on *Yorktown*. A little later, 24 Dauntlesses sent *Hiryu* to the bottom, for the loss of just three of their number. Bereft of air cover, the Japanese fleet conceded defeat.

Midway was a famous victory which firmly established air power as the supreme arbiter in naval warfare. The cost was high: American aircraft losses were 85, a considerable number of which ran out of fuel and ditched, and one fleet carrier. The Japanese losses were much heavier. Many experienced and battle-hardened flyers were lost, and these were irreplaceable. Almost as vital were the casualties among the veteran mechanics. Japanese naval aviation commenced an irreversible decline from this point.

A handful of fighter pilots became aces at Midway, while others added to their scores. Among them were Wildcat pilots John S. Thach, inventor of the Thach Weave which did so much to offset the superiority of the Zero, and Scott McCuskey, who claimed five victories of his eventual total of 14 on 4 June. For the Japanese, Iyozo Fujita claimed three victories and seven shared during the battle.

From this point on, the Allies took the offensive in the Pacific. The first crack in the Japanese perimeter came when Guadalcanal was captured. This was the shape of things to come, as island after island was taken or by-passed. Constant fighting bled the Japanese air arms almost to death; they could not make good their losses. The crunch came during the 'Great

126

Marianas Turkcy Shoot' in June 1944. Seven fleet and eight light carriers of the USN were opposed by nine IJN carriers. A significant number of Japanese land-based aircraft were taken out even before the start. The IJN carriers hurled 328 aircraft into the fray. They lost 243, against American losses of just 28. This was the fifth and last great carrier action of the war.

Why so great a discrepancy? The reasons lay in Japanese deficiencies. Recruitment standards had to be lowered to cope with the demand. Training schools could not cope with the extra influx. And, for the most part, in 1945 IJN pilots were flying a fighter little better than the same old 1940-vintage Zero. By contrast, the USN used a well-honed fighter direction system in defence, while the new and potent Hellcat and Corsair were freely available. With the exception of a handful of surviving veterans, Japanese Navy fighter pilots were outclassed and outflown.

A single example will suffice. The Vought Kingfisher floatplane was a single-engine two-seater, capable of just 164mph. It took 12.1 minutes to reach 5,000ft, and its fixed forward-firing armament consisted of a single .30 calibre machine gun. Against a Zero it was duck soup. Or was it . . .? On 16 February 1945 Kingfisher pilot D. W. Gandy was spotting for ship's gunfire on northern Iwo Jima at 1,500ft:

> . . . I sighted a lone Zero 52 break through the clouds about 500 yards ahead. The Zero sighted me about the same time, turned towards me on a reverse course, and commenced a high side pass from the right. I increased throttle and rpm to maximum and made a quick climbing turn to the right into him, forcing him to make a diving, head-on run. The Zero fired one short burst which missed me completely, passed about 50ft on my left and made a tight turn to the right.
>
> I made a tight, diving left turn and then a right turn, which put me on his tail about 500ft astern, and commenced firing long bursts from my .30-caliber nose gun into his cockpit, engine and right wing root. He weaved to the left, emitting a thin stream of grey smoke from either the engine cowl or right wing root, and his right landing gear lowered. Now he tried a very tight turn to the right, but I was able to turn inside him again while closing at 155mph indicated, and continued firing into his right wing root. The Zero 52 did a diving roll to the right, burst into flames, and crashed on a bluff. . .

In what was technically a grossly unequal contest, pilot quality, added to a modicum of luck, had once more proved the supreme arbiter in air combat.

The island-hopping campaign by the USN and USMC was half of a two-pronged attack. The USAAF, supported by the RAAF and RNZAF, thrust up through New Guinea to the Philippines. Equipped in the early stages mainly with the P-40, most American units converted to the P-38 Lightning.

No Japanese fighter could match the speed and altitude performance of this aircraft, and Zeros and Hayabusas fell in droves before its guns. Other USAAF fighters used against the Japanese were the P-47 Thunderbolt and the P-51 Mustang, while the RAAF and RNZAF for the most part employed the P-40 Warhawk and the Spitfire V.

By now the Japanese had abandoned the 'manoeuvrabilty above all' doctrine, and most new fighters had self-sealing fuel tanks, armour protection and a heavy armament. The Nakajima Ki-61 Hien and Ki-44 Shoki led the way for the Army, while the Ki-84 Hayate was in many ways superior to any Allied fighter. For the Navy, the Kawanishi N1K1 Shiden was outstanding, if tricky to fly. But few of these entered service.

The top scorers for the USAAF in the Pacific, and in fact top American scorers of the war ,were Richard Bong (40 victories) and Tommy McGuire (38). Both were P-38 pilots, and both used dive-and-zoom tactics with considerable success. McGuire was killed in the Philippines on 1 July 1945 when he tried to turn with a Zero at low level. Bong died in a flying accident in a P-80 jet just five weeks later.

'Top Gun' for the US Navy was Hellcat pilot David McCampbell, with 34 victories. A master of mass slaughter, he claimed seven on 19 June 1944 and nine on 24 October of that year. Navy runner-up was Cecil Harris with 24. For the US Marines, 'Swivel-Neck Joe' Foss scored 26, all with the Wildcat. He was followed by Corsair pilot Bob Hanson with 25, 20 of which were claimed in sixteen days in January 1944. He was shot down and killed by ground fire on 3 February 1944. Pappy Boyington was credited with 28; six of these were scored with the AVG, the rest with USMC Corsairs of the Black Sheep Squadron VF-213. The top scorer with the Thunderbolt was Neel Kearby with 22. He was shot down in flames on 5 March 1944.

Most of the high-scoring IJN pilots were active in the early part of the war. Hiroyoshi Nishizawa claimed his first victory on 3 February 1942, and his score rose rapidly. Five Wildcats over Guadalcanal followed, and by 30 November he had been credited with 30. After two spells in Japan, he claimed his 86th and 87th victories on 25 October 1944. He was killed the following day when the DC-3 transport in which he was a passenger was shot down by Hellcats. The runner-up was Tetsuzo Iwamoto, credited with 80 victories in the Pacific and 14 in China, but many of these were shared or 'probables'.

The top-scoring Japanese Army pilot of the war was Satoshi Anabuki, with 51. With his score at three, he converted to the Ki-43 Hayabusa and

(Above) Oswald
Boelcke, the 'Father of
Air Fighting' and the
greatest fighter ace,
leader and tactician of
the early World War I
period. His untimely
death in action meant
that he was over-
shadowed by his star
pupil, Manfred von
Richthofen. (Bruce
Robertson)

(Right) Albert Ball was
an inspiration to British
flyers in both world
wars. A schoolboy by
temperament, he disliked
killing, but he fought
hard until his fatal crash
in May 1917. (Bruce
Robertson)

(Above) Georges Guynemer was at first rejected by the *Aviation Militaire* as too frail. His combat reports were irreverent, frequently referring to his opponents as *fiacres* (taxis). (Collection SHAA via Bruce Robertson)

(Right) James McCudden (left) specialised in the solo stalk of high-flying reconnaissance machines. He is seen here with Gerald Constable-Maxwell (centre) and Lieutenant Zinc (right). (Bruce Robertson)

(Above) Charles Nungesser, the Flying Hussar, seen here in December 1916. His Nieuport already carries his distinctive if macabre *insigne*. He was arguably the most indomitable pilot of the war, and his survival is no less than amazing. (Collection SHAA via Bruce Robertson)

(Above) Alexandr Kazakov (far left) was the leading Russian ace of the Great War with 17 victories. He is seen here with other fighter leaders: (left to right) Zemitan, Kruten and Kulvinski. (Bruce Robertson)

(Below) The Albatros series of fighters had the cleanest lines of all. Seen here is the D.III in the spring of 1917. (Alfred Price)

(Above) René Fonck, 'the commercial traveller booking his orders', although lacking glamour, was probably the greatest ace of the war. His SPAD VII carries a rear-vision mirror. (Collection SHAA via Bruce Robertson)

(Left) The diminutive Ernst Udet became the ranking surviving German ace of the Great War. Between the wars he was a noted test pilot and stunt flyer. (Bruce Robertson)

(Above) The Sopwith Camel was the most manoeuvrable fighter of the war. This night-adapted version is flown by Gilbert Murlis-Green (20 victories). (Philip Jarrett)

(Below) The agile Fiat CR.32 was flown by Spanish Civil War top-scorer Garcia Morato. These aircraft belong to the Italian Asso di Bastogni (Ace of Clubs) Squadron. (Philip Jarrett)

(Above) Used by the Republicans (and Soviet 'volunteers') in the Spanish Civil War, the Polikarpov I-16 was the most advanced fighter of its era. It was also used by Russia against Japan on the Chinese border, against Finland in the Winter War, and against Germany in 1941. (Philip Jarrett)

(Left) Jim Lacey pictured prewar. He became an ace in the Battle of France, and went on to become one of the top scorers in the Battle of Britain. (Lacey via Richard Bickers)

(Left) Robert Stanford Tuck in the cockpit of his No 257 Squadron Hurricane in late 1940. He was considered one of the best marksmen in the RAF. (Maurice Allward)

(Right) Hiroyoshi Nishizawa, nicknamed 'The Devil' by his comrades, was the leading Japanese ace of the war. He was lost while returning to Japan in an unarmed transport. (Bruce Robertson)

(Above) 'Sailor' Malan, one of the great fighter tacticians and leaders in the 1940–42 period. (Philip Jarrett)

(Above) Dick Bong, seen here in his P-38 Lightning in New Guinea on 6 March 1943, was the top scorer for the Allies in the Second World War. (Jeff Ethell Collection)

(Right) Among his other decorations, Ivan Kozhedub, the leading Soviet ace of the Great Patriotic War, wears the Hero of the Soviet Union Star. He later flew MiG-15s in Korea, but with what result is not known. (Bruce Robertson)

(Above) High-scoring USAAF ace Don Gentile warms up his P-51B Mustang prior to a long-range escort mission over Germany. (Bruce Robertson)

(Below) A defecting North Korean pilot delivered this MiG-15bis to the Americans in September 1953. The aircraft number has been blanked out by the censor. Exhaustive combat trials against the Sabre revealed many weaknesses. (USAF via Philip Jarrett)

(Right) The F-86 Sabre achieved an enviable record of victories over Soviet-built and flown MiG-15s in Korea. This is the F-86F variant. (Philip Jarrett)

(Right) Pakistani Sabre pilot Mohammed Alam was credited with shooting down five Indian Hunters in a single mission in 1965. He is seen here after the war, by which time he was flying Mirage IIIPs. (John Fricker)

(Below) The workhorse of both the USAF and USN in Vietnam was the F-4 Phantom. Powerful but unmanoeuvrable, and initially without a gun, its success depended on correct tactics. The Phantom was also used by Israel against Egypt and Syria.

(Above) Robin Olds, seen here without his trademark handlebar moustache, as a Brigadier-General and Commandant of the Air Force Academy at Colorado Springs. Twenty-two years after becoming an ace in World War II, Robin Olds became the USAF top-scorer in Vietnam with four victories. His combination of aggression and situational awareness was legendary, as attested to by those who flew with him. (USAF via Duane Reed)

(Above) Although the MiG-17F had no supersonic capability, its agility made it a formidable opponent if well handled. It was widely used in the Middle East and Vietnam. (Philip Jarrett)

(Right) Fourth-ranking Israeli ace Asher Snir, who amassed his total of 13½ in the Six-Day War of 1967, the War of Attrition, and the October War of 1973.

(Above) Thirteen kill markings adorn Israeli Mirage IIICJ No 159. They are, however, the aircraft kills, scored while it was flown by several different pilots. It is not widely known that some aircraft performed much better than others, both in the Middle East and in Vietnam, mainly due to the radar and avionics systems being more reliable.

(Right) Ezra Dotan, a fighter squadron commander who, when switched to Skyhawk attack aircraft, shot down two Syrian MiG-17s in one sortie. Faced with overshooting the second, he said, 'I throttled back. I extended my dive brakes. I lowered my flaps. Had it been possible I would have stuck my ears outside the cockpit!'

(Above) The F-15 Eagle has long been the world's pre-eminent air superiority fighter. In Israeli service it scored more than 40 victories in the Beka'a action of 1982, and, with the USAF, 34 of 39 victories in the Gulf War in 1991. (Shlomo Aloni)

(Below) The F-16 has a remarkable record. In Israeli service it claimed 44 Syrian aircraft over the Beka'a in 1982. Subsequently, border violations by Afghan intruders have resulted in several victories for Pakistani F-16s. In the Gulf War of 1991 it was used as a bomb truck by the USAF, and did not add to its air combat score. Since then it has claimed Iraqi victims over the 'No-Fly Zones', and Serbian aircraft over Bosnia and Yugoslavia. (Lockheed Martin)

was sent to Burma, where in the space of 17 months he claimed 28 RAF and 13 USAAF aircraft, including the first B-24 to fall in the region. On his return to Japan in February 1944 he claimed six Hellcats while ferrying Ki-84 Hayates to the Philippines. His final victory was a B-29, in June 1945.

Few Allied flyers were able to do much in the China/ Burma/India theatre, mainly due to lack of opportunity. Seven Americans reached double figures, topped by Pappy Herbst with 18. Several of the American top-scorers in the CBI theatre, notably Charles Older (18½) and Tex Hill (18¼) were formerly with Chennault's AVG, with which they scored the majority of their victories. For the RAF, Bob Cross claimed nine over Burma, seven of them Hayabusas, while flying Hurricanes and Spitfires between January 1943 and March 1944. For the Japanese Army, Goichi Sumino claimed 27 over Burma before his death in action on 6 June 1944.

Like the *Luftwaffe*, the Japanese also faced a considerable heavy bomber threat, but, whereas in Europe the Boeing B-17 Flying Fortress was the main opponent, in the Far East the Consolidated B-24 Liberator took the honours. Equally heavily armed, it had a lower ceiling but was faster than the B-17, which made it more difficult to intercept for the lightly-armed and under-powered Japanese fighters. Lack of an effective early warning and ground control system did little to aid the defenders.

To make matters worse, the huge Boeing B-29 Superfortress appeared over Japan on 15 June 1944. Fast, high-flying and with a very heavy defensive armament carried in remotely-controlled barbettes, it was a formidable opponent. The nearest the Japanese came to the heavily armoured FW 190 was the Mitsubishi J2M Raiden. It was fast and climbed well, but lacked manoeuvrability. Against American carrier fighters, or when from April 1945 long-range Mustangs appeared in the skies over Japan, Raiden pilots were disadvantaged. Only the swashbuckling Saadaki Akamatsu (27 victories) was successful in the Raiden against Mustangs and Hellcats, accounting for at least eight.

Against the big bombers, two Hien pilots did well. Teruhiko Kobayashi claimed 12 B-29s in his total of 20-plus, while Chiuchi Ichikawa claimed nine B-29s out of ten victories. In the twin-engine Ki-45 Toryu night fighters, Totaro Ito claimed nine B-29s and four B-24s, while Isamu Kashiide claimed seven B-29s in his total of nine. But these were the exceptions. To intercept these monsters was to run the gauntlet of a hail of fire. Even to attempt to intercept them was, in the final months of the war, to be swamped by Mustangs.

British naval aviation failed to produce any high-scoring aces during the entire war. When they operated in target-rich environments, they were handicapped by low-performance fighters, with the result that a high proportion of their victories were shared. Typically we have Fulmar pilot Graham Hogg, who was credited with four confirmed and eight shared victories in the Mediterranean between September 1940 and May 1941. He died in a flying accident in March 1942.

In the Pacific in the late-war period, when the skies swarmed with hungry American pilots, there were simply not enough Japanese victims to go around. For example, the top-scoring Seafire pilot was Richard Reynolds, with two and three shared – and both confirmed victories (two Zeros) came on the same day.

Summary

By definition, a fighter ace is a pilot with at least five confirmed victories, but, to quote Napoleon the Pig in George Orwell's Animal Farm, 'Some are more equal than others!' This poses the question: where were victories most difficult to obtain? Obviously not on the Russian Front, nor against Japan in the later stages of the war. As a purely personal opinion, the writer would suggest against the Germans on the Western Front, or against the Japanese in 1942. But the reader must judge.

British and Commonwealth Aces

The selection of representative aces for the Second World War has been made difficult by sheer lack of space, complicated by the fact that sixty of them have already been profiled in the two companion volumes to this work: *Luftwaffe Fighter Aces* and *Allied Fighter Aces of World War II*. Repetition has largely been avoided.

James Harry 'Ginger' Lacey Jim Lacey joined the RAF Volunteer Reserve in 1937, and took an instructor's course during the following year. Called up on the outbreak of war, he joined No 501 Squadron and went to France with them in May 1940. Flying alone on 13 May, he encountered the enemy for the first time – an He 111 escorted by a Bf 109. These he carefully stalked and shot down from very close range. He returned to England on 19 June having raised his score to five.

Lacey flew almost continuously throughout the Battle of Britain, his squadron being kept in the front line longer than any other. An above-average pilot and a first-class shot, he became one of the leading exponents of the Hurricane. Between July and the end of October he claimed 18 destroyed, 13 of them Bf 109s, with five 'probables' and six damaged, although he himself was twice shot down during this period. No 501 Squadron then converted to Spitfires, with which he added another four to his tally. After a 'rest' as an instructor, when his pupils included future Malta ace George Beurling, he briefly returned to operations with No 602 Squadron, where he damaged two FW 190As, before a series of testing and instructional postings, culminating in India, where he commanded No 17 Squadron. On 19 February 1945 he encountered Japanese aircraft in the air for the first and only time, and picked off a straggling Hayabusa with just five cannon shells. He later became the first Spitfire pilot to fly over Japan.

Although Lacey stayed in the RAF after the war, he was not high command material. Legends about him abound, particularly of his Far Eastern service. He retired from the RAF in 1967 and became an instructor at the Grindale Flying Club. His final score was 28 destroyed, five 'probables' and nine damaged.

James Ghillies (Ben) Benson Ben Benson flew night fighters almost throughout the war. He joined No 141 (Defiant) Squadron in July 1940 and survived the daylight massacre of the type. In October the Squadron converted to night fighting, and on 22/23 December of that year he scored the first night victory for the type. Ten months later No 141 converted to Beaufighters and Benson teamed up with radar operator Lewis Brandon. There was little trade around at this time, and their sole success was one Do 217 shot down and another damaged. They then joined the Mosquito-equipped No 157 Squadron, at first on home defence and later on intruder and bomber support missions.

The night of 11/12 September 1944 saw Benson and Brandon patrolling, rather unhopefully, off south-eastern Denmark, when Lewis Brandon picked up a contact:

> A contact it was. It was travelling fast, but I was able to lead Ben up to it with little difficulty. We saw it was a Junkers Ju 188, and it appeared to be orbiting a German fighter beacon. Ben eased the Mosquito's nose up a little and dropped back slightly. The Junkers drifted into his gunsight and he gave a four-second burst. We saw strikes and flashes come from the starboard wing root. The German gave a great lurch and lost much of its flying speed. Ben had to pull up to avoid collision. Then a pinpoint of flame spluttered from its starboard engine and grew larger as we watched it going earthward.

147

Within seconds Brandon gained another contact, which was also sent down in flames from close range. On return to base they found that their Mosquito was covered in German oil and had been scratched by debris.

Benson ended the war with ten destroyed, four damaged, and six V-1s sent down, all except the first shared with Brandon. Their final victim was an He 219 on 5/6 January 1945.

Evan Dall 'Rosie' Mackie So named because of his florid complexion, Rosie Mackie was a New Zealander. He first saw action over France early in 1942, where he shared a Bf 109 and claimed an FW 190A as a 'probable'. He was posted to Tunisia in March 1943, and by 8 May he had claimed six victories. He then started to operate over Sicily and Italy, where he gained another nine, six of them fighters. Rested in February 1944, he returned to England and converted to Tempests.

He joined No 122 Wing in Holland on 13 December, and between then and the end of the war added another five, to become one of the few Tempest aces. His war total was 20 and three shared destroyed, two 'probables' and 10 and one shared damaged.

American Aces
George S. 'Ratsy' Preddy Had Fate been kinder, Preddy would probably have emerged as the USAAF's top scorer in Europe. He made his combat début in the defence of Darwin, northern Australia, where he flew P-40s against the Japanese. He was not very successful: in over a year, he managed to damage one fighter and one bomber. He was posted to Europe in the summer of 1943, his first claim, a Bf 109, being made on 1 December of that year. On 29 January 1944 he claimed a FW 190A as his third victory, but the engine of his Thunderbolt was hit by flak and he ditched in the English Channel, from which he was rescued by the RAF.

From April 1944 the 352nd Fighter Group re-equipped with Mustangs, and George Preddy went on to become the top scorer with this type. Between then and returning to the USA on leave in August, he claimed 18 whole and four shared victories. Six of these came on 6 August. Preddy, leading the Group, was about to rendezvous with the USAAF bomber stream south of Hamburg when he spotted 30-plus Bf 109s in tight formation at 28,000ft, obviously intent on the same task:

> I went right in for the pack and shot down five, starting with the tail-end Charlie. Only one of the five managed to bale out; the rest went down in flames. After

splitting them up I got on the tail of the sixth and chased him down to 5,000ft. The first five never had a chance – not one of them fired a shot at me – but the sixth gave me a real dogfight.

By this time *Jagdflieger* pilot quality was falling fast; Preddy and his wingman seem to have encountered a unit of novices. For the USAAF fighter pilots, the difficulty was in knowing whether or not they had engaged one of the few surviving *Experten*, who were still deadly and difficult opponents.

Preddy returned from leave in October 1944 and added two more to his score. On 25 December he shot down two more Bf 109s near Bonn, but, returning at low level in poor visibility, he was shot down and killed by 'friendly' ground fire near Liège in Belgium. In 143 sorties, averaging 3¾ hours each, he had claimed 25 confirmed victories and four shared.

Robert W. Hanson 'Butcher Bob' Hanson of the US Marine Corps was the top-scoring Corsair pilot of the war. Like many Marines, he was of the 'get stuck in' school of tactics. He arrived in the Pacific Theatre of Operations in mid-1943 with VMF-214 and opened his account with two victories in August. He then transferred to VMF-214's 'chummy' squadron, VMF-215, and on 1 November shot down two Zeros and a torpedo bomber over Bougainville before being shot down himself. He survived, and he returned to the Squadron after an absence of four days.

VMF-215 returned to action in January 1944 after a brief rest, and 'Butcher Bob', who had by now found his 'shooting eye', went through a purple patch. Fighting over Rabaul between 14 and 30 January, and utilising the superior performance of his Corsair to the full, he claimed 20 Zeros in just six sorties. His score at 25, he was hit by ground fire on 3 February and tried to ditch. The Corsair was notoriously allergic to water landings: the wingtip hit first and it cartwheeled. Thus died Bob Hanson.

A Czech Ace

Karel 'Old Kut' Kuttelwascher Karel Kuttelwascher qualified as a fighter pilot with the Czech Air Force in 1934 but on the German occupation of his country in 1938 escaped to France via Poland. There he was accepted for the *Armée de l'Air*. He flew Morane MS. 406s, then Dewoitine D.520s, during the French campaign, in which he was credited with two shares and a 'probable'. After the capitulation he escaped to England and joined the RAF, where he flew Hurricanes.

After a few daylight fighter sweeps in 1941, during which he accounted for three Bf 109s and scored a 'probable', he found his *métier* when his squadron was switched to night intruder missions. Now flying the four-cannon Hurricane IIc, fitted with long-range tanks, he patrolled *Luftwaffe* airfields in France looking for trade. His first night intruder victory came on 1/2 April 1942 when he watched a Ju 88 take off from Melun. Having stalked it and shot it down, he returned to Melun in time to see another Ju 88 preparing to take off. Diving to the attack, he badly damaged it while it was still on the ground.

By 1/2 July his score had risen to 15 victories on intruder missions, all bombers. Later in the war he flew Typhoons and Mosquitos, but with no further success. His final tally was 18 destroyed, plus two shared in France, two 'probables' and five damaged. He survived the war to become an airline pilot.

A Finnish Ace

Nils Katajainen Katajainen was eighth in the list of Finland's aces but arguably first in the survival stakes. He survived no fewer than ten forced landings or crashes, making him a double 'Chinese Ace'. The first came in the uneasy period between the Winter War and the Continuation War, when he badly damaged his Brewster Buffalo on take-off and was forced to land on one main wheel.

His first victory, on 28 June 1941, was marred when his engine was hit and he was forced to nurse his stricken aircraft back to base. On 12 August his third and fourth victories, over Polikarpov I-15s, saw him hit in the fuel tank. After two more victories, the engine of his Buffalo was damaged by ground fire. Once more he limped back to base.

The Buffalo, responsive but underpowered, and with a derisory rate of climb, had proved a failure with the RAF and the USMC. Against the Soviet Union, where most fighting took place at medium and low levels, it proved adequate in the hands of a good pilot. However, after 13 victories, Nils was posted to fly bombers!

Not until April 1943 did he return to fighters. More victories followed, but on 6 June he was wounded. On his return his score continued to rise, reaching 17½ by February 1944, making him the fourth-ranking ace with the Buffalo. Conversion to the Bf 109G brought two more crashes, but in ten days from 23 June he claimed 17 destroyed, although two Il-2s on 3 July saw him force-land his damaged fighter once more. Four days later his 109 was damaged by ground fire and he was badly injured in the ensuing forced landing. His war total was 35½.

A French Ace

Marcel Albert In the French campaign Marcel Albert flew Dewoitine D.520s, with which he had been credited with one shared victory and one 'probable'. In October 1941 he flew to Gibraltar to join the Free French element of the RAF, but after a short sojourn with No 340 Squadron he chose to join the Normandie-Niemen Regiment in Russia. Conditions in the East were very different: so close to the front were the squadrons based that a bell was rung when German artillery moved within range. For the most part, the unit's aircraft flew without radio, and as most fighting took place at comparatively low level little time was spent grabbing for altitude after a scramble. Flying Yak-9s, then Yak-3s, Albert claimed 22 victories in the East, which made him the top-scoring French fighter pilot of the war.

German and Austrian Aces

Edmund 'Paule' Rossmann Paule Rossmann flew Bf 109s with *JG 52* from 1940 to 1943. He was in very distinguished company: high-scoring *Experten* Gerd Barkhorn (301), Gunther Rall (275), Hermann Graf (212), Helmut Lipfert (203), Walter Krupinski (197), Johannes Steinhoff (176) and many others all flew with this unit.

Rossmann claimed six victories over France and Britain in 1940. He accompanied *JG 52* to the Eastern Front in 1941, but was wounded in the right arm at an early stage. Although he returned to the cockpit of his Bf 109, his weakened arm left him unable to horse his fighter around in hard manoeuvres. To compensate, he developed tactics to suit, attacking only when he was sure of achieving surprise so as to ensure a non-manoeuvring target. At the same time he became an outstanding long-range marksman.

A *Rottenführer* by late 1942, Rossmann was given a singularly gifted *Kacmarek*. This was Erich Hartmann, who ended the war as the top-scoring fighter ace of all time, with 352 victories. It was Rossmann who taught Hartmann to hang back and evaluate the situation before attacking – something which stood the young man in good stead in the battles to come.

Rossmann's inability to manoeuvre hard made it just a question of time before a Russian fighter pilot cornered him. He was shot down and captured during heavy fighting over Orel on 9 July 1943, his total 93.

151

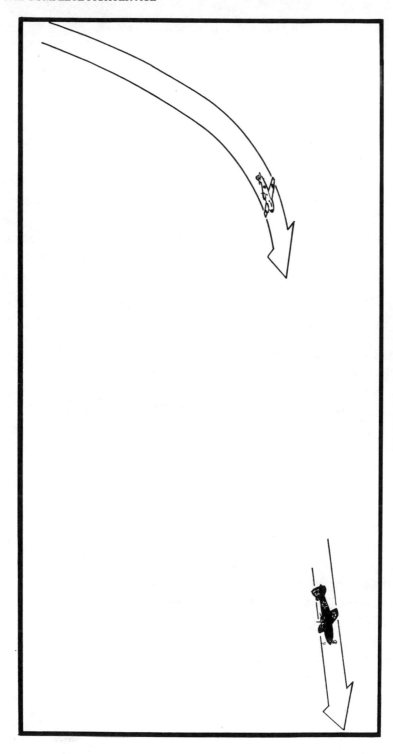

Fig. 10. Rossmann's Attack

His right arm weakened by wounds, Edmund 'Paule' Rossmann (93 victories) was unable to haul his Messerschmitt through hard manoeuvres and he developed a technique of long-range shooting to compensate.

Gordon Mc Gollob Born in Vienna, and named after an American friend of his parents, Gordon Gollob commenced the war as a *Zerstörer* pilot flying the Bf 110 with *ZG 76*, with which he claimed one victory in Poland and five in France and the Battle of Britain. Gollob converted to the Bf 109, and flew with *JG 3* on the Eastern Front. On 18 October 1941 he claimed nine victories in a day, a record at that time. Gollob's 100th victory came on 20 May 1942; on 29 August he reached 150 – the first pilot ever to do so.

Although he later flew with *JG 77*, Gollob failed to add to his score. Promoted to become Fighter Leader in the West, he succeeded Adolf Galland as *General der Jagdflieger* in January 1945. He was described by 'Macky' Steinhoff, who commanded the new *Luftwaffe* post-war, as 'an ambitious and humourless man'.

Ludwig Becker A pioneer night fighter, Ludwig Becker scored the first *Luftwaffe* ground-assisted night victory on 16 October 1940. Ten months later he gained the first *Nachtjagdflieger* victory with the aid of airborne radar, when his radar operator, Josef Staub, steered him to the target using his new *Liechtenstein* radar. Becker perfected a method of attack in which he came in low – which outlined his quarry against the sky – then hauled back on the stick and fired, raking the target from nose to tail.

Ludwig Becker, who should not be confused with the later *Nachtjagdflieger Experte* Martin Becker (58 victories), was squandered on a daylight mission against USAAF Liberators on 26 February 1943. Lost with him was Josef Staub, who had shared in 40 of his 46 night victories.

A Hungarian Ace

György Debrödy A graduate of the Hungarian Air Force Academy, György Debrödy arrived on the Eastern Front early in 1943, but before his unit joined combat it was overrun on the ground and its Italian-built Reggiane Re 2000 *Héja* fighters destroyed. Having escaped the disaster, Debrödy converted to the Bf 109 and gained his first victory, a Soviet Lavochkin La-5, on 5 July.

Early in September he was one of two Hungarians escorting He 111 bombers when they were bounced by six Yak-9s. He downed one for his seventh victory, but was immediately hard hit by another and crash-landed in enemy territory. Having eluded his pursuers, he swam the wide Dniepr river and eventually returned to his unit.

His score at 16, Debrödy was once again downed behind Russian lines, but his friend Miklós Kenyeres landed his 109 close by and somehow they

153

both squeezed into the tiny cockpit. Ironically Kenyeres (19 victories) was shot down by ground fire just two days later and taken prisoner.

Having added two more to his score, Debrödy was recalled for home defence. His first two USAAF victims were Lightnings, on 14 and 16 June 1944. July saw him add two bombers and a fighter to his tally, but then came a hiatus. A Liberator fell to his guns early in November, then on the 16th of the month Debrödy took off for his 204th and final combat sortie. After downing a Yak-9, he engaged another head-on. The Yak disintegrated under his fire, but not before it had hit and seriously wounded Debrödy, who barely managed to nurse his damaged fighter back to base. He survived, but saw no more combat. His final score was 26, which made him the second-ranking Hungarian ace of the war.

An Italian Ace

Adriano Visconti Originally a reconnaissance pilot, Adriano Visconti opened his score with a Gladiator over Libya in 1940. Shortly afterwards he converted to fighters, flying Macchi MC.202s, then MC.205s. He was credited with two Hurricanes and two Blenheims over Malta. Operating over Tunisia, then Sicily, he added 14 more to his tally before the armistice in August 1943. He then fled from Sardinia and joined the *Aeronautica Nazionale Repubblicana*, in which he commanded the *Asso di Bastogni Gruppo*. Fighting on with the Axis cause, he accounted for three Thunderbolts, one Lightning and three bombers, to bring his score to 26. In the final days of the war he was murdered by Italian partisans.

Franco Lucchini also claimed 26 victories, but five of these were during the Spanish Civil War. He was shot down and killed by escorting Spitfires when attacking Flying Fortresses over Sicily on 5 July 1943.

Japanese Aces

Yasuhiko Kuroe A graduate of the Imperial Military Academy, Kuroe made his combat début over China in 1938 and, flying the slow but agile Nakajima Ki-27 against the Russians over Khalkin Gol in 1939, claimed his first two victories. The entry of Japan into World War II found him leading an experimental flight of Nakajima Ki-44 *Shoki* fighters. The *Shoki* was a departure for the Japanese: performance took precedence over manoeuvrability, and it carried armour protection, while wing loading was nearly half as much again as that of its *Hayabusa* stablemate.

Kuroe claimed three victories with the *Shoki* before moving to command the *Hayabusa*-equipped 64th *Sentai* in Burma. Here, between April 1942 and January 1944, he claimed 22 more victories, including two P-51 Mustangs and two Mosquitos. He returned to Japan as a test pilot, and in the late spring of 1945 flew the experimental twin-engined Kawasaki Ki-102A against American B-29s, claiming three, to bring his tally to 30. It was not all easy going: his various aircraft were hit by more than 500 bullets, and he was shot down three times and wounded three times. In January 1944, he did what he described as 'a silly thing'. He became target-fixated, and followed a Spitfire for about thirteen minutes. This gave plenty of time for another Spitfire to come to the rescue, and Kuroe's machine was badly hit. He only just made it back to an emergency landing field, with a perforated fuel tank, damaged landing gear and no propeller pitch control. He survived the war as the third-ranking Japanese Army ace.

Saburo Sakai The most famous Japanese fighter ace of the war was Saburo Sakai, whose name is forever linked with the days when the Zero seemed invincible. Remarkably, he never lost a wingman in combat, although it was touch-and-go at times. He was severely wounded over Guadalcanal, and his safe return to base was an epic of flight and endurance. Then, at a late stage in the war, he returned to a fighter cockpit, although he was blind in one eye. It is the stuff of legend.

Prior to Pearl Harbor, Sakai had opened his account with two victories over China, although he was wounded there and spent an entire year recovering. With Japan's entry into World War II, his unit was assigned to attack air bases in the Philippines. The nearest Japanese airfields were on Taiwan, about 500 miles away – an unprecedented distance for single-engine fighters.

With constant practice, the Zero pilots reduced their fuel consumption, Sakai setting a record figure of just 17 gallons an hour. On 8 December 1941 the attack took place and Sakai recorded the first air victory in the Philippines, a Curtiss   P-40. Two days later he was one of ten Zero pilots who combined to shoot down a B-17. He recorded:

> This was our first experience with the B-17, and the airplane's unusual size caused us to misjudge our firing distance. In addition, the bomber's extraordinary speed, for which we had made no allowance, threw our rangefinders off.

The action then moved to Java, where Sakai recorded victories over Dutch fighters, but illness then intervened. He recovered in time to transfer to Lae,

155

Fig. 11. Gladych's Ruse

Outmanoeuvred and boxed by two FW 190s, 'Mike' Gladych was escorted down to a *Luftwaffe* fighter airfield. At the last moment he opened fire at targets on the ground; anti-aircraft guns replied and shot the FW 190s off his tail.

on the eastern coast of New Guinea, with his unit, arriving on 8 April. The Lae pilots were a hand-picked bunch, probably the nearest thing the Japanese Navy ever had to an élite unit.

On the far side of the island, separated by the jungle-clad Owen Stanley mountain range, was the US/Australian air base at Port Moresby. Action was soon almost continuous as both sides struck at each other. With so many opportunities, Sakai's score mounted rapidly, mainly Curtiss P-40s and Bell P-39s but with some twin-engine bombers among the victims. By 8 August his tally had climbed to 58, making him Lae's most successful pilot.

It was on this day that he flew his fateful mission to Guadalcanal, where the epic fight against a Dauntless dive-bomber, described earlier, took place. The American gunner was killed but pilot Dudley Adams survived. Sakai was then badly wounded by the gunner of another bomber, and returned to base partially paralysed and blind in one eye.

Months in hospital followed, and Sakai, classed as unfit for combat, was posted to home defence as an instructor. But as the American ring of steel contracted around Japan, times changed. On 20 June 1944 he arrived on Iwo Jima. Within days he had his first encounter with American Hellcats. His restricted vision proved a terrible handicap, and, flying the outclassed and outnumbered Zero, he barely survived. In the days that followed, the pattern was repeated. An occasional Hellcat fell to his guns, but the Lae days were gone forever.

Returned to the home islands once more, Sakai began test-flying new fighter types. Only one more combat sortie remained. On the night of 13/14 August 1945 he and another pilot took off without orders and managed to claim a B-29. Shortly after this, Japan surrendered. Credited with 64 victories in rather more than 200 combats, Saburo Sakai was the fourth highest scoring Japanese pilot of the war.

A Polish Ace

Boleslaw 'Mike' Gladych In many ways the operational career of Mike Gladych was pure Hollywood. When in 1939 Germany invaded Poland, he flew PZL P.11c fighters against the *Luftwaffe*. When Poland fell, he escaped to France and flew Morane-Saulnier MS.406s. On the capitulation he fled to England and flew Spitfires, then transferred to the USAAF early in 1944 where he flew Thunderbolts with Hub Zemke's 'Wolfpack'. These are the established facts; as to the rest, myths and legends abound!

Gladych is reported to have claimed victories with the Poles and French, but the record does not bear this out. He is also supposed to have flown

157

Mustangs with a USAAF Group and shot down an Me 262 jet, but this cannot be confirmed either. One of the strangest stories concerned a German pilot who flew a fighter which carried the number '13' in white, who often declined to finish off a badly damaged opponent. This happened to Gladych on 3 June 1940, when he was bounced from astern and the elevator of his Morane jammed, leaving him unable to manoeuvre. The Bf 109 came in for the kill, but after a short burst, pulled alongside. The pilot waved, then broke off. Was he out of ammunition?

Flying Spitfires with the all-Polish No 303 Squadron RAF, Gladych claimed his first victories on 23 June 1941. A Bf 109 fell to his guns near St Omer; on his second sortie of the day, he claimed three 109s and a probable near Desvres. He rammed a fourth, then, injured by debris, limped back to force-land at Manston.

Gladych flew two tours with the RAF, claiming eight victories and two 'probables', all fighters. Once again he had encountered 'White 13', been damaged, then allowed to escape. He was not unique: other pilots had experienced the same thing.

March 8, 1944, found him flying a bomber escort mission with the US 56th Fighter Group. A furious dogfight with FW 190As ended with his being separated from his flight, and cornered at low altitude by two 190s. A long and exhausting chase ensued, but there was no escape. Boxed in, he gave up. Ahead was the *Luftwaffe* airfield at Vechta, and one of the German pilots pulled alongside and signalled him to land. It was of course 'White 13'!

Obediently Gladych dropped the nose of his Thunderbolt, but then, at the last moment, slammed his throttle forward and opened fire. The German gunners responded instantly, surrounding him and the two Focke-Wulfs with flak. 'White 13' was hit, while Gladych made his escape in the confusion.

He claimed ten more victories while flying with the USAAF, to bring his war total to 18 destroyed and two 'probables'. But what of 'White 13'? By sheer chance Gladych met him again several years later. He was *Experte* Georg-Peter Eder, credited with 78 victories, in the course of which he had been shot down seventeen times and wounded on twelve occasions.

Soviet Aces

Boris Safonov Unlike many Russian pilots, Boris Safonov was meticulous in his approach to combat aviation. Graded 'above average', he graduated from training in November 1934, and for the next few years flew Polikarpov

I-15s and I-16s in the far north of the country. Meanwhile he studied every aspect of his trade and became a master craftsman. He is believed to have taken part in the Winter War against Finland, but in what capacity and with what results are not known.

When, on 22 June 1941, the Third Reich attacked the Soviet Union, Safonov was an experienced and accomplished fighter pilot. His first victory – which was also the first Soviet victory on the northern front – came on 24 June when he shot down a Heinkel He 111 over Zalentsa Bay using what were described as 'experimental rockets'. Air-to-air rockets were, of course, not new: RS 82s had been used over Khalkin Gol, though with little success. Be this as it may, Safonov's succeeding victories were all scored with guns.

North of the Arctic Circle summer days are extremely long and the nights are never completely dark. This made a heavy workload for the defenders, as with no early warning system they were forced to fly standing patrols. Even though flying five or six sorties a day, Safonov still made time to analyse tactics and capabilities, and pass his conclusions to his pilots. His main rule was, 'Long range – short bursts; short range – long bursts.'

Unlike many Russian units, the I-16s in Safonov's outfit carried radios, which enabled him to direct the fight. If the aircraft were bounced from astern by 109s, the agility of the I-16 enabled it to turn through 180 degrees quickly enough to enable a head-on pass to be made, in which the heavy armament and less vulnerable radial engine of the Russian fighter gave it a slight edge. The one essential, provided by Safonov, was to call the break at precisely the right moment. Ruses were another tactic tool for him. On at least one occasion he simulated the manoeuvres of a panic-stricken novice to lure German pilots into a false position. As one finally got on his tail, he throttled back, then blasted it as it overshot.

September 1941 was an eventful month. A triple victory on the 15th brought Safonov's score to 16 and was marked by the award of the red ribbon and gold star of the Hero of the Soviet Union. At about the same time RAF Hurricanes arrived at Vaenga; Safonov was the second Russian pilot to convert to the type.

The long nights, short days and foul weather of the Arctic winter curtailed air activity, and Safonov added only a few to his score with the Hurricane. Then, in spring 1942, the faster Curtiss P-40 Kittyhawks arrived.

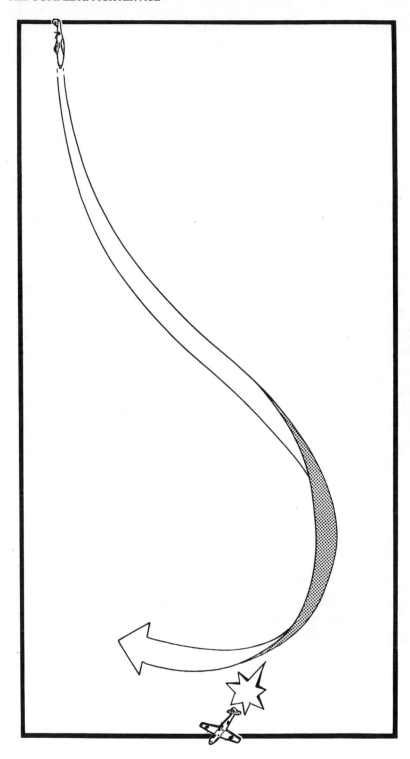

Fig. 12. Pokryshkin's Method

Leading Soviet ace Alexandr Pokryshkin developed a method of 'height, speed, manoeuvre and fire' which brought him success with the Bell P-39 Airacobra.

Engine failures were common, and the aircraft was never popular with the Russians.

On May 30 1942 Safonov led three Kittyhawks to provide air cover for Murmansk convoy PQ.16. As they arrived, the convoy was under heavy air attack. Wading straight in, Safonov had shot down two Ju 88s and damaged a third when he was attacked by a Bf 109 – possibly that flown by 94-victory *Experte* Rudolf Müller – and his engine was hit. He ditched near a Soviet minelayer, but his aircraft went straight down, taking him with it.

Boris Safonov had flown 234 missions, taken part in 34 air combats, claimed 25 victories and shared in 14 others. An inspiring leader, he was the first major Soviet ace to be lost.

Alexandr Pokryshkin Down the years, a handful of fighter leaders have become outstanding tutors and mentors. Oswald Boelcke and Mick Mannock in World War I and Werner 'Vati' Mölders in World War II are typical examples. Alexandr Pokryshkin belongs in their company.

A career officer since 1933, Pokryshkin had made a close study of aerobatics – of which he was an outstanding exponent – and fighter manoeuvres. By June 1941 he was flying MiG-3 interceptors in the Odessa Military District. On the first day of the war he led his *zveno* down at an unfamiliar shape, only to spot at the very last moment that it carried red stars. It was a Sukhoi Su-2, and tragedy was averted by a hairsbreadth. Next day brought success: in a two-versus-five combat he downed a Bf 109, although his own aircraft was damaged in the process. Shortly after this he was shot down by ground fire while on a reconnaissance mission. He returned from behind the German lines on foot.

In 1942 he was transferred to command an *eskadril* in the 16th Guards Regiment, flying Bell P-39 Airacobras, locally known as *Britchiki*. In USAAF service this aircraft had been regarded as a 'turkey', but in Pokryshkin's hands it proved deadly. Gradually his score rose, and he achieved 48 victories with it. Under his leadership, many other pilots achieved high scores with the Airacobra, notably Grigorii Rechkalov (44), Nikolai Gulayev (36) and Aleksandr Khubov (31).

Pokryshkin's particular forte was fighting in the vertical plane, of which he was an absolute master. His formula for success was 'Altitude – speed – manoeuvre – fire.' In all, he flew 360 sorties, took part in 156 air combats and was credited with 59 victories. He was shot down four times in total, and ended the war flying the Yakovlev Yak-9.

161

Leading Aces and Their Scores

British and Commonwealth
Shared victories are added as fractions. 'Probables' are not included

Score	Name	Remarks
50.67	M. T. St J. 'Pat' Pattle (SA)	Approx. only; KIA 20.4.41
36.92	J. E. 'Johnnie' Johnson (Brit)	
31.50	W. 'Cherry' Vale (Brit)	
31.33	G. F. 'Screwball' Beurling (Can)	
29.50	A. G. 'Sailor' Malan (SA)	Plus 2 unconfirmed
29.00	J. R. D. 'Bob' Braham (Brit)	PoW 25.6.44
28.50	C. R. 'Killer' Caldwell (Aust)	
28.00	J. H. 'Ginger' Lacey (Brit)	
27.70	Colin F. Gray (NZ)	
27.67	R. R. S. 'Bob' Tuck (Brit)	PoW 28.1.42
26.83	Neville F. Duke (Brit)	
26.50	Frank R. Carey (Brit)	
26.00	E. S. 'Sawn-Off' Lock (Brit)	MIA 3.8.41
21.83	Douglas R. S.Bader (Brit)	PoW 9.8.41
21.67	Donald E. Kingaby (Brit)	
21.50	E. D. 'Rosie' Mackie (NZ)	
21.00	Branse A. Burbridge (Brit)	
21.00	Michael N. Crossley (Brit)	
21.00	H. W. 'Wally' McLeod (Can)	KIA 27.9.44
20.83	G. 'Sammy' Allard (Brit)	KAS 13.3.41
20.50	W. V. 'Bill' Crawford-Compton (NZ)	
20.00	John Cunningham (Brit)	

The top-scoring Fleet Air Arm pilot was Jackie Sewell with 8.50 victories, all while flying naval aircraft. KIFA Sept. 1943.

'Doodlebug' Aces
'Doodlebugs', the forerunners of modern cruise missiles, were very small and difficult targets which, if they exploded, could easily destroy their attackers.

59½	Joseph Berry (Brit)	Plus 1 aircraft; KIA 2.10.44
53	P. del Brooke (Brit)	
51	W. Nowoczyn (Pol).	
51	A.F. Osborne (Brit)	
39	F. R. L. Mellersh (Brit)	Plus 8 aircraft
36½	Remy van Lierde (Belg)	Plus 5 aircraft
30	Roland Beamont (Brit)	Plus 6½ aircraft; PoW 12.10.44
22½	A. R. Moore (Brit)	Plus 3½ aircraft
21	R. F. Burgwal (Holl)	
21	Edward Crew (Brit)	Plus 12½ aircraft

20¾	R. W. Cole (Brit)	
20½	R. J. Cammock (NZ)	
20	O. D. Eagleson (NZ)	Plus 2½ aircraft

American – USAAF

40.00	R. I. 'Dick' Bong	Pacific; KIFA 6.8.45
38.00	Thomas B. McGuire	Pacific; KIA 1.7.45
28.00	F. S. 'Gabby' Gabreski	Europe; plus 6.50 in Korea
28.00	R. S. 'Bob' Johnson	Europe
27.00	Charles H. McDonald	Pacific
26.83	G. E. 'Ratsy' Preddy	Europe; KIA 25.12.44
25.00	John C. Meyer	Europe; plus 2 in Korea
23.00	L. C. 'Wildcat' Wade	N. Africa/Italy; all with RAF; KAS Jan. 1944
22.59	R. S. 'Ray' Wetmore	Europe
22.50	D. C. 'Dave' Schilling	Europe
22.00	Gerald R. Johnson	Pacific; KIFA 1945
22.00	W. H. 'Bud' Mahurin	Mainly Europe; plus 3.50 in Korea
22.00	Jay T. Robbins	Pacific
21.80	D. S. 'Don' Gentile	Europe; inc. 2 with RAF
21.50	F. J. 'Rat-Top' Christensen	Europe
21.00	John J. Voll	Italy
20.00	Thomas J. Lynch	Pacific; KIA 9.3.44
20.00	Robert B. Westbrook	Pacific; KIA 22.11.44
19.50	Glenn T. Eagleston	Europe; plus 2 in Korea

American – USN and USMC (all Pacific)

34	David McCampbell	USN.
28	G. 'Pappy' Boyington	USMC (6 with AVG); PoW 3.1.44
26	J. J. 'Joe' Foss	USMC
25	R. W. 'Bob' Hanson	USMC; KIA 3.2.44
24	Cecil E. Harris	USN
23	E. A. 'Gene' Valencia	USN
21	Kenneth A. Walsh	USMC
20	Donald N. Aldrich	USMC

Belgian

| 11.50 | Rodolphe de Hemricourt de Grunne | 10 in Spain, 1½ with RAF; KIA 21.5.41 |
| 8.00 | Yvan du Monceau de Bergandael | All with RAF |

Bulgarian (points system, actual victories unknown)

| 14 | Stoyan Stoyanov | |

Croatian

36	Cvitan Galic	KIA 1944
34	Mato Dubovak	
18	Mato Culinovic	KIA
18	Dragutin Ivanic	

Czech

18.48	K. M. 'Old Kut' Kuttelwascher	18 with RAF
17.00	Josef Frantisek	All with RAF; KAS 8.10.40

Danish

10.50	Kaj Birksted	All with RAF

Finnish (Winter War and Continuation War)

94.17	Eino I Juutilainen	
78.00	Hans 'Hasse' Wind	WIA 28.6.44
56.00	Eino A. Luukkanen	
44.50	Urho S. Lehtovara	
44.00	Oiva E. Tuominen	
42.00	Risto O. Puhakka	
36.00	Kauko O. Puro	
35.50	Nils E. Katajainen	
32.25	Kyösti K. Karhila	
32.25	Lauri V. Nissinen	KIA
31.08	Jorma Karhunen	
29.50	Emil O. Vesa	
28.50	Tapio T. Järvi	
26.00	Klaus J. Alakoski	
23.25	Alto K. Tervo	KIA
23.00	Jorma K. Saarinen	KIA
21.50	Antti J. Tani	
21.50	Eero A. Kinnunen	KIA
21.00	Urho P. Myllylä	

French

23	Marcel Albert	1 shared with *A de l'A*, rest Normandie-Niemen
20	Pierre Le Gloan	Approx. 5 plus 7 shared with *A de l'A*, 6 plus 2 'probables' with Vichy in Syria; KAS 11.9.43
20	Edmond Marin la Meslée	4 destroyed plus 12 shared and four 'probables', all with *A de l'A*; KIA Feb. 1945
18	Jean-François Demozay	All with RAF
18	Roland de la Poype	1 destroyed and 1 'probable' with RAF; 6 destroyed and 9 shared

		destroyed, plus 1 shared 'probable' with Normandie-Niemen
17	Michel Dorance	14 plus 3 'probables' with *A de l'A*; KIA 1940
17	Pierre Clostermann	All with RAF, but confusion between aircraft destroyed in air and those on ground
16	Jacques André	All with Normandie-Niemen
16	Louis Delfino	8 plus 2 'probables' with *A de l'A*, rest with Normandie- Niemen
16	Roger Sauvage	2 with *A de l'A*, rest with Normandie-Niemen
16	Albert Littolf	6 shared destroyed and one shared 'probable' with *A de l'A*; 5 destroyed with RAF, 2 destroyed and 2 shared with Normandie-Niemen
15	Georges Valentin	Mainly with *A de l'A*
14	Camille Plubeau	All with *A de l'A*, inc. 4 'probables'

N.B. See earlier comment on French system of scoring, which may include shared victories and 'probables' as whole victories. For example, the Czech ace Alois Vasatko flew with the *Armée de l'Air* in 1940 and took part in actions which resulted in 12 victories, but, of these, only three were wholly credited to him, while the fractions from the other nine add up to a mere 2.32, averaging barely ¼ each. Yet some lists credit him with 15 victories during this period!

German and Austrian (all victories are on the Eastern Front unless otherwise stated)

352	Erich 'Bubi' Hartmann	
301	Gerhard Barkhorn.	
275	Günther Rall	3 WF
267	Otto Kittel	KIA 14.2.45
258	Walter 'Nowi' Nowotny	3 WF; KIA 8.11.44
237	Wilhelm Batz	5 WF
222	Erich Rudorffer	60 WF, 26 NA
220	Heinz 'Pritzl' Baer	96 WF, 45 NA and Med
212	Hermann Graf	10 WF
209	Heinrich Ehrler	10 WF; KIA 4.4.45
208	Theodor Weissenberger	33 WF
206	Hans Philipp	1 Pol, 33 WF; KIA 8.10.43
206	Walter Schuck	8 WF
204	Anton Hafner	20 NA and Med; KIA 17.10.44
203	Helmut Lipfert.	
197	Walter 'Graf Punski' Krupinski	20 WF
192	Anton Hackl	87 WF
189	Joachim Brendel	
189	Max Stötz	16 WF; MIA 19.8.43
188	Joachim Kirschner	21 Med; KIA 17.12.43

180	Kurt Brändle	20 WF; KIA 3.11.43
178	Günther Josten	
176	Johannes Steinhoff	28 WF and Med
174	Ernst-Wilhelm Reinert	51 NA, 20 Med and WF
174	Günther Schack	
173	Emil Lang	25 WF; KIA 3.9.44
173	Heinz Schmidt	MIA 5.9.43
166	Horst Adameit	1 WF; MIA 8.8.44
162	Wolf-Dietrich Wilcke	25 WF, 4 Med; KIA 23.3.44
158	Hans-Joachim Marseille	7 WF, 151 NA; KAS 30.9.42
157	Heinrich Sturm	KAS 22.12.44
157	Gerhard Thyben	5 WF
152	Hans Beisswenger	
150	Gordon Gollob	1 Pol, 5 WF

Another 68 *Experten* claimed between 100 and 149 victories, and a further 128 claimed between 60 and 99. It will be noted that, with the exception of Marseille and Baer, both already listed, few scored heavily against the Western powers. Some that did were:

112	Kurt Bühligen	Inc. 40 NA
104	Adolf Galland	
102	Werner Schroer	Of 114, inc. 61 NA
102	Egon Mayer	KIA 2.3.44
101	Josef Priller	
97	Gustav Rödel	Of 98, inc. 52 in NA and Med
95	Siegfried Lemke	Of 96, inc. 21 heavy bombers
93	Josef Wurmheller	Of 102

German and Austrian Night Fighter Aces
The *Nachtjagdflieger* operated in a target-rich environment which enabled them to outscore their RAF opposite numbers:

121	Heinz-Wolfgang Schnaufer	
110	Helmut Lent	8 by day; KAS 5.10.44
83	Heinrich zu Sayn-Wittgenstein	29 EF; KIA 21.1.44
72	Wilhelm Herget	15 by day
66	Werner Streib	1 by day
65	Manfred Meurer	KIA 21.1.44
65	Günther Radusch	1 by day in Spain
64	Rudolf Schönert	
64	Heinz Rökker	1 by day

Hungarian

34	Deszö Szentgyörgyi	
26	György Debrödy	WIA 16.11.44
25	Laszlo Molnar	KIA autumn 1944
24	Lajos Toth	

19	Miklos Kenyeres	PoW Feb. 1944

Italian

26	Adriano Visconti	7 with ANR; killed by partisans 29.4.45
26	Franco Lucchini	5 in Spain; KIA 5.7.43
23	Teresio Martinoli	1 with Allies; KIFA Aug. 1944
22	Leonardo Ferrulli	1 in Spain; KIA 5.7.43
20	Mario Visentini	KAS 1941
19	Franco Bordoni-Bisleri	

Japanese

Official lists of Japanese scores were not kept, and virtually all the following include shared victories and 'probables'. This listing includes only those who became aces in World War II, although victories over China and Khalkin Gol are included in the totals where applicable.

94	Tatsuzo Iwamoto	Navy; inc. 14 in China
87	Hiroyoshi Nishizawa	Navy; KIA 26.10.44
70	Shoichi Sugita	Navy; KIA 15.4.45
64	Saburo Sakai	Navy; inc. 2 in China
54	Takeo Okumura	Navy; inc. 4 in China; KIA 22.9.43
51	Satoshi Anabuki	Army
38	Isamu Sasaki	Army
34	Toshio Ohta	Navy; KIA 21.10.42
32	Kazuo Sugino	Navy
30	Yasuhiko Kuroe	Army; inc. 2 over Khalkin Gol
29	Shizuo Ishii, Navy	Inc. 3 in China; KIA 24.10.43
28	Kaneyoshi Muto	Navy; inc. 5 in China; KIA 24.7.45
27	Junichi Sasai	Navy; KIA 26.8.42
27	Goichi Sumino	Army; KIA 6.6.44
26	Moritsugo Kanai	Army; inc. 7 over Khalkin Gol
25	Naoshi Kanno	Navy; KIA 1.8.45
24	Nobuo Ogiya	Navy; KIA 13.2.44
20	Tetsuo Kikushi	Navy
20	Shigeo Sugio	Navy
20	Teruhiko Kobayashi	Army

Norwegian

14.33	Svein Heglund	All with RAF
10.33	Helner Grundt-Spang	All with RAF

Polish

21.00	Stanislaw Skalski	6 in Poland, remainder RAF, plus 3 unconfirmed with RAF
18.00	B. M. 'Mike' Gladych	8 with RAF, 10 with USAAF

18.00	Witold Urbanowicz	1 Soviet a/c in 1936, 15 with RAF, 2 with USAAF over China
16.50	Eugeniusz Horbaczewski	All with RAF; KIA 18.8.44
12.67	Jan Zumbach	1 shared with *A de l'A*, rest with RAF
11.50	Michal Maciejowski	All with RAF; PoW 9.8.43

Romanian (points system, actual victories unknown)

60	Constantine Cantacuzene	Defected to Allies Aug.1944
50	Alexandre Serbanescu	KIA 18.8.44
40	Florian Budu	Approx. only

Slovakian

33	Jan Gerthofer
32	Jan Reznak
29	Isidor Kovarik

Spanish (EF WWII only)

| 12 | Gonzala Hevia Alvarez-Quinones |
| 10 | Mariano Cuadra Medina. |

Soviet

62	Ivan Kozhedub.	
59	Aleksandr Pokryshkin.	
57	Nikolai Gulaev	Inc. 4 prior to WWII
56	Grigoriy Rechkalov	Plus 5 shared
52	Arseniy Vorozheikin	Inc. 6 over Khalkin Gol
52	Kirill Yevstigne'ev	
50	Dimitri Glinka	KIFA Nov. 1944
50	Aleksandr Khubov	
48	Ivan Pilipenko	
46	Vasiliy Kubarev	
46	Nikolai Skomorokhov	
43	Vladimir Bobrov	Inc. 13 in Spain
43	Georgiy Kostilev	
42	Sergei Morgunov	
41	Vitaly Popkov	
39	Viktor Golubev	
38	Vasiliy Gulubev	
37	Sergei Lugansky	Plus 6 shared
37	Mikhail Pivovarov	
36	Anatoliy Dolgikh	
36	Grigoriy Gul'tyaev	
36	Aleksandr Koldunov	
36	Nikolai Kuznetsov	May inc. 15 shared victories
35	Ivan Babak	PoW but escaped
35	Pavel Kamozin	

35	Vladimir Lavrinenkov	Plus 11 shared
35	Nikolai Pavlushkin	
34	Aleksandr Chislov	
34	Fedor Chubukov	
34	Piotr Gnido	
34	Aleksandr Kotchekov	
34	Sergei Luk'yanov	
34	Ivan Sytov	
32	Andrey Borovykh	
32	Viktor Kirilyuk	
32	Mikhail Komel'khov	
32	Nikolai Krasnov	
32	Mikhail Ryazanov	Plus 16 shared
32	Ivan Stepanenko	
32	Mikhail Zelenkin	
31	Pavel Golovachev	
30	Sultan Akhmet-Khan	Plus 19 shared
30	Fedor Arkhipenko	
30	Boris Glinka	
30	Ivan Likhobabiyiy	
30	Piotr Likholetov	
30	Valentin Makharev	
30	Piotr Pokhryshev	Inc. 8 shared
30	Aleksei Khlobystov	Inc. 3 by ramming
29	Pavel Kiriya	
29	Ivan Kravtsov	
29	Vladimir Merkulov	
29	Vasiliy Merkushev	
29	Nikolai Naidenov	
29	Konstantin Novikov	
29	Mikhail Pogorelov	
29	Ivan Romanenko	
28	Lazar Chapchakhov	
28	Mikhail Ignate'ev	
28	Igor Kaberov	
28	Konstantin Kovalov	
28	Boris Kobzan	Inc. 4 by ramming
28	Andrey Kulagin	
28	Pavel Murave'ev	
28	Vasiliy Osipov	
28	Yevgeniy Selyanin	
28	Vladimir Serov	
28	Piotr Vostrukhin	
28	Vasiliy Zaitsev	
28	Nikolai Zotov	
27	Piotr Bazanov	
27	Mikhail Garam	

27	Mikhail Grinev	
27	Aleksandr Karpov	
27	Pavel Klimov	
27	Vasiliy Klimov	
27	Anatoliy Kozhevnikov	
27	Sergei Kuznetsov	
27	Aleksandr Maiorov	
27	Spartak Makovsky	
27	Viktor Merenkov	
27	Aleksei Smirnov	
27	Viktor Talalikhin	Inc. 1 by ramming
26	Mikhail Baranov	Inc. 1 by ramming
26	Arseniy Bastrakhov	
26	Andrei Chirkov	
26	Ivan Golosov	
26	Vasiliy Kharitonov	Inc. 1 by ramming
26	Nikolai Kita'ev	
26	Nikolai Lavitskiy	
26	Ivan Leonovitch	
26	Vasiliy Mikhailev	
26	Mikhail Sachkov	
25	Chichiko Bendeliani	
25	Ivan Borisov	
25	Viktor Borodachev	
25	Aleksei Gubanov	
25	Vasiliy Markov	
25	Boris Safonov	Plus 14 shared; KIA 30.5.42
25	Viktor Subirov	
25	Vladimir Shikunov	
25	Igor Vasilevskiy	

Except for the very few, casualties in the above listings are not known. There may also be many cases where shared victories are included in the totals as whole victories. Several hundred Soviet fighter pilots claimed between 5 and 24 victories during the Great Patriotic War.

Major British Fighters of World War II

Type	*Hurricane I*	*Spitfire Vb*	*Spitfire IX*	*Tempest V*
Span	40ft 0in	36ft 10in	36ft 10in	41ft 0in
Length	31ft 5in	29ft 11in	30ft 6in	33ft 8in
Height	13ft 2in	12ft 7in	12ft 7in	16ft 1in
Wing area	258 sq ft	242 sq ft	242 sq ft	302 sq ft
Power	RR Merlin, 1,030hp	RR Merlin, 1,440hp	RR Merlin, 1,710hp	Napier Sabre II, 2,420hp
				contd . . .

Loaded wt	6,600lb	6,650lb	7,500lb	8,500lb
Wing ldg	26lb/sq ft	28lb/sq ft	31lb/sq ft	38lb/sq ft
Power ldg	0.156hp/lb	0.217hp/lb	0.228hp/lb	0.285hp/lb
Vmax	316mph	374mph	408mph	435mph
Service ceiling	33,200ft	37,000ft	44,000ft	36,000ft
Rate of climb	2,300ft/min	3,650ft/min	4,150ft/min	4,700ft/min
Range	425 miles	470 miles	434 miles	740 miles

Polish and French Fighters of World War II

Type	PZL P.11c	Morane MS.406	Dewoitine D.520	Bloch MB.152
Span	35ft 2in	34ft 10in	33ft 6in	34ft 7in
Length	24ft 9¼in	26ft 9in	28ft 9in	29ft 10in
Height	9ft 4¼in	9ft 4in	8ft 5in	9ft 11in
Wing area	193 sq ft	172.22 sq ft	172 sq ft	186.43 sq ft
Power	Bristol Mercury, 640hp	Hispano-Suiza 12Y, 860hp	Hispano-Suiza 12Y, 930hp	GR 14N 1,000hp
Loaded wt	3,968lb	5,610lb	5,900lb	6,173lb
Wing ldg	20.6lb/sq ft	33lb/sq ft	34lb/sq ft	33lb/sq ft
Power ldg	0.161hp/lb	0.153hp/lb	0.158hp/lb	0.162hp/lb
Vmax	242mph	304mph	332mph	316mph
Service ceiling	c26,000ft	32,800ft	33,600ft	c31,000ft
Rate of climb	2,440ft/min	2,559ft/min	5.8min to 13,125ft	3.4 min to 6,560ft
Range	435 miles	603 miles	550 miles	335 miles

Major German Fighters of World War II

Type	Bf 109E-3	Bf 109G-6	FW 190A-3	FW 190D-9
Span	32ft 4in	32ft 7in	34ft 5½in	34ft 5½in
Length	28ft 4in	29ft 7in	29ft 0in	33ft 5in
Height	11ft 2in	11ft 2in	13ft 0in	11ft 0in
Wing Area	174 sq ft	173 sq ft	197 sq ft	197 sq ft
Power	DB 601, 1,100hp	DB 605, 1,800hp	BMW 801Dg, 1,700hp	Jumo 213A, 2,240hp
Loaded wt	5,523lb	6,945lb	7,652lb	9,480lb
Wing ldg	32lb/sq.ft	40lb/sq.ft	39lb/sq.ft	48lb/sq.ft
Power ldg	0.199hp/lb	0.259hp/lb	0.222hp/lb	0.236hp/lb
Vmax	354mph	387mph	399mph	426mph
Service ceiling	36,091ft	38,550ft	33,800ft	39,372ft
Rate of climb	3,281ft/min	4,560ft/min	c.4,100ft/min	c.4,200ft/min
Range	412 miles	450 miles	644 miles	520 miles

contd . . .

Major Italian Fighters of World War II

Type	Fiat CR.42 Falco	Fiat G.50bis Freccia	Macchi MC.200 Saetta	Macchi MC.202 Folgore
Span	31ft 10in	36ft 0¼in	34ft 8½in	34ft 8½in
Length	27ft 1½in	25ft 7in	26ft 10½in	29ft 0½in
Height	11ft 9½in	9ft 8½in	11ft 5¾in	9ft 11½in
Wing area	241 sq ft	196 sq ft	181 sq ft	181 sq ft
Power	Fiat A 74R, 840hp	Fiat A 74R, 870hp	Fiat A 74R, 870hp	RA Monsoni, 1,175hp
Loaded wt	5,033lb	5,963lb	5,597lb	6,459lb
Wing ldg	21lb/sq ft	30lb/sq ft	31lb/sq ft	36lb/sq ft
Power ldg	0.167hp/lb	0.146hp/lb	0.155hp/lb	0.182hp/lb
Vmax	267mph	294mph	312mph	370mph
Service ceiling	33,465ft	29,000ft	29,200ft	37,730ft
Rate of climb	c.2,500ft/min	c.2,600ft/min	3,125ft/min	c.3,750ft/min
Range	482 miles	620 miles	354 miles	475 miles

Major Russian Fighters of World War II

Type	MiG-3	LaGG-3	La-5FN	Yak-9
Span	33ft 6in	32ft 2in	31ft 9in	32ft 10in
Length	27ft 1in	28ft 11in	28ft 7in	28ft 1in
Height	10ft 10in	11ft 9in	11ft 9in	9ft 10in
Wing area	188 sq ft	188 sq ft	188 sq ft	185 sq ft
Power	Mikulin AM-35, 1,350hp	Klimov 105PF, 1,310hp	Shvetsov ASh-82fn, 1,850hp	Klimov VK-105PF 1,240hp
Loaded wt	7,385lb	7,032lb	7,407lb	6,747lb
Wing ldg	39lb/sq ft	37lb/sq ft	39lb/sq ft	36lb/sq ft
Power ldg	0.183hp/lb	0.186hp/lb	0.25hp/lb	0.184hp/lb
Vmax	398mph	348mph	403mph	367mph
Service ceiling	39,400ft	31,495ft	31,150ft	36,100ft
Rate of climb	5.7m/16,405ft	5.6m/16,405ft	4.7m/16,405ft	4.5m/16,405ft
Range	510 miles	404 miles	475 miles	565 miles

British and German Night Fighters of World War II

Type	Beaufighter VIf	Mosquito XIX	Bf 110G-4	Ju 88G-6
Span	57ft 10in	54ft 2in	53ft 5in	65ft 11in
Length	41ft 8in	41ft 2in	41ft 7in	51ft 1in
Height	15ft 10in	15ft 3in	13ft 1in	15ft 11in

contd . . .

Wing area	503 sq ft	454 sq ft	413 sq ft	587 sq ft
Power	2 × Hercules,	2 × Merlin,	2 × DB605B,	2 × Jumo 213A,
	1,670hp	1,620hp	1,475hp	1,750hp
Loaded wt	21,600lb	20,600lb	20,732lb	28,900lb
Wing ldg	43lb/sq ft	45lb/sq ft	50lb/sq ft	49lb/sq ft
Power ldg	0.155hp/lb	0.157hp/lb	0.142hp/lb	0.121hp/lb
Vmax	333mph	378mph	297mph	389mph
Service ceiling	26,500ft	29,000ft	26,248ft	32,800ft
Rate of climb	1,850ft/min	2,700ft/min	2,165ft/min	1,655ft/min
Range	1,480 miles	1,400 miles	491 miles	1,398 miles

USAAF Fighters of World War II

Type	*P-40 Kittyhawk*	*P-47D Thunder-bolt*	*P-38J Lightning*	*P-51D Mustang*
Span	37ft 4in	40ft 9in	52ft 0in	37ft 0in
Length	31ft 2in	36ft 1in	37ft 10in	32ft 3in
Height	10ft 7in	14ft 2in	12ft 10in	13ft 8in
Wing area	236 sq ft	300 sq ft	328 sq ft	233 sq ft
Power	Allison V-1710,	Double Wasp,	2 × Allison V-	Merlin V-1650,
	1,600hp	2,300hp	1710, 1,425hp	1,695hp
Loaded wt	8,500lb	14,600lb	17,500lb	10,100lb
Wing ldg	36lb/sq ft	49lb/sq ft	53lb/sq ft	43lb/sq ft
Power ldg	0.188hp/lb	0.158hp/lb	0.163hp/lb	0.167hp/lb
Vmax	362mph	429mph	420mph	437mph
Service ceiling	30,000ft	40,000ft	40,000ft	40,000ft
Rate of climb	c.2,700ft/min	2,780ft/min	2,850ft/min	3,475ft/min
Range	700 miles	950 miles	1,240 miles	1,650 miles

USN and USMC Fighters of World War II

Type	*F2A Buffalo*	*F4F Wildcat*	*F6F-3 Hellcat*	*F4U-1 Corsair*
Span	35ft 0in	38ft 0in	42ft 10in	41ft 0in
Length	26ft 0in	29ft 0in	33ft 7in	33ft 4in
Height	12ft 1in	12ft 1½in	11ft 3in	16ft 1in
Wing area	209 sq ft	260 sq ft	334 sq ft	314 sq ft
Power	Cyclone,	Twin Wasp,	Double Wasp,	Double Wasp
	1,100hp	1,200hp	2.000hp	2,000hp
Loaded wt	6,840lb	7,975lb	12,186lb	12,694lb
Wing ldg	33lb/sq ft	31lb/sq ft	36lb/sq ft	40lb/sq ft
Power ldg	0.161hp/lb	0.15hp/lb	0.164hp/lb	0.158hp/lb
Vmax	292mph	320mph	376mph	417mph
Service ceiling	30,500ft	34,000ft	37,500ft	37,900ft

contd . . .

Rate of climb	3,070ft/min	2,190ft/min	3,240ft/min	2,890ft/min
Range	650 miles	830 miles	1,085 miles	1,015 miles

Japanese Fighters of World War II

Type	*Ki 43 Hayabusa*	*A6M Zero*	*Ki 84 Hayate*	*N1K1 Shiden*
Span	37ft 6½in	39ft 4½in	36ft 10in	39ft 3in
Length	29ft 2½in	29ft 9in	32ft 7in	30ft 8in
Height	10ft 1½in	9ft 2in	11ft 1in	13ft 0in
Wing area	237 sq ft	242 sq ft	226 sq ft	253 sq ft
Power	Sakae, 975hp	Sakae, 975hp	Homare 45, 1,900hp	Homare 45, 1,990hp
Loaded wt	5,320lb	5,134lb	7,965lb	9,039lb
Wing ldg	22lb/sq ft	21lb/sq ft	35lb/sq ft	36lb/sq ft
Power ldg	0.183hp/lb	0.19hp/lb	0.239hp/lb	0.22hp/lb
Vmax	320mph	346mph	388mph	370mph
Service ceiling	36,800ft	35,100ft	34,450ft	39,700ft
Rate of climb	3,240ft/min	3,140ft/min	3,400ft/min	3,350ft/min
Range	1,006 miles	1,130 miles	1,025 miles	1,069 miles

4. HIGHER AND FASTER

By the end of World War II the performance of the piston-engine fighter was close to its practical limits. The previous three decades had seen maximum speeds and rates of climb quadruple and ceilings triple. These improvements had, however, been achieved at the expense of manoeuvrability: sustained rates of turn were down by almost two-thirds, while turn radii were much larger. For the moment, the performance-versus-manoeuvrability controversy had been decisively settled in favour of the former.

At the same time, altitude advantage had become the supreme arbiter in battle, to be sought above all else. Altitude could be converted into speed for the attack, which could in turn be converted back into altitude afterwards. Future fighters needed to fly faster and climb higher than their opponents. But even as piston-engine fighter performance reached a plateau, jet-powered fighters began to enter service.

Operational from late in 1944, their numbers were too few to have any great impact on the war. The early jet engines were prone to malfunction, acceleration was poor, and they were so thirsty that endurance was extremely limited. On the other hand, they offered a speed advantage over conventional fighters of the order of 100mph, and an excellent rate of climb.

The main operational problem arose from compressibility. At the normal flying speeds of the time, the air in front of the aeroplane moved smoothly out of the way. But as the local speed of sound was approached, the air could not move fast enough and became compressed in an uneven manner. This 'lumpy' air reacted on the aircraft to cause buffeting, which often resulted in loss of control or, in extreme cases, structural failure.

Tactically, the result was that altitude was less of an advantage for the early jet fighters, as they quickly reached their limiting Mach numbers in quite shallow dives. As more was discovered about compressibility postwar, various aerodynamic measures were taken to offset it. These included speed brakes, thinner wings and swept wings, the sweep angle of which

---

The speed of sound varies with air density, and thus with altitude. At the tropopause, a theoretical 36,090ft, it is 659.8mph; at sea level it increases to 761mph. These figures are, however, modified by air temperature, which affects density. To rationalise this, the speed of sound is referred to as Mach 1; aircraft speeds are given as decimal fractions, e.g. 0.83.

---

helped to delay its onset. At the same time, structures were made stronger to cope with the increased aerodynamic loads. This had a spin-off effect: it made fighters tougher, and more difficult to shoot down.

The typical aircraft weapon of 1915 was the Lewis gun – 7.7mm in calibre, firing a projectile weighing 0.4oz, and with a cyclic rate of fire of about 600 rounds per minute and a muzzle velocity of 2,240ft/sec. By 1945 the best aircraft gun was the German Mauser MG 213, a revolver cannon which spewed out 1,200 20mm shells of 7.4oz each per minute, with a muzzle velocity of 3,300ft/sec. The USAAF largely stayed with the 12.7mm Browning, six of which fired 120 1.17oz projectiles per second with a muzzle velocity of 2,750ft/sec.

Other weapons had been tried. Electrically fired Le Prieur rockets had been effective against observation balloons from 1916, but the latter were large and static targets and against relatively small and agile aircraft they were insufficiently accurate. The Russians used RS 82 rockets against the Japanese at Khalkin Gol in 1938, and against the *Luftwaffe* hordes in 1941, with little result, and for the same reason. The *Luftwaffe*, faced with four-engine heavy bombers of the USAAF from 1943, tried the 210mm mortar, the Nebelwerfer 42, carried underwing in 'stovepipes'. The low velocity of these weapons required an aiming point some 200ft above the target, and they were time-fuzed to explode at a pre-set range. This proved almost impossible to judge with any precision. Accuracy was once again the problem. The end of the war saw the German R4M rocket in service, a salvo of which could blanket an area of sky big enough to give a good chance of hitting a heavy bomber, but in practice it achieved little.

Dropping bombs on formations of aircraft appeared to offer a viable alternative. Both the Germans and the Japanese experimented with this, but the aiming and ranging problems proved intractable. Successes were spectacular but few. The gun reigned supreme.

In the space of 30 years, effective shooting ranges had more than tripled, while hitting power had increased by a factor of 50 or more. Aiming accuracy also increased. The gyroscopic computing gun sight had entered service in 1943. The pilot set the wingspan of his adversary, then adjusted the circle of diamonds to touch them. The sight automatically set up the correct deflection angle for the shot. All the pilot had to do was to track his opponent for a couple of seconds, then open fire. This enabled him to score hits at angles which were previously the exclusive preserve of gifted marksmen. It should, of course, be observed that while the number of victories doubled, this was only from two to four per cent per burst! The next advance was the radar-ranging gun sight, which gave accurate ranging on a target. This was fine when it worked, which was not all that often.

Battle in the Stratosphere
The first conflict involving jet fighters on both sides took place in Korea between 1950 and 1953. War broke out in June 1950, when the communist North invaded the South. The recently formed United Nations Organisation was invoked, and, with its blessing, the American Far Eastern Air Force swept the small and obsolete North Korean Air Force from the skies. With total air supremacy, UN ground forces overran the North and by November had almost reached the Chinese border.

At this point the People's Republic of China intervened, backed in the air by the Soviet Union. The two major communist states, spurred by their shared ideal of world domination, had at that time a close relationship, so much so that two regiments of the latest and best Russian fighter, the swept-wing MiG-15, were deployed to China early in 1950, barely two years after the first flight of the prototype on 30 December 1947 and only months after the type first entered service. Russian-flown MiG-15s went into action over Korea within the year. One can only assume that aerial intervention had been anticipated by the USSR.

This was the first of many covert clashes between the major powers. While the USAF flew openly under the United Nations banner, the Soviet pilots carried Chinese or North Korean insignia on their fighters and wore Chinese flying overalls. They were forbidden to operate over the sea, where if shot down they might have been captured, and when operating over land were restricted from venturing too far south for the same reason.

The one thing that could not be disguised was the language. The communist pilots communicated with each other and with the ground in Russian, and this must have immediately been discovered by the UN listening service. But neither superpower was keen on advertising the fact that they were

177

at war with each other, for fear of escalating the conflict. There was, however, a single instance in the entire war where American jets were confronted by Soviet Air Force MiGs. On 18 November 1952, USN Panthers attacked targets near Hoeryong, near the border. They were intercepted by MiG-15s based near Vladivostok, two of which were shot down and others damaged.

The MiG-15

In the immediate post-war period, the perceived threat to the Soviet Union was an air attack by nuclear-armed American strategic bombers, specifically the Boeing B-29. To oppose this threat, a fighter was required with a maximum speed of Mach 0.9, a high rate of climb, good manoeuvrability at high altitude, a minimum endurance of one hour and an exceptionally heavy armament to inflict lethal damage with just a few hits.

The result was the MiG-15, a small, 'no-frills', swept-wing fighter, armed with two 23mm NS-23 cannon with 80 rounds each and a single 37mm N-37 cannon with 40 rounds. Soviet armament experts had calculated that, on average, two hits by 37mm shells or eight hits by 23mm shells were enough to destroy a B-29.

A single hit from either was potentially devastating to a fighter, but scoring hits was less than easy. The N-37 pumped out about seven shells per second each weighing 1.62lb; the NS-23 had double this rate of fire with a projectile weight of 0.44lb. But the real problem lay in aiming. Muzzle velocities for both cannon were the same, 2,264ft/sec, but the ballistic qualities, and therefore the trajectories of the projectiles, varied widely. Against a large, non-manoeuvring target like a B-29 this was no real problem, but against a small, hard-manoeuvring fighter it made accurate aiming very difficult.

Although the MiG-15 had been publicly displayed at Tushino in the summer of 1948, the West knew very little about it and it was widely assumed to be just another inferior Soviet product. But when it appeared over Korea in November 1950 its high-altitude performance came as a nasty shock to its adversaries.

The MiG-15 was powered by a British-designed engine, the Rolls-Royce Nene, examples of which had been supplied to the Soviet Union by the British Labour government of the time. With the addition of water injection, the Nene became the RD-45F (*Forsirovanni*, or boosted). A centrifugal- rather than an axial-flow engine, the Nene was arguably the best jet engine in the world at that time, and it gave the light and austere MiG-15 an outstanding high-altitude performance.

178

Straight-Wing Jet Fighters, Korea

Type	Lockheed F-80C Shooting Star	Grumman F9F-2 Panther	Republic F-84E Thunderjet	Gloster Meteor F.8
Span	38ft 9in	38ft 0in	36ft 5in	37ft 2in
Length	34ft 5in	37ft 3in	38ft 6in	44ft 7in
Height	11ft 3in	11ft 4in	12ft 10in	13ft 10in
Wing area	237.6 sq ft	250 sq ft	260 sq ft	350 sq ft
Take-off wt	16,856lb	19,494lb	16,685lb	19,100lb
Power	J33-A-23, 5,400lb	J42-P-6, 5,000lb	J35-A-17D, 5,000lb	2 × Derwent, 3,600lb
Wing ldg	71lb/sq ft	78lb/sq ft	64lb/sq ft	55lb/sq ft
Thrust ldg	0.32lb/lb	0.26lb/lb	0.30lb/lb	0.38lb/lb
Vmax	522kt	473kt	519kt	512kt
Climb rate	c.5,000ft/min	5,140ft/min	5,800ft/min	6,950ft/min
Ceiling	46,800ft	44,600ft	40,750ft	44,000ft

NB. At about this time the statute mile was abandoned in favour of the nautical mile, as a measure which made long-distance navigation easier. Consequently miles per hour were replaced by knots. A nautical mile is 1.1515 statute miles.

Swept-Wing Jet Fighters, Korea

Type	NA F-86A Sabre	NA F-86F Sabre	MiG-15	MiG-15bis
Span	37ft 1¼in	39ft 1½in	33ft 0in	33ft 0in
Length	37ft 6in	37ft 6½in	33ft 1¾in	33ft 1½in
Height	14ft 9in	14ft 9in	11ft 1¾in	11ft 1½in
Wing area	288sq ft	313sq ft	222sq ft	222sq ft
Take-off wt	16,223lb	15,198lb	11,913lb	13,458lb
Power	J47-GE-13, 5,200lb	J47-GE-27, 5,910lb	RD-45F, 5,000lb	VK-1, 5,952lb
Wing ldg	56lb/ sq ft	48lb/ sq ft	54lb/ sq ft	61lb/ sq ft
Thrust ldg	0.32lb/lb	0.39lb/lb	0.42lb/lb	0.44lb/lb
Vmax	588kt	604kt	567kt	598kt
Climb rate	7,470ft/min	9,300ft/min	8,265ft/min	9,055ft/min
Ceiling	48,000ft	48,000ft	49,871ft	50,856ft

A MiG-15bis evaluated by the United States shortly after the war was taken up to 55,600ft by Chuck Yeager, although this is believed to the absolute rather than the service ceiling.

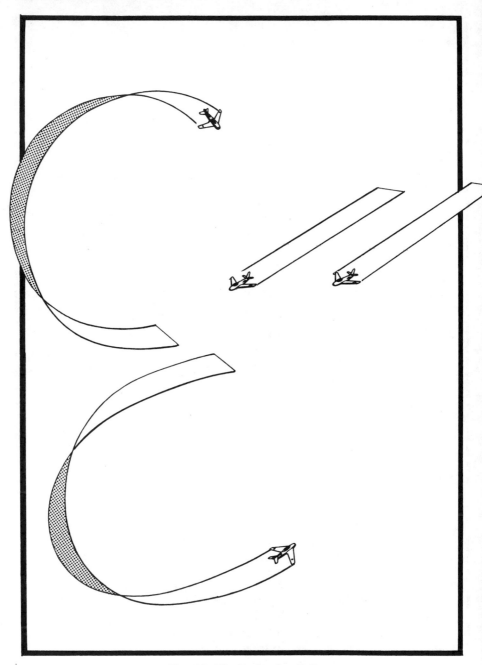

Fig. 13. The Defensive Split
*The superb climb performance of the MiG-15 in Korea allowed this
manoeuvre. When bounced from astern, one aircraft in the element
broke hard; the other broke upwards and manoeuvred for
an attacking position.*

At this time, only two UN jet fighters were in the theatre, both straight-winged. The standard USAF fighter was the Lockheed F-80 Shooting Star; the USN fielded the Grumman F9F Panther carrier fighter. Shortly afterwards, the Republic F-84E Thunderjet entered the arena, but none possessed the performance to force combat on the swept-winged Soviet fighter.

By the end of 1950 Chinese and North Korean pilots were being trained on the MiG-15, but not until the following summer did they become proficient enough to join combat. Even then, the undernourished Chinese and North Koreans were far more prone to blacking-out in hard manoeuvres than their Russian allies. For most of the war, Russian pilots carried the main burden of combat. Even then they were disadvantaged. Whereas the Americans had g-suits and 'bone domes', the Soviets wore standard Chinese-style flying overalls and leather helmets.

The MiG-15 made its combat début on 1 November 1950, when a flight of piston-engined Mustangs was attacked by six of the swept-wing Soviet fighters. No damage was caused to either side. This set an oft-repeated pattern when jets met propeller-driven fighters. Even when surprise was achieved, the speed differential was too high to allow more than a fleeting firing opportunity, whilst if the jets slowed up they could be out-turned. Over the next three years about two dozen MiG-15s were claimed by Mustang, Corsair and Sea Fury pilots, although it must be admitted that the MiGs had rather the better of things.

The first ever jet-versus-jet victory occurred on 8 November 1950 when six MiG-15s bounced eight F-80 Shooting Stars near the Chinese border, marked by the Yalu River. The F-80s saw them coming and turned into them for a head-on pass which did no damage to either side. Five MiGs disengaged up and back across the Yalu, but the sixth, having dumped too much speed with a hard pull-out, set off for home in a shallow dive. Shooting Star pilot Russell Brown set off in pursuit and pumped a five-second burst into the MiG, which caught fire and crashed near the Yalu. This victory notwithstanding, the F-80 was badly outperformed by its Russian opponent, and Brown's success was largely a matter of being in the right place at the right time. On the following day, carrier pilot Bill Amen unleashed the four 20mm cannon of his Panther to score the first jet victory for the USN.

Alarmed by the performance of the Russian-built fighter, the USAF imported their 'latest and greatest', the North American F-86 Sabre. First flown almost three months earlier than the MiG-15, by test pilot and Pacific ace

'Wheaties' Welch, the XF-86 went supersonic in a dive on 26 April 1948 – something that the MiG-15 was never to emulate.

With similar installed power, the Sabre was rather larger and heavier than its opponent, which in part accounted for its inferior high-altitude perform- ance. However, handling was far superior, notably in transients in pitch and roll. Roll rate peaked at Mach 0.60 at 210deg/sec – considerably faster than its opponent. Both aircraft suffered from severe pitch-up (up to 8g) at tran- sonic speeds, although this was largely cured on later Sabres by an all-flying tail. The Sabre's greatest weakness was its firepower: six .50-calibre ma- chine guns had been adequate for World War II, but it was less so in Korea. This was aggravated by the lack of oxygen in the stratosphere: even though badly hit, many MiGs stubbornly refused to burn!

The MiG-15 handled less well. As a gun platform it was unstable, with a tendency to snake laterally at speeds above Mach 0.86, while the speed brakes deployed automatically at Mach 0.92, when heavy buffeting started. Whereas the Sabre was benign at the stall, the MiG-15 gave little or no warning; spun at the slightest provocation and snap-rolled from accelerated stalls. So bad was this that a white line was painted vertically down the instrument panel to aid centring the control column.

Swept-Wing Combat

The first clash between Sabres and MiG-15s was not long in coming. On 17 December 1950 Bruce Hinton led a flight of four F-86As towards the Yalu, call-sign 'Creature Baker' (CB). Nearing the Yalu at 25,000ft, the pilots eased their speed back to that of cruising F-80s, hoping to be mistaken for Lockheed fighters. As they turned north-east, parallel to the Yalu, the bait was taken. Pitts, flying the No 2 position, called four bogeys at 9 o'clock low. Janeczek at No 3 identified them as having swept wings. Hinton turned his flight into the MiGs to engage. What follows is taken from the combat report.

> En A/C [enemy aircraft] were in battle formation [finger four], went into climb- ing right trail; continued turn as [CB] flight began out-turning MiGs in turn pulling approx. 5gs, en A/C seemed to lose integrity as en observed friendly [CB] flight coming in. En levelled out on a heading par to Yalu River, [CB] flight was closing in, air speed approx. 410kt at 20,000ft. En A/C dropped tips [tanks] with white thick foam coming from tips. A/C began to dive then started climbing left to turn. Air speed at this point was above red line [Mach 0.95]. En flight began spreading out with their No 4 man breaking left with friendly No 3 and 4 [Janaczek and Bryce] chasing en 1 and 2. Fl Ldr [Hinton] gave en wg

[wing] man a burst and sprung leaks from right wg approx. 1½ft out [from the fuselage]. Leaks from fuselage from various places observed as many API [armor-piercing incendiary] strikes were seen to hit fuselage. En No 2 man appeared to be in trouble while in gentle turn to left he popped speed brakes for approx. 2 secs then pulled them back in. After first burst he started smoking. Friendly flight leader [Hinton] maneuvred out of jet wash approx 800 to 1,000ft gave en A/C long burst, observed fire coming from tail pipe and profuse smoke coming from entire A/C obstructing him from view. Flight leader [Hinton] then pulled up as MiG began to decelerate and fired another long burst, whereas smoke was replaced by long violent flames enveloping entire rear of A/C. A/C then slowed down terrifically with the flight leader pushing out his dive brakes and throttling back giving him another long burst. Small pieces observed coming from A/C at the same time smoking and on fire badly, then MiG did a reverse turn, got on his back, was very slow and started losing altitude rapidly in a violent dive. Flight leader saw smoke trail going down towards ground approximately 10 mi SE of border below 10,000ft. No explosion seen. Friendly No 3 and 4 man chased No 4 man gaining on him slightly at 0.98 Mach; MiG made slight turn to the left and then went straight down towards river. 3 and 4 then left area and observed 1 MiG spinning slowly and awkwardly at 3,000 to 5,000ft going down smoking, then rejoining formation. Friendly No 2 [Pitts] fired 3 second burst from 2,000ft [range] at en No 3. MiG then went into steep dive and headed for border.

This was the first of over 750 Sabre victories over Korea. It does however underline the inadequacy of the .50in Colt-Browning: Hinton fired nearly 1,500 rounds to bring down his MiG.

The Korean War was fought out by ground forces, supported by air power. To enable the latter to be effective, close air support and interdiction had to operate free from interference, which in turn called for air superiority. Had it not been for the Sabres, the Russian-manned MiGs could have cut a deadly swathe through the UN attack aircraft, but with Sabres as top cover they were at risk if they operated at the low levels required. The MiGs were therefore forced ever higher, to the point where air combat became largely divorced from the ground fighting.

Jet combat in the stratosphere posed unique problems. The thin air gave little lift, and at 40,000ft stalling speeds more than doubled. Turn capability reduced proportionately: in anything other than a gentle turn the pilot risked 'dropping it', with embarrassing consequences. This was of course on the level; diving turns posed fewer problems, although the loss of altitude could be tactically serious. By the same token, maintaining formation posed equal problems: if a wingman lagged even slightly during a turn, he was often

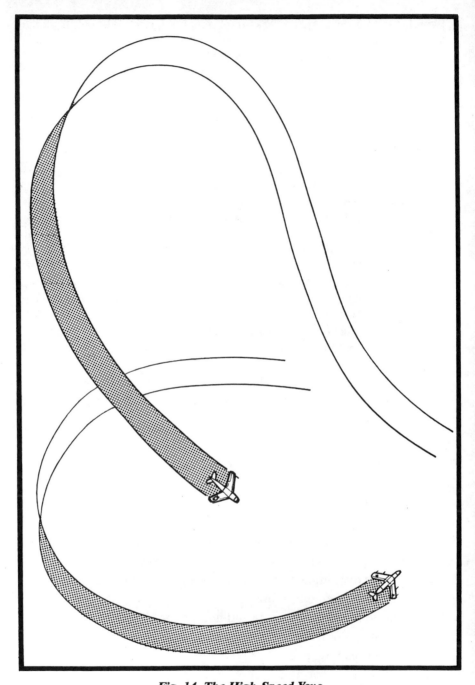

Fig. 14. The High-Speed Yoyo
The bounce from above frequently made the attacker too fast to turn with its target. The answer was to pull high and use the vertical plane to cut the corner.

unable to catch up. The cross-over turn was modified – both outside men went under, not over.

Also as a result of the thin air, large throttle movements had to be avoided as these could easily result in the engine flaming out. Engineless flight over 'MiG Alley' was not a good situation in which to be. With closing speeds often of the order of 1,000kt, a small fighter which only became visible at about five nautical miles would reach firing range in barely 20 seconds – little enough time in which to line up for a shooting chance or an evasion. Sighting was also a problem: with nothing to give perspective, a pilot's eyes were too often focused at short range. Often the only clue was the distant glint of the sun on a canopy. Sabre ace George Jones recorded:

> I spotted a glint in the sky, about 3 o'clock high. I wagged the stick, rocking my wings to get my wingman's attention. He looked across and I silently signalled 'drop tanks'. Again a silent signal for full military power, and we started a slow turn under that glint in the sky. Now there were many other flashes in the sun up ahead. All of a sudden I saw them. First there was nothing, then they jumped into focus.

Ten-victory ace 'Boots' Blesse, author of the tract *No Guts, No Glory*, added a cautionary note: 'Avoid staring at contrails or the only aircraft in sight. There are a dozen around for every one you can see!'

Even when a sighting was made, identification remained a problem, compounded by the similar appearance of the Sabre and MiG-15. Both were single-engine, swept-wing fighters with a shiny aluminium finish. To overcome this, Sabres carried first black and white stripes, then later broad yellow bands. Many Sabre pilots used binoculars to assist them with long-range identification.

Tactical circumstances differed widely. Whereas the MiGs were based in China just north of the Yalu, the Sabres were 200nm south of the battle area. This not only reduced their time on patrol, it gave ample early warning to communist radar stations, which was amplified by the prevailing winds at high altitude, blowing from the north at 80kts or more, which delayed the arrival of the Sabres. This was, however, turned to advantage: it was not unusual for Sabres to shut down their engines to conserve fuel on the return trip, coasting on a strong tail wind. Given ample early earning, MiGs could take off, form up and gain altitude on the inviolate Chinese side of the frontier. Only when they had a height advantage did they turn south to seek battle.

Initially the Sabres flew in squadron formation, but this proved unwieldy. It was progressively reduced to two flights of four, then finally four-ship

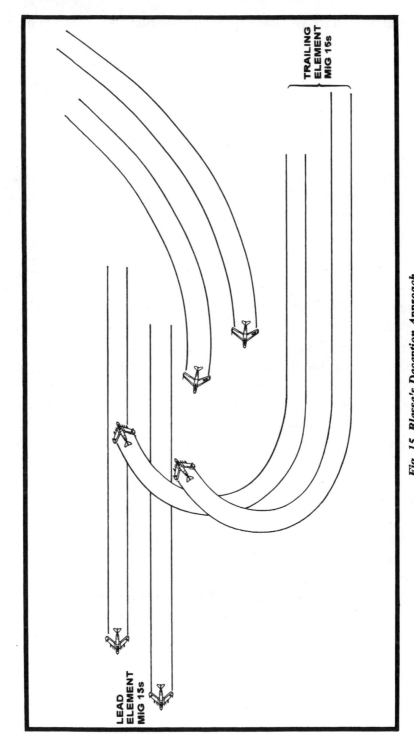

Fig. 15. Blesse's Deception Approach

When attacking a four-ship formation, Frederick 'Boots' Blesse developed an approach which, like the discovered check in chess, confused his opponents as to the true target.

flights at three-minute intervals. This gave maximum flexibility, ensured that support was never very far away and provided cover for aircraft low on fuel to withdraw. Efforts were made to keep out of the contrail belt, which made them visible from many miles away. However, as the contrail belt varied in height, this was not always easy.

Sabre pilots often felt heavily outnumbered. The reality was rather more complex. From July 1951, when detailed records began to be kept, to the end of the war, Sabre sorties outnumbered those of the MiGs by almost 2 to 1. In only five months, from October 1951 to February 1952, did MiG sorties exceed those of the Sabres. On the other hand, when the MiGs were up, they were up in large numbers, often fifty or more.

The Russians also used the basic four-ship flight, and prior to February 1951 they tended to operate in regimental strength. This was typically seven or eight flights of four in line astern, stepped down. They were on occasion stepped up, but this made station-keeping far more difficult. Like the Americans, they found large formations too unwieldy, and reverted to saturating an area with flights of four, often operating two regiments in the same area at the same time.

The outstanding altitude performance of the MiG-15 gave its pilots the initiative. They could sit on a high perch, beyond the reach of the Sabres, and pick their moment to attack. This generally consisted of a single pass, followed by disengagement back upstairs. For the Sabre pilots, this was frustrating, and not a little frightening. To be shot at by a MiG was rewarded by admission to the exclusive 'Six o'Clock Club'. This carried a certificate giving details of the encounter, and illustrated by a cartoon of a worried-looking Sabre pilot hotly pursued by a ferocious MiG-15 spraying shells in all directions!

Fortunately for the F-86 drivers, it was not always like this. Sometimes the MiGs were found at lower altitudes, where the Sabre was superior in most respects. On other occasions they might manage to lure their opponents down, while in some cases the Russians stayed to fight. But much depended on pilot quality. Both sides had a leavening of fighter pilots from the Second World War who passed on their experience to the novices, but the greatest difference lay in the method of replacement. In the Sabre wings, pilots were replaced gradually, generally after 100 missions. This meant that at all times the new boys were introduced to combat by experienced leaders. By contrast, the Russians rotated entire units, and often a combat-hardened group was replaced by one of very middling worth. When this

187

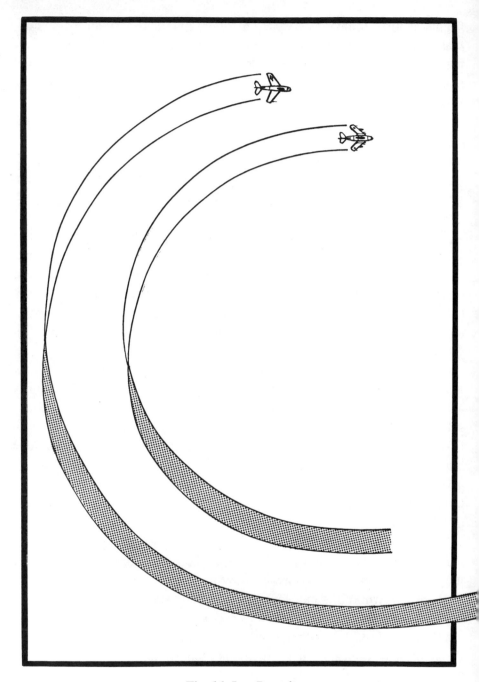

Fig. 16. Lag Pursuit
*Against a slower but better-turning opponent, matching its rate of turn
while staying outside its radius prevented an overshoot and allowed
speed to be bled off while maintaining an offensive position.*

happened, the MiGs at first tended to stay high and not engage. After a little experience was gained, they started to send small units down to nibble briefly at the Sabres before disengaging. Gradually they became more aggressive, but just when they started to 'mix it' in earnest they were replaced and the whole cycle, which was obvious even to their opponents, began again.

There was however one tactic used by the MiGs which was very hard to counter. This was the defensive split, or yoyo. When bounced from astern, the most threatened MiG broke hard into the attack while the other pulled high. Given the extraordinary rate of climb of the Russian fighter, it was a waste of time for the Sabres to attempt to follow the high man. If they assailed his hard-turning companion, they became vulnerable to the second fighter, who by pulling through an oblique loop could quickly reach an attacking position. 'Boots' Blesse found a partial answer to this. He recommended taking up an attack vector which not only allowed him to switch targets quickly but made the MiGs uncertain which of them was the real target. The resulting confusion often caused delay, which in turn increased vulnerability.

More often the Sabres were forced onto the defensive. The favoured 'last-ditch' manoeuvre was a steep spiral dive which Russian pilots could rarely match and made accurate gunnery almost impossible. Once established in the spiral, a snap roll in the opposite direction left the pursuing MiG floundering.

In fighter-versus-fighter combat over Korea, even World War II aces had difficulty in scoring at first, and the first jet ace of the conflict was a long time coming. The reason lay in the speed/altitude combination: speeds were 50 per cent and altitudes 33 per cent greater. Turn rates fell away sharply, while in extreme cases turn radii more than tripled. But the basic weaponry, and its effective firing range, remained the same. To achieve a firing solution, judgement of space and time had to be far more precise. A USAF study concluded that only about one in every ten sightings resulted in an attack, and that only a small proportion of attacks were converted into shooting opportunities.

American Aces

James 'Jabby' Jabara Credited with 1½ victories against the *Luftwaffe*, 'Jabby' Jabara started slowly against the MiGs and his first victory did not come until 3 April 1951. After adding three more that month, he was due to return to Japan, but his tour was extended. The Korean War was unpopular in the United States, where few understood what it was about. As the USAF desperately needed an ace to improve public relations, Jabara was allowed to stay on, and he was put up front on all likely missions.

The fifth victory was also slow in coming – almost a month passed. Then on 20 May a huge multi-bogey fight developed over 'MiG Alley' at 35,000ft. Jabara tried to jettison his drop tanks, but one hung up. Undeterred, he hastened into the fray and latched on to a MiG. Following its every evasive move, he finally got into position and fired three bursts from a range of 1,500ft, hitting the fuselage and port wing. The MiG snap-rolled and spun. By now detached from the main fight, Jabara and his wingman followed it down and saw the pilot eject. Climbing back towards the furball, Jabara sneaked in behind another MiG, sending it down on fire. Once again he defied the rules and followed his victim down, only to be bounced by two MiGs at 6,500ft. For two minutes he pulled every trick in the book to escape, then finally two Sabres came to his aid. He had become the first American ace in Korea.

Jabara returned to Korea in January 1953 but was unsuccessful for five months. Then once again he found his touch and accounted for nine more MiGs between mid-May and mid-July. His 15 victories made him the second highest American scorer in Korea.

Joe McConnell Joe McConnell had been a bomber navigator over Europe in World War II – an unlikely start for the man who became the ranking USAF ace of the Korean War. He trained as a fighter pilot post-war, and arrived at the 51st FIW late in 1952. Once through the initial induction phase common to 'rookie' pilots, his career was meteoric – five victories in 33 days. His eighth victory, on 12 April, was marked by his being shot down into the sea. Rescued by helicopter, he was soon back in action. A purple patch of six victories in six days followed, shortly after which he was posted home. McConnell's tally of 16, achieved in 106 sorties, equalled the jet total of Heinz Baer during World War II and made him the top-scoring Sabre pilot of the Korean War. Back home he became a service test pilot, but he died in a crash on 25 August 1954.

Robinson 'Robbie' Risner Robbie Risner's most memorable day in combat was 4 December 1952. Normally the Chinese side of the Yalu River was off-limits, but the demands of this mission took the Sabres right over the Chinese base at Antung, where they encountered four MiGs. Risner, with

190

Joe Logan flying his wing, got behind the No 4 MiG and fired a burst which shattered its canopy. Undeterred, the enemy pilot reversed his turn, but Risner turned inside him. The MiG pilot then began to roll to throw him off, only to be hit once more and start to burn:

> This MiG pilot was the toughest guy I ever flew against . . .
>
> When I did that [hit him the second time] he split-S'd. And we were low! Like 2–3,000ft, and he didn't have a prayer of makin' it . . . And he pulled out down a dry river bed – rocks and dust just flew. He just barely made it! I'm talkin' about feet!

With his wing-tips almost scraping the ground, the MiG pilot went into a series of maximum-rate turns. Each time Risner tried to line up his sight, the MiG pushed his stick forward for a negative-g turn. On one occasion he flew inverted up the side of a hill with the remains of his canopy almost scraping the bushes, then pulled through and down the other side. Sometimes he chopped his throttle and deployed his speed brakes in an attempt to force the American to overshoot. Once he nearly succeeded:

> I did a high-g roll across the top and ended up in a tight wing position. And he looked over and shook his fist at me . . . He certainly was the most amazing pilot that I've ever run into! I got the number four man . . . I wonder what the lead would have been like.

The combat ended over the Chinese airfield at Fencheng, when Risner, using the last of his ammunition, sent the MiG down. But the day's excitement was not yet over. As the two Sabres climbed away, Joe Logan's aircraft was hit by ground fire. By the time he reached 20,000ft he was out of fuel, and a prison camp was looming. He had just one slim chance. Risner was going to try to push him to safety with his nose in Logan's tailpipe:

> So I eased in behind Joe Logan and it took several tries because the turbulence was really bad. Even without his engine running, he's going through the air at 170 in a glide. I found if I could find a finite point between the top and bottom turbulence coming off his wing then I could maintain that position . . . And I certainly didn't make it all in one run. There were many hook-ups and many times I got pitched out . . .

Finally they reached the island of Cho Do, where rescue services were based, and Logan parachuted down into the sea. It had been an epic performance.

Robbie Risner was credited with eight MiG-15s over Korea. He flew again over Vietnam, but was shot down and taken prisoner.

Russian Aces

For years, little was known about Russian air operations over Korea, and what has recently become available generally fails to tie in with Western records. But as the scores of fighter aces are hedged around with controversy anyway, a little more will not hurt us. Just one thing must be borne in mind: the Korean fighting took place in the lifetime of Stalin. As we all know, 'Uncle Joe' was extremely unforgiving of failure, or what he regarded as failure. As recorded earlier, many Russian leaders who fought in Spain were purged (a rather more severe process than that carried out by an English public school matron) on their return. Given the choice, would we rather face the KGB and the Gulags, or tweak the results?

Eugeny Pepelyaev The outbreak of the Great Patriotic War saw Pepelyaev flying I-16s in the Far East, but his only taste of action was against the Japanese in August 1945, for which no details are available. In Korea he commanded the 196th Fighter Air Regiment, which, with the 176th FAR, made up the 324th Fighter Air Division commanded by Great Patriotic War ace Ivan Kozhedub. (Kozhedub had gained 62 victories in the previous conflict; it is known that he flew in Korea, but whether he added to his score is unclear.)

According to Pepelyaev, some 90 per cent of the pilots in his 196th FAR were veterans of the Great Patriotic War, with one or more victories. The High Command seemed to feel that flight safety was paramount, but Pepelyaev introduced a programme of intensive and realistic combat training. He first led his men into battle in April 1951, in an inconclusive skirmish with no victories and no losses, but found out the hard way that the Sabre could out-turn the MiG-15. Neither was it long before he discovered the survivability of the MiG-15 against the American .50in machine guns; it was not unusual for MiGs to return with 40–50 bullet holes in them.

Gradually Pepelyaev's score mounted, and by the beginning of 1952 he had claimed 23 victories, three of which he gave to wingman A. Rozhkov, in 108 sorties. They consisted of 12 Sabres, six Shooting Stars, four Thunderjets and one F-94B Starfire.

According to Pepelyaev – and this is confirmed by five victory ace Boris Abakumov, who flew on the same mission – eight Starfires penetrated into China as far as Mukden (now Shenyang) in heavy cloud conditions during July 1951. They were intercepted by ten MiG-15s, and seven of them were shot down.

This is a strange claim. The Starfire was a radar-equipped night fighter so overweight as to be a 'turkey' in close combat. Its range was such that it would have been hard-pressed to reach Mukden and return. The type did not deploy to Korea until March 1952, and even then it was not released to operate over the North until November for fear of compromising its top-secret radar. Finally, only two were lost in combat during the war, both at night, although another 28 were written off to other causes. But obviously the MiGs intercepted something. Soviet aircraft recognition was far from perfect, as evidenced by a certain Muraviev, who mistakenly added two Chinese MiG-15s to his four Sabres and one Thunderjet. It is highly unlikely that these aircraft were Starfires. But what were they? Pepelyaev is quoted as saying, 'Not everything that was scored was actually shot down!'

Sergei Kramarenko An ace of the Great Patriotic War, with 12 victories to his credit, Kramarenko served as a squadron commander under Pepelyaev from December 1951 and claimed another 12 victories, two of which were Australian Meteors. He observed:

> The fight, as a rule, was decided in the first attack. It did not matter whether it was successful: after the first attack, MiG-15s reached for altitude, while Sabres rushed towards the ground. Each tried to get to the altitude where it held a distinct advantage and thus the air battle, having scarcely begun, faded at once.

A frequently used Soviet evasion manoeuvre was the oblique loop, a difficult manoeuvre for a pursuer to gain a firing solution. On his own, Kramarenko was cornered by three Sabres:

> I made ten or twelve oblique loops. With ultimate g-loads. Everything went dark in my eyes. But I constantly watched the situation and terrain, gradually pulling away from the Sabres and towards the Yalu River . . . A half-roll. Diving. My direction was towards the bridge, protected by anti-aircraft gunners.

Sergei Kramarenko was shot down once and ejected safely. He retired in 1981 as a Major-General.

During the entire war, the Russians acknowledged losses of 345 MiGs, but their claims totalled over 1,300. Given that loss figures are generally fairly accurate, and with the knowledge that the combined Chinese and North Korean Air Forces took a significant part of the action, and that their losses, although undisclosed, were heavy, the claims of the Sabre pilots look remarkably accurate.

The same cannot be said for their opponents, although stated USAF losses are conflicting. *Saber Measures (Charlie)*, the USAF official study, shows 103 air-to-air fighter losses from July 1951 to the end of the war. Extrapolate this to take in the period from December 1950, and this becomes about 130. To this we must add losses of fighter-bombers, reconnaissance aircraft, heavy bombers etc., plus aircraft of the USN, USMC, RAAF, FAA and SAAF. Taking all these into account, losses to all causes probably exceeded 2,000, although the vast majority of these fell to ground fire.

No North Koreans became aces, although a handful of Chinese are believed to have done, two of whom claimed nine victories.

Aces and Their Scores

American (all USAF unless otherwise stated)

Score	Name	Remarks
16	Joseph McConnell	KIFA 25.8.54
15	James Jabara	Plus 1½ in WWII; died 1967
14½	Manuel Fernandez	
14	George Davis	Plus 7 in WWII; KIA 10.2.52
13	Royal Baker	Plus 3½ in WWII
10	'Boots' Blesse	Author of *No Guts, No Glory*
10	Harold Fischer	PoW 7.4.53
10	Vermont Garrison	Plus 7 in WWII
10	James Johnson	Plus 1 in WWII
10	Iven Kincheloe	Inc. 4 Yak-9s; KIFA post-war
10	Lonnie Moore	KIFA 10.1.56
10	Ralph Parr	
9	James Low	
8	Robbie Risner	
7	Clifford Jolley	
7	Leonard Lilley	
7	Henry Buttelman	
6½	Donald Adams	KIFA 1952
6½	'Gabby' Gabreski	Plus 28 in WWII
6½	James Hagerstrom	Plus 6 in WWII
6½	George Jones	
6½	Winton Marshall	
6	Robert Love	
6	John Bolt	USMC; plus 6 in WWII
6	James Kasler	
5½	William Whisner	Plus 15½ in WWII
5	Robert Baldwin	
5	Richard Becker	Second Sabre ace
5	Stephen Bettinger	Plus 1 in WWII

5	Guy Bordelon	USN; night kills in Corsair
5	Richard Creighton	Plus 2 in WWII
5	Clyde Curtin	
5	Cecil Foster	PoW 1953
5	Ralph Gibson	
5	Robert Latshaw	KIFA 20.4.56
5	Robert Moore	
5	Dolphin Overton	
5	George Ruddell	
5	Harrison Thyng	Plus 5 in WWII
5	William Westcott	

Among several other World War II aces who added to their scores in Korea were Bud Mahurin with 3½ MiGs and John C. Meyer and Glenn Eagleston with two apiece. Mahurin was shot down by ground fire and taken prisoner on 13 May 1952. Several British and Canadian pilots flew Sabres alongside the Americans, but so far as is known, none were credited with more than three victories. There were no non-Sabre aces in the conflict.

Russian

This list, compiled from the best available sources, is almost certainly incomplete.

23	Eugeny Pepelyaev	Includes three given to or shared with his wingman; in 108 sorties
21	Nikolai Sutyagin	In 150 sorties
15	Dmitri Os'kin	In 150 sorties
15	Lev Schukin	In 212 sorties; shot down twice
15	Aleksandr Smurchkov	In 191 sorties
15	Serafim Subbutin	
14	Mikhail Ponomarev	In 140 sorties
14	A. Sherberstov	Doubtful
13	Sergei Kramarenko	In 149 sorties; plus 12 in WWII
11	Stepan Bakhaev	In 166 sorties
11	Nikolai Dokaschenko	In 148 sorties
11	Mikhail Mikhin	
11	Grigory Okhay	In 122 sorties, in which he was hit only once; plus 6 in WWII
10	Dmitri Samoylov	In 161 sorties
10	Arkady Boytsov	At least
9	Grigory Ges'	In 120 sorties
8	V. Alfe'ev	
8	L. Inanov	
8	Grigory Pulov	In 120 sorties
7	B. Bokach	
7	Muraviev	Inc. two Chinese MiG-15s in error
6	Fedor Shebanov	In 150 sorties
6	Nikolai Zameskin	In 135 sorties (36 combats)

6	I. Zaplavnev	Plus 6 in WWII
5	Boris Abakumov	WIA 7.1.52
5	Anatoliy Karelin	In 50 sorties, all B-29s at night

General Georgey Lobov flew 15 combat missions over Korea and claimed four victories to add to his World War II score of 19 plus eight shared. Details of combats by the ranking Soviet ace of the Great Patriotic War, Ivan Kozhedub (62 victories), are not available; the obvious inference is that he did nothing special.

Chinese

9	Chao Bao Tun
9	Kim Tsi Oc
8	Fan Van Chou

5. MACH 2 AND MISSILES

The nuclear weapons demonstrated at Hiroshima and Nagasaki in 1945 clearly showed the dangers of a full-scale confrontation between the super-powers. The price of waging such a war was far too high, even for the winners. The mushroom cloud of a nuclear detonation was actually umbrella-shaped, and for the next four decades the world sheltered beneath it.

Relations between the superpowers became a game of bluff based on a precarious balance of power. For this to work, the threat had to be credible. Both sides had at least to appear willing to use nuclear weapons if the necessity arose, and had to possess an effective means of delivery. It was far from cheap. The direct confrontation thus turned into an economic war, which only the richest, most technically advanced and most determined nation would win. Later, when 'nukes' became miniaturized, so that they could be restricted to the battlefield, the risk of escalation remained too high for their use to be feasible.

There were two main delivery systems. Ballistic missiles were the swiftest and surest, but these were single-shot weapons: once launched they could not be recalled, and they also invited instant retaliation. The alternative was the fast jet bomber. While weapons delivery took hours rather than minutes, and they were far more vulnerable to defensive measures, bombers were flexible. At the first sign of danger they could be scrambled and enter a holding pattern, awaiting further orders. If needed, they could be diverted to other targets; while deployed to forward areas, they became an unmistakable signal of national resolve.

Little could be done to defend against the ballistic missile, but bombers were a different matter entirely. Spurred by the threat of nuclear annihilation, the major industrial powers, the USA, the USSR, Britain and France, started to produce interceptors. The common denominator was an outstanding rate of climb and an exceptional turn of speed. In less than five years, maximum speeds attainable doubled from the supersonic to something in

197

excess of Mach 2, with designs on the drawing board capable of Mach 3 or more. Radical advances in avionics brought in semi-automatic interception, while the quest for greater killing power resulted in homing missiles and fast-firing multi-barrelled cannon.

This was the 'worst case' war scenario. It was of course expected that other, smaller and more localised conflicts would occur, but it was considered that the most advanced fighters in existence, designed to fight 'The Big One', would easily be able to cope with smaller conflicts, in which the opposition would almost certainly be less well equipped. In the event, the 'worst case' war failed to materialise.

Faced with mutually assured destruction, with the apt acronym of MAD, communism, bent on world domination, adopted a new strategy. Some countries could be bought into the communist sphere of influence by a liberal supply of arms and military advisers. If their neighbours leaned towards the West, they would be destabilised, perhaps with the aid of cross-border guerrillas, until conditions were right for a *coup*. In this way, communist influence would gradually spread across the globe with little risk of causing a confrontation between the superpowers. In the West, this strategy was known as the Domino Effect.

The fact that Russian air units with the latest equipment were in China several months before North Korea invaded the South suggests that hostilities were planned, and the need for air power foreseen, long in advance. Be that as it may, it set a pattern of indirect confrontation which persisted for more than three decades. So far as is known, Korea was the only conflict where Russians flyers directly fought Americans, although there were other wars where one side or the other was directly engaged. More often the locals fought it out using American or Russian equipment. The result was a series of regional wars which were usually, but not always, of short duration.

Homing Missiles

Homing missiles had many advantages over guns. They were much longer-ranged (in some cases they could even be launched from beyond visual distance), they could follow their targets in flight, and they carried a warhead which could inflict lethal damage with a near miss. As first advertised, they seemed to have made close combat redundant. In practice this was far from the case.

All early missiles had a long minimum range, typically half a mile or more, which was determined by the time taken to arm themselves and start to guide. Any opponent closer than this was therefore safe from their attentions. Secondly, they were not instantly available: they needed the right switch settings to be made, followed by a short settling time prior to launch. Thirdly, they could not be launched in anything more than a mild turn, 2g or so. Fourthly, the impressive brochure speeds and ranges were modified by altitude and launch aircraft speed; at sea level these reduced by more than half. Fifthly, they had been designed to track only a non-manoeuvring, or gently manoeuvring, target; hard evasive manoeuvres would generally defeat them. Sixthly, the homing heads were confused by clutter near the ground. Finally the new missiles were prone to malfunction.

Two basic missile types entered widespread service prior to 1973; semi-active radar homers (SARH), and infra-red (IR) or heat homers. The former was a large weapon with an impressive brochure range. In theory it would destroy an opponent at far beyond visual distance. In action it was limited by two factors. The first was the need for positive identification, which was not always readily available. The second was the effective range of the parent radar, which against small targets was often far less than the stated brochure range. The classic example was the F-4 Phantom radar, which could not lock on to the MiG-21 from head-on until the range had closed to about twelve nautical miles, although this was still beyond visual distance. As at typical closing speeds this gave less than one minute before the merge, there was limited time in which to identify and attack.

IR (heat) missiles were essentially short-ranged, visual distance weapons. Intrinsically more accurate than the SARH type, they had smaller warheads, but were only capable of homing on a hot engine efflux and so could only be launched from the classic astern position. In the gun-only era, a standard evasion move was to accelerate away out of range. The reach of the Sidewinder now made this potentially disastrous. It is an interesting point that, whereas air-to-air missiles were popularly supposed to eliminate manoeuvre combat, heat homers, with their dual need of manoeuvre to attain the astern launch position, and hard manoeuvring to evade, actually made manoeuvre more important than ever.

Like the gun, although for different reasons, IR missiles could not be used in cloud or mist, and in a confused situation care had to be taken that the missile would not switch targets to a nearby friendly. Close to the ground, the difference between minimum range and effective range became marginal.

The next generation of fighter pilots went to war only able to guess what the future held. Time and hard-won experience would tell.

Limited Wars, 1953–73

In the two decades which followed the end of the Korean conflict, there were several 'brushfire' wars. They included the secession of Katanga from the Congo in 1960; that of Biafra from Nigeria in 1968; and the totally ridiculous World Cup War between El Salvador and Honduras in 1969. Only in the last of these was there any air combat. This was between World War II-vintage Mustangs and Corsairs. It produced no aces and little of interest.

In the Far East, there were occasional clashes between aircraft of the People's Republic of China and the Chinese Nationalists based on Taiwan. Again no aces emerged, but on 24 September 1958 Nationalist F-86F Sabres armed with Sidewinder heat-seeking missiles claimed four MiGs shot down. This was the first ever use of homing missiles in combat.

India versus Pakistan

India and Pakistan fought two very brief territorial wars, the first in 1965 and the second in 1971. While the gun remained the primary fighter weapon, the nature of the air fighting was totally different from that in Korea. The borders between the two countries were long, spreading the available air power thinly. Most missions were flown in support of the ground forces, where dust and haze restricted visibility. Nor was radar coverage comprehensive. Consequently encounter battles at medium and low levels, between numerically small forces, were the rule.

In 1965, the main Indian fighter component consisted of 118 British-built Hunters and 80 Gnats, backed by a mere ten Mach 2-capable MiG-21s. It was opposed by about 90 Pakistani F-86F Sabres, plus a dozen Mach 2-capable F-104A Starfighters. The Hunter was a rather more modern design than the Sabre. It was faster and accelerated better, while its four 30mm Aden cannon packed a destructive punch. The Gnat was a nod in the direction of affordability – a small, lightweight and austere fighter, armed with two 30mm Aden cannon. The idea, repeated many times down the years, was to produce a machine which was affordable in greater numbers than the orthodox fighters of the day, while lacking little in capability. In practice it had just one real advantage: its tiny size made it difficult to see at any distance, and Gnats often succeeded in surprising Sabres.

The Sabres had one outstanding advantage. About a quarter of their number carried Sidewinder missiles. Although few Sabres actually carried Sidewinders, Hunter pilots had to assume that they did until they could prove otherwise. This forced them into a turning fight, and, in the turn, the low-aspect ratio Hunter bled off speed rapidly, negating its speed and acceleration advantages over the Sabre.

The 1965 war produced only one ace, which was hardly surprising considering the numbers involved and the consequent lack of opportunity. This was Sabre pilot Mohammed Alam, who had flown Hunters with the RAF and thus knew his opponents well. He flew roughly 40 sorties during the 22-day war. His first combat came on 6 September, when he claimed two Hunters downed near Adampur. On the following day, while defending his base at Sargodha, he and his wingman encountered six Hunters. Diving to the attack, he launched a Sidewinder, which failed to guide. His second hit, and the Hunter pilot ejected. He had lost sight of the other five, but continued the chase in their general direction:

> . . . my wingman called out, 'Contact, Hunters 1 o'clock', and I picked them up at the same time – five Hunters in absolutely immaculate battle formation. They were flying at about 100–200ft, at around 480 knots and when I was within gunfire range they saw me. They all broke in one direction, climbing and turning steeply to the left, which put them in loose line astern . . .

This was a bad tactical error. A horizontal or vertical split might quickly have sandwiched Alam and forced him to disengage. As it was, it allowed him to turn inside the Hunters, firing at one after the other like ducks in a shooting gallery. Pulling in excess of 5g, about 12deg/sec, Alam hit four of them in less than 25 seconds.

> My fifth victim of this sortie started spewing smoke and then rolled on to his back at about 1,000ft. I thought he was going to do a barrel roll, which at low altitude is a very dangerous manoeuvre for the opponent if the man in front knows what he is doing. I went almost on my back and then I realised that I might not be able to stay with him so I took off bank and pushed the nose down. The next time I fired was at very close range – about 600ft or so – and his aircraft virtually blew up in front of me.

Five victories in one sortie, four of them in less than half a minute, against better-performing aircraft, sounded like the tallest of tall stories, especially as Indian Air Force records show only two Hunter pilots missing on this date. Air Marshal Sir John Nicholls, who scored two victories in Korea flying the Sabre, and later commanded the Air Fighting Development Squadron of the RAF, commented to the effect that while poor Indian tactics lined the Hunters up perfectly, the Sabre gun sight had insufficient settling time to track properly. However, if the sight had been used in fixed mode it was

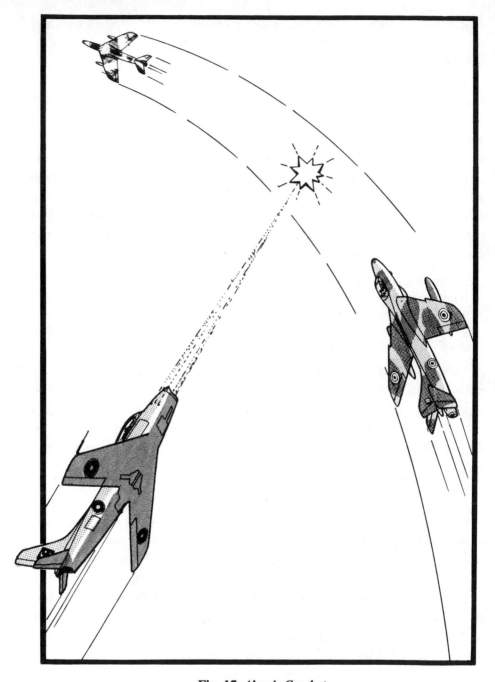

Fig. 17. Alam's Combat
Pakistani ace Mohammed Alam once shot down four out of five Indian Hunters
in a single pass. They had all broken in the same direction, setting themselves
up like ducks in a shooting gallery.

possible. As Alam commented, '. . . they just slid back into my sights one by one'. Alam's eighth and ninth victories came on 14 September – two Hunters, one with gunfire and the other with a Sidewinder.

In 1965 both the F-104A and the MiG-21 had opened their scores, but the only encounter between the two proved indecisive. The year 1971 saw the first real confrontations between the two. Four F-104As were lost to the Indian fighter, one with guns, one with guns and a K-13A 'Atoll' missile and two with K-13As only. All three encounters took place at low level, where the Starfighter was easily out-turned and, to a lesser degree, out-accelerated.

Pakistani Sabre pilot Sayed Sa'ad Hatmi had claimed two victories in the 1965 conflict. Flying a Shenyang J.6 (a reverse-engineered MiG-19) in the later conflict, he added a Hunter and two Sukhoi Su-7s to bring his tally to five in the two conflicts to become the second Pakistani ace.

Middle East Wars

The story of the state of Israel, formed in 1948, is one of uneasy peace, interspersed with generally short but intense periods of war. The first quarter-century of Israel's existence was a fight against odds, surrounded as she was by hostile Arab neighbours – Egypt, Jordan, Lebanon, Syria and Iraq.

In its early years, the Israeli Air Force consisted of a pot-pourri of native and mercenary pilots, Canadians and Americans among them, and aircraft from whatever source they could be obtained. In the early days there were no IAF aces as such, although at least two mercenary pilots added enough to their World War II scores to qualify.

By 1955 both Israelis and Egyptians were equipped with jets. First blood was drawn by Israeli Meteor pilot Aharon Yoeli, who shot down two intruding Egyptian Vampires on 1 September. But by this time the Israeli and the Arab air forces had started to equip. The former wanted American fighters, but, as these were unavailable due to political considerations, they were forced to settle for French aircraft – Dassault Ouragans, Vautours and Mystère IVs. The Egyptians and their Arab allies were, with the exception of Jordan, which had close connections with Britain, supplied by the USSR, firstly with MiG-15 and -17 fighters, later supplemented with Ilyushin Il-28 bombers.

The nationalisation of the Suez Canal by Egypt in 1956 gave Israel two unlikely allies, Britain and France. There was, however, little air combat during this war, in which the Egyptian Air Force was largely destroyed on

203

the ground by the British and French. The first Israeli ace was still eleven years in the future.

Over the next ten years, the combatants re-equipped with far more advanced aircraft. Israel bought the supersonic Super Mystère B.2 and the Mach 2-capable Mirage IIICJ tailless delta from France; Egypt and its allies were supplied with transonic MiG-17s, supersonic MiG-19s and Mach 2-capable MiG-21s by the Soviet Union. These were backed up by Sukhoi Su-7 fighter-bombers and Tupolev Tu-16 jet bombers.

The next few years saw the occasional skirmish, but the only one worthy of note came on 28 November 1966 when a Mirage shot down an Egyptian MiG-19 with a Matra 530 – the first (and probably only) victory credited to this missile. Finally international tensions made war inevitable. Israel was a small and narrow country; its geographical constraints meant that defence in depth was impossible. By June 1967 the Israel Defence Force could muster just 90 modern fighters, 72 of which were Mirage IIICJs, plus 18 lesser types. It was opposed by a total of about 220 MiG-21s and 110 MiG-19s, plus about 300 subsonic and transonic types. At more than 6:1, the odds were heavy.

The Six-Day War

Just over a quarter of a century earlier, with no warning, the Imperial Japanese Navy had launched a devastating strike against Pearl Harbor, which was dubbed 'The Day of Infamy!' On the morning of 5 June 1967, the Israeli Air Force followed suit with the now-famous pre-emptive strike called 'A Great Tactical Victory!' As USAF Lt-Col 'Boots' Boothby wryly commented, 'It all depends whose side you're on!'

By cratering runways and destroying aircraft on the ground, the Israelis reduced the Egyptian Air Force to manageable proportions and then quickly turned their attention to Syria and Jordan, with similar results.

Over the six days that the war lasted, the Israelis claimed 58 air combat victories, nearly half of them on the first day. Israel air combat losses amounted to ten, including a Mirage which fell to an Iraqi Hunter. Another 36 aircraft were lost to ground fire, or to operational causes. Mirage pilot Giora Rom became the first Israeli ace, and the only ace of the Six-Day War. He shot down two Egyptian MiG-21s on the first morning, a Syrian MiG-21 that afternoon and two Egyptian MiG-17s on day three. All were scored with guns. In fact, all the Israeli air combat victories were scored with gunfire, even though the heavy and largely ineffective R.530 was available. The

Fighters of the Limited Wars

Type	Hawker Hunter F.6	Mikoyan MiG-17F	Vought F-8E Crusader	Mikoyan MiG-19/J.6
Span	33ft 8in	31ft 7in	35ft 2in	29ft 6½in
Length	45ft 10½in	36ft 11½in	54ft 6in	34ft 6½in
Height	13ft 2in	12ft 5½in	15ft 9in	13ft 2½in
Wing area	340 sq ft	253.3 sq ft	350 sq ft	269 sq ft
Take-off wt	17,750lb	11,770lb	29,000lb	16,275lb
Power	1 × RR Avon, 10,000lb	1 × VK-1F, 7,452lb	1 × P&W J57, 18,000lb	2 × AM-9B, 6,700lb ea
Wing ldg	52lb/sq ft	46lb/sq ft	83lb/sq ft	61lb/sq ft
Thrust ldg	0.56lb/lb	0.63lb/lb	0.62lb/lb	0.82lb/lb
Vmax	Mach 0.94	Mach 0.97	Mach 1.70	Mach 1.38
Climb rate	c.5,500ft/min	12,800ft/min	21,000ft/min	c.22,640ft/min
Ceiling	c.50,000ft	54,450ft	58,000ft	54,800ft
Armament	4 × 30mm Aden	1 × 37mm N-37D, 2 × 23mm NR-23	4 × 20mm Colt, 2/4 AIM-9	2 × 23mm NR-23, 2 × K-13A
Combat with	India, Iraq, Jordan, Lebanon	China, Egypt, Iraq, Syria, Vietnam	USN	Egypt, Vietnam

Fighters of the Limited Wars *continued*

Type	Lockheed F-104A	Mikoyan MiG-21F	Dassault Mirage III	MDD F-4E Phantom
Span	21ft 11in	23ft 5½in	27ft 0in	38ft 4in
Length	54ft 9in	44ft 2in	48ft 5½in	63ft 0in
Height	13ft 6in	13ft 5½in	13ft 11½in	16ft 3in
Wg area	196.1 sq ft	247.6 sq ft	377 sq ft	530 sq .ft
Take-off wt	19,200lb	16,245lb	19,000lb	45,750lb
Power	1 × GE J79, 14,800lb	1 × R11-F-300, 12,654lb	1 × Atar 9B, 13,320lb	2 × GE J79, 17,900lb ea
Wing ldg	98lb/sq ft	66lb/sq ft	50lb/sq ft	86lb/sq ft
Power ldg	0.77lb/lb	0.78lb/lb	0.70lb/lb	0.78lb/lb
Vmax	Mach 2.2 plus	Mach 2.05	Mach 2.15	Mach 2.20
Climb	50,000ft/min	34,450ft/min	16,400ft/min	28,000ft/min
Ceiling	58,000ft	62,300ft	54,100ft	55,000ft
Armament	1 × 20mm M61, 2 × AIM-9	1 × 30mm NR-30, 2 × K-13A	2 × 30mm DEFA, 2 × Shafrir, AIM-9 or R550	1 × 20mm M61, 4 × AIM-7 and 4 × AIM-9
Combat with	Pakistan	Egypt, Syria Iraq, India, Vietnam	Israel, Libya	Israel, USA

smaller, home-brewed Shafrir I proved no better: it was used by a Mirage to damage an Iraqi Tu-16 near Netanya, but the big bomber flew on until finished off by ground fire.

A major factor in the Middle Eastern Wars was the clear, almost unlimited visibility, which allowed manoeuvre combat to commence at unprecedented ranges. This was just as well: the MiG-21s had a very small radar cross-section, and the Mirage Cyrano radar often failed to pick it up until the range had closed to seven or eight miles, by which time it was clearly visible.

The Mirage gained an enviable reputation in the Six-Day War, but to what extent was this justified? The tailless delta layout gave a moderate wing loading, but at the same time speed loss in hard turns was very high. In certain areas its main adversary, the MiG-21, was superior. The real difference lay in pilot quality: with few exceptions, the Soviet-trained Arabs were no match for their Israeli opponents.

An illustration is given by Mirage ace Oded Marom (11 victories). On 8 June he and another pilot encountered two Egyptian MiG-19s south of El Arish and shot them both down. He later commented, 'You never saw such a miserable aircraft as a MiG-19, like a big cigar. Fat fuselage, short wings like a bug, and it flew the same – like a bug!'

This is a reflection on the pilots rather than the aircraft. The MiG-19 was one of the first two supersonic fighters to enter service (the other was the American F-100 Super Sabre). Its twin engines made it the first fighter with a thrust/weight ratio to exceed unity. Five years later American Phantom pilot Bill Ridge barely escaped from one over Vietnam. His assessment, made via his cockpit voice recorder: 'Boy . . . those [expletives deleted] can turn!'

The War of Attrition

The Arab air forces had their Six-Day War losses replaced by the USSR. Meanwhile France refused to sell replacement kit to Israel. As it turned out, this was a blessing in disguise. The United States agreed to supply A-4 Skyhawk light attack bombers and F-4E Phantom multi-role fighters, while an attempt to achieve independence resulted in the Neshr and Kfir, both basically home-built Mirages, the latter with the American J79-GE engine.

On the ground, the War of Attrition was static. It began with Egyptian artillery fire across the Suez Canal in June 1969 but quickly escalated into a series of air strikes by both sides. Israeli losses to surface-to-air missiles (SAMs) were heavy, but in the air they generally had the best of things. Amos Amir claimed six of his seven victories in the War of Attrition.

The game changed from April 1970 when Soviet 'volunteers' arrived in Egypt to fly MiG-21MFs. At first, both sides held back from a confrontation for fear of escalation, but when in July of that year a Skyhawk was damaged by a Russian-flown fighter it could no longer be delayed. On the final day of the month, the Israeli Air Force laid a trap. The bait was four Mirages on a reconnaissance mission. They were covered by four more Mirages and four Phantoms, flown by selected Israeli pilots credited with 59 victories between them. It has never been specifically stated, but it seems probable that the three Israeli flights flew very close formations, to appear as single blips on Egyptian radar. As Soviet Colonel V. Dubrov wrote in 1978, concerning air combat in the Middle East, 'They were counting not on the enemy failing to spot fighters in the air, but on preventing the enemy from promptly figuring out the engagement intentions.'

Twenty MiG-21s scrambled to intercept and a huge air battle took place. In the space of four minutes five MiGs went down, two to Phantoms and three to Mirages, with no Israeli losses. At least two established aces added to their scores in this encounter; Asher Snir and Iftach Spector. Even the Egyptians were pleased with the outcome. They had been heavily criticised by the Russians, who had now proved no better. Eight days later the War of Attrition ended.

The October War, 1973

Although the War of Attrition had ended, border skirmishes had not. Eitan Peled downed a Syrian MiG-21 late in 1970 for the first of his eventual five victories, whilst Avihu Bin-Nun, later the Israeli Chief of Staff, missed his fifth victory by a whisker when on 13 September 1973 a Sidewinder launched by a Mirage impacted a Syrian MiG-21 fractionally ahead of his Sparrow. Iftach Spector added his tenth and eleventh victories during this same encounter, one being made with gunfire. Trouble was brewing, and it came to a head on 6 October.

On this occasion the Arab nations had to be seen as the aggressors; the Israelis could only wait to be attacked. At Ophir, in the extreme south of the Sinai peninsula, two young Phantom pilots scrambled under a hail of bombs. A fight against an estimated 28 Egyptian MiGs followed, and at the end of it Amir Nahumi was credited with four victories, his wingman, S——, with three. Taking into account the relatively poor manoeuvrability of the Phantom, this says little for the air combat capability of its opponents.

Nahumi's fifth victory, a Syrian MiG, came on 13 October, then two Egyptian MiGs on the following day, his last of the conflict. But Nahumi was far from finished. Flying an F-16 on 14 July 1981, he downed a Syrian MiG-21 with a Sidewinder. In the Beka'a action of June 1982 he brought his tally to 14 to become the first F-16 ace. But that is outside the scope of this chapter.

Israeli victory claims in the October War amounted to no fewer than 335, 101 by Phantoms and the remainder by Mirages and Neshrs. About 60 victims fell to gun attacks and the rest to missiles. The Shafrir was reportedly the most successful missile, with over 200 kills claimed.

Although Israeli sources credit a handful of Arab pilots as being exceptional, not one is known to have become an ace. On the other hand, something like 35 Israelis are believed to have scored five or more victories. Officers still operational are protected by anonymity, and for this reason the following list must be regarded as incomplete.

Israeli Aces

Score	Name	Remarks
17	Giora Epstein	Mirage/Neshr; ret. 20.5.97
15	Iftach Spector	Mirage/Phantom
14	Amir Nahumi	Phantom/F-16; ace both types
13½	Asher Snir	Mirage/Phantom; died 1986
13½	Abraham Shalmon	Mirage
11½	Ya'acov Richter	Mirage
11	Oded Marom	Mirage
11	Israel Baharov	Mirage
10½	Yehuda Koren	Mirage
9	Eitan Karmi	Mirage/Neshr
9	Shlomo Levi	Mirage
8	Ilan Gonen	Mirage/Neshr
8	Shlomo Egozi	Phantom
7½	M——	Phantom/F-15; 1st F-15 kill
7½	Uri Gill	Mirage/F-16
7	Amos Amir	Mirage
7	Ran Ronen	Mirage
7	Yirmiahu Kadar	Neshr
6½	Moshe Hertz	Mirage/Neshr
6	Uri Even-Nir	Mirage
6	Yoram Agmon	Mirage/Phantom
5	Eitan Peled	Phantom
5	Ariel Cohen	Neshr
5	Giora Rom	Mirage; 1st Israeli ace

5	Ben-Ami Peri	Phantom
5	Itamar Noiner	Mirage

At modern jet speeds, nowhere in Israel is more than a few minutes' flying time from the border. Defence in depth is not an option. While never specifically stated, the air defence of Israel has traditionally started above hostile airfields. This has naturally led to an extremely aggressive attitude on the part of its flyers, which in turn accounts at least in part for their success in air combat. Other factors are superior training, good (if not necessarily better) aircraft and equipment, and the knowledge that defeat would result in the end of their country.

Historically, just five per cent of fighter pilots become aces. Given 35 Israeli aces, this indicates a total of about 700 fighter pilots. This seems a little low, but we must remember that all Israeli fast-jet pilots were extensively employed on attack, interdiction and close air support missions, which obviously reduced their chances in the air-to-air arena. The Israelis have always been close-mouthed about their methods and exploits, and much more remains to be revealed. Profiles of two of their leading aces follow.

Giora Epstein In 1956 eighteen-year-old Giora Epstein was found to have an unusual heart rhythm and was rejected for flying training. He was, however, allowed to become a paratrooper, and over the next three years made 495 jumps. Still set on becoming a pilot, he persevered, and almost six years later was accepted – to fly helicopters! After an appeal to the commander-in-chief, this was reversed, and in 1964 he joined a Super Mystère squadron. By the time of the Six-Day War he was a Mirage pilot with 101 Squadron.

His only victory in the war came on 7 June 1967 and was an Egyptian Su-7, which he caught at low altitude south of El Arish. Then, in the War of Attrition, he accounted for a MiG-17, another Su-7 and two MiG-21s, to become an ace. All were downed with gunfire.

The October War saw Epstein attached to headquarters. Not until 18 October did he see action, when he downed an Egyptian Mi-8 helicopter. On the following day he downed two Su-7s with Shafrir missiles, then two Su-20s later that afternoon. On the following day, flying a Neshr, he accounted for three MiG-21s in a single mission, at least two with Shafrirs. His final three victories came on 24 October. Flying a two-seat Mirage IIIB, in a huge multi-bogey dogfight, he again shot down three MiG-21s, two with

Sidewinders and one with cannon. His tally of 17 jet victories is widely accepted as a record, although two Russian MiG-15 pilots in Korea have claimed more.

Epstein, who has hebraicised his name to Aven, retired from the Air Force Reserve on 20 May 1997 with the rank of Colonel. At the time of writing he flies for the Israeli airline El Al.

Asher Snir In the Six Day War Asher Snir flew Mirages with 119 Squadron. His first victory came on the first day of the war – a Syrian MiG-21. Two more victories followed, and more during the War of Attrition. Two were notable, one in 1970 when Snir and his squadron commander, Amos Amir, scrambled to intercept a Syrian MiG-17 over the Golan. At first the contest seemed unequal – two Israeli aces flying supersonic Mirages against an obsolescent transonic MiG-17 – but, as Snir later wrote, '. . . in certain turning conditions, and at low to medium speeds, the MiG-17 is actually superior to the Mirage, and whoever dares to be enticed into these conditions will get screwed right royal.'

The Syrian pilot saw the Mirages in time, evaded their first attacks, dived to ground level and put up a virtuoso display of defensive flying. For the next eight and a half minutes the Mirages carried out a series of co-ordinated gun attacks, but the Syrian foiled every one. Finally his route took him across a wide valley, deep enough to allow Snir to launch a Sidewinder without it impacting the ground. A last-minute break was not enough, the MiG's wing was ripped off and the aircraft hit the ground. Snir's other notable victory in the War of Attrition was a Russian-flown MiG-21, in the July 1970 ambush recorded earlier. In the October War Snir flew Phantoms and brought his tally to 13½. He attained high command in the air force but died of cancer on 5 October 1984.

North Vietnam, 1965–73

Air combat over North Vietnam was for the most part of low intensity. It was also, from the American point of view, very 'high-tech', with more force multipliers than had ever been used previously. The latter included airborne early warning, countermeasures, signals intelligence and specialised defence-suppression aircraft, and a well-honed rescue and recovery organisation.

USAF units used against the North were for the most part based in Thailand, several hundred miles to the west. They were backed by USN carriers in the Gulf of Tonkin, thus presenting a two-pronged threat. Against this the North Vietnamese could pit a mere handful of fighters – MiG-17s and -21s at first, then later Shenyang F.6s – all of which were theoretically outclassed by American Phantoms with medium-range missiles. In practice this was offset by a comprehensive North Vietnamese ground radar and control system. This could detect inbound American strikes well back, often during in-flight refuelling.

The heavily outnumbered NVAF made no attempt to gain air superiority. Instead it opted for a policy of air deniability, using the triple threat of anti-aircraft artillery, SAMs and fighters to disrupt American raids. Of these, the guns caused by far the greatest number of losses, and the fighters the fewest!

It was of course not necessary for the NVAF MiGs to actually shoot down American aircraft. If they could take up an attacking position which forced their opponents to jettison their ordnance or abort their attack runs, the object of the exercise had been achieved. Often the MiGs failed to rise at all, leaving American escort fighters with little to do except provide extra targets for the SAMs. When they were scrambled, ground control directed them to a favourable position at low altitude, where the Phantom radars could not detect them. Once there, they climbed to altitude for a swift, often supersonic bounce from astern.

That the air fighting was not very effective or intense is demonstrated by the loss figures. Between mid-1965 and January 1973, with a hiatus between mid-1968 and early 1972, the combined USAF, USN and USMC lost a maximum of 78 aircraft in air combat, seven of which were 'probables'. In the same period they claimed just 200 victories. It was a far cry from Korea!

There were many reasons for this paucity of results. A couple of unfortunate incidents with medium-range missiles in the early days caused visual identification to be made mandatory. At a stroke, the beyond-visual-range kill capability of the Phantom was negated. This made close combat more likely, and the huge F-4 was disadvantaged in a turning fight against the agile NVAF sports cars. This was aggravated by the lack of a gun; not until 1968 did the first gun-armed Phantom appear. Even when they could be used, the Sparrow and Sidewinder were less than reliable, achieving a kill only every eight or ten launches.

Prior to 1969, the USN fielded the Vought F-8 Crusader. An agile single-seater, the Crusader was known as 'the last of the gunfighters', but while it achieved the best kill/loss ratio of all with 5:1, 17 of its 20 victims were the inferior MiG-17, most of which fell to Sidewinders. But the most crucial

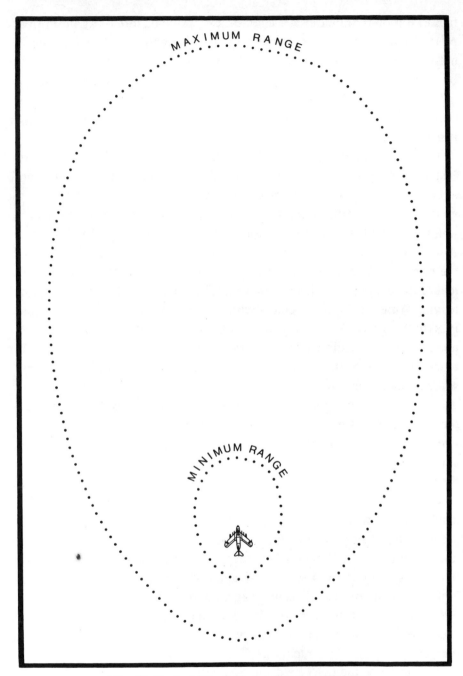

Fig. 18. Typical Missile Launch Range Envelope
This is of course completely variable, depending on missile performance,
altitude and angle and the relative speeds of attacker and target.
One thing is certain: head-on attacks give longer effective range.

factor of all was training. Hard to believe though it may be, the Americans had largely abandoned the art of air combat. Most of their training concentrated on forward interception, for which the Phantom had originally been designed, or the high-speed, low-level delivery of tactical nuclear weapons!

Air combat over Vietnam proved one thing conclusively. Forward interception apart, Mach 2 speeds had little value. Post-war analysis revealed that Mach 1.6 was never exceeded; time at or above Mach 1.2 could be measured in minutes, and that in the entire conflict, supersonic flight time totalled just hours.

Only two American pilot aces emerged during the entire war, while three back-seaters were similarly credited. But the most influential figure was an elderly colonel, an ace from World War II, more than two decades earlier.

Robin Olds Robin Olds made his combat début flying P-38 Lightnings from England in the summer of 1944. He claimed nine victories with the P-38, a remarkable achievement against the *Luftwaffe* with an aircraft widely regarded as a 'turkey', before converting to the P-51D Mustang, with which he added another three. In his post-war career he gained the reputation of being a maverick, and general officer rank had become most unlikely. Late in 1966 Colonel Olds arrived in Thailand to command the 8th ('Wolfpack') TFW.

The NVAF was at this time becoming increasingly troublesome. China was by now a fully-fledged nuclear power, and confrontation had to be avoided. The obvious solution, bombing NVAF airfields, might drive the MiGs north to China in a reprise of the Korean War, making confrontation a distinct possibility.

With no other alternative, Olds initiated Operation 'Bolo', a plan to reduce the NVAF in the air. In essence it consisted of simulating a full-scale bombing raid to draw the defenders into the air, using missile-armed F-4C Phantoms in lieu of F-105 fighter-bombers. Having penetrated North Vietnamese airspace, the Phantoms, in flights of four spaced at five-minute intervals, set up combat air patrols over all NVAF airfields, with a blocking force along the Chinese border to prevent MiGs from escaping.

After a cancellation due to weather, 'Bolo' was launched on 2 January 1967, even though conditions were still far from suitable. Ralph Wetterhahn, an 80-mission veteran, flew as Olds' wingman. He commented on his leader: 'It was his first mission to Hanoi, and up to this point he had controlled the flight with a coolness I had never experienced . . . The man was either the ultimate intrepid warrior or a foolhardy novice.'

Shortly afterwards, several MiG-21s came bursting up through the undercast, and, to quote Wetterhahn, 'total confusion set in!' After two abortive attacks, Olds latched on to a MiG at his 10 o'clock, crossing from right to left. Knowing it to be useless to attempt to turn with a MiG, he started a vector roll:

> . . . he was turning around to the left, so I pulled the nose up high and rolled to the right . . . I got up on top of him and half upside down, hung there, and waited for him to complete more of his turn and timed it so that as I continued to roll down behind him I'd be about 20 degrees angle off . . . When I got down low and behind and he was outlined by the sun against a brilliant blue sky, I let him have two Sidewinders, one of which hit and blew his right wing off.

To defeat the better-turning MiG-21, Robin Olds used the vertical manoeuvre plane, an art largely lost by many fighter pilots of the Vietnam era. He also tended to launch missiles in pairs in the hope that at least one would work as advertised.

Olds' phenomenal ability to keep track of a fast-moving combat became legendary. Future Aggressor pilot Bill Lafever, his back-seater on 4 May, takes up the story:

> Pascoe [future General Richard M.; 2 victories], our No 2 on the right side, called two MiGs [-21s] at 10 o'clock. Olds says, 'OK, I got 'em.' So we do a vector roll attack and the MiGs did a defensive split. We followed one and launched two Sparrows at him. One went ballistic; the other passed behind and failed to detonate. The MiG was really hauling about, and we hassled with him for a good five minutes every which way, upside down, all the good things. We fired three Sidewinders at him, one of which went off just under his tailpipe and started a fire, but he kept going. While all this was going on, the other MiG had extended out, then come back. I picked him up coming back over us. I said: 'We got the other MiG 12 o'clock high!' Olds says: 'I got him.' He knew; he actually knew where the other MiG was in the middle of all the hassle.

Two more victories, both MiG-17s, followed sixteen days later, making Olds the top-scorer in South-East Asia for the next five years. He summed it up as follows:

> The key is what you can see, retain, anticipate, estimate in a three-dimensional movement of many aircraft. Can you look at an enemy aircraft and know the odds – to get him before somebody else – if he can get behind you first, and so on? It's a three-dimensional impression; you must get it in seconds. This is essential in aerial combat. The guy you don't see will kill you. You must act instantly,

anticipate the other fellow's motives, know that when you do this, he must do one of several things.

Promoted to Brigadier-General, Robin Olds was appointed Commandant of the US Air Force Academy at Colorado Springs before retiring to Steamboat Springs. He is widely regarded as the greatest fighter leader of the war.

American Aces, Vietnam

Only two American pilots scored five victories in South East Asia, one from the USAF and the other from the USN, and both achieved their victories in 1972, the final full year of the war. For the USAF at least, a major player during this year was a piece of kit known as 'Combat Tree'. This was an IFF interrogator, which positively identified MiGs as hostile before they reached visual distance. Used only by the 432nd TRW, it allowed Sparrows to be used without fear of scoring 'own goals'.

The US also credited back-seaters with victories. At first each victory was shared between pilots and operators; later this was amended to a full victory for each. The justification for this is obscure. With kills scored with Sparrows the back-seater arguably made a considerable contribution, but with Sidewinder and gun kills, and in the few cases where an opponent was outmanoeuvred to the point where he lost control and crashed, the pilot was fully responsible. On the other hand, once close combat was joined, the back-seater became a second pair of eyes checking six o'clock, which allowed the pilot to concentrate exclusively on bringing down an opponent. It is a matter of record that some 40 per cent of initial sightings were made by the guy in the back. It is also not widely realised that certain aircraft were more effective than others, mainly because their radar and systems were far more reliable. This was not only the case with USAF Phantoms: Israeli Mirages and North Vietnamese MiGs have exhibited the same trait.

Score	Name	Remarks
6	Chuck DeBellevue	WSO, 432 TRW USAF; 4 × MiG-21s with Sparrows; 2 × F.6s with Sidewinders; 4 with Ritchie, 2 with John Madden
5	Steve Ritchie	Pilot, 432 TRW USAF; 5 × MiG-21s, all with Sparrows; 4 with DeBellevue
5	Jeffrey Feinstein	WSO, 432 TFW USAF; 3 × MiG-21s with Sparrows, 2 × MiG-21s with Sidewinders; 2 with Carl Bailey

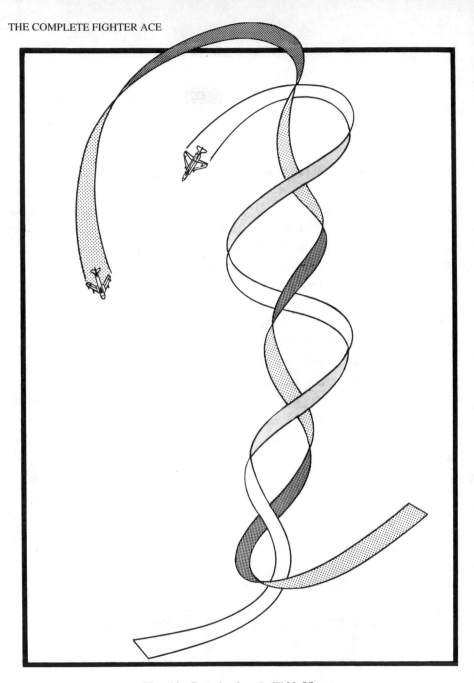

Fig. 19. Cunningham's Fifth Victory
*Twice Randall Cunningham had pulled up into a vertical rolling scissors,
only for his heavy Phantom to overshoot the much lighter MiG-17 and
become a guns target. On the third occasion he chopped the throttles on
the way up, forcing the MiG to overshoot. With it out in front,
he launched a Sidewinder to destroy it.*

| 5 | Randall Cunningham | Pilot, VF-96 USN; 1 × MiG-21, 4 × MiG-17s, all with Sidewinders, all with Driscoll; 3 × MiG-17s 10.5.72 |
| 5 | Willie Driscoll | RIO, VF-96 USN; all as above |

Richard 'Steve' Ritchie Whereas most fighter aces were determined to become pilots from a young age, Steve Ritchie was an exception. At High School he had not even considered a flying career. But life tends to take over, and he joined the USAF and qualified as a pilot in late 1962. His first experience of Vietnam was as a 'Stormy' fast-mover forward air controller, flying Phantoms. Then, in 1972, with nearly 3,000 hours' flying time, he returned for a second Phantom tour with the 'Combat Tree'-equipped 432nd TRW.

His first two victories were MiG-21s, on 10 and 31 May. Then on 8 July he led the egress flight, briefed to protect the strike force as it came out. Up ahead, a Phantom had been damaged by a K-13 missile; at much the same time another Phantom broke formation with a fire warning light. Returning, both announced their position, course and altitude – not a good idea, as the NVAF were certain to react. Ritchie turned his flight in their general direction to assist, while dropping from 15,000ft to 5,000ft. As his flight neared Banana Valley, some 30 miles south-west of Hanoi, he was informed by 'Disco', an RC-121 over Laos which monitored NVAF radio traffic, that MiGs two miles north had them in sight and were cleared to fire. Ritchie pulled hard left and gained visual contact at 10 o'clock level. Just a few seconds later and the MiGs would have swung in behind him:

> . . . we passed canopy to canopy about a thousand feet from each other, doing about 600mph each. He was a spit-polished silver MiG-21 with bright red stars on his wings and tail . . . I didn't see the number two MiG. But I knew he was in trail.

Ritchie rolled level, stayed in full afterburner and headed downward to wait for the second MiG, which duly arrived 8,000ft astern of the leader. As they passed he entered a nose-low slicing turn with a 135-degree overbank, rolled out and picked up the trailing MiG as it turned hard right. Ritchie vector-rolled left, coming out at 5 o'clock low and 6,000ft astern. Chuck DeBellevue in the back seat confirmed a good radar lock; Ritchie went through the obligatory count of 'four potatoes' settling time for the Sparrow, then squeezed the trigger twice. Another second and a half before the

217

Fig. 20. The Vector Roll Attack
*Yet another way of defeating a better turning opponent by using the vertical.
On 2 January 1967 a MiG-21 emerged from cloud at Robin Olds' 10 o'clock,
travelling fast from right to left. Rolling away from it, he came up and under,
ending in a missile launch position at about 20 degrees' deflection.*

missiles launched, by which time the MiG was approaching the 60 degree angle-off limit.

The first Sparrow hit, and the second went through the fireball. Following Ritchie's gyrations, his flight had fallen into trail, and by now the shiny lead MiG-21 had turned and was coming in behind Tommy Feezel, flying the No 4 position. Feezel had been on Ritchie's wing for his first victory on 10 May. The MiG had to be to Ritchie's right, although the future ace was initially unable to see it:

> . . . as I came over the top of the fireball, I unloaded in full 'burner . . . essentially what I did was cut across the circle to where the MiG was. Came across the circle and, sure enough, picked them both up in sight.

The MiG lost interest in Feezel, 'flat-plated' through almost 180 degrees and started down into Ritchie. Pulling 5g, the American pilot launched a Sparrow at the very edge of the envelope, 60 degrees off-boresight and at a range of 3,000ft. Remarkably, it hit! The engagement had lasted 1 minute 29 seconds. Two more MiGs were headed their way, but Ritchie disengaged, being by that time, as he graphically put it, 'Out of missiles, fuel and guts!'

Just 15 minutes later, the radar on Ritchie's Phantom went down. Had this happened earlier, he would not have become the only USAF pilot ace of the conflict. His fifth victory, another MiG-21, again with Chuck DeBellevue, came on 28 August.

In spring 1974 he left the USAF, but his attempt to enter politics failed. After various business ventures, he is, at the time of writing, a front-runner for the position of Secretary of the Air Force.

Randall 'Duke' Cunningham The US Navy was quick to realise that air combat training was deficient. In 1969 they initiated the Postgraduate Course in Fighter Weapons, Tactics and Doctrine, which involved air combat manoeuvring against dissimilar, or adversary, aircraft. 'Duke' Cunningham – the nickname was adopted in homage to film star John Wayne's all-American principles – was an early graduate of Top Gun, as it quickly became known, and when the air war hotted up in 1972 he put its lessons to good use.

With regular back-seater Willie Driscoll, his first two victories were a MiG-21 on 19 January and a MiG-17 on 8 May, both with Sidewinders. His big day came on 10 May, when Carrier Wing 9 attacked the Hai Duong rail depot in force. Cunningham's role was flak suppression.

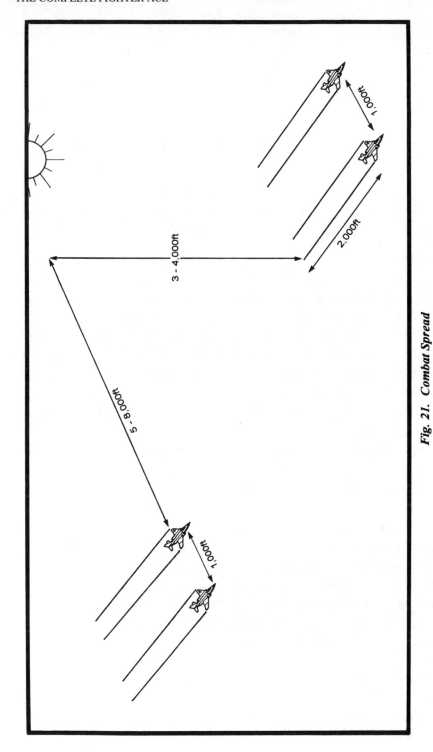

Fig. 21. Combat Spread

The standard US fighter formation in Vietnam, with two elements of two 1,000ft apart, spaced a mile or more horizontally and 3 - 4,000ft vertically. The lead element flew low and down-sun, about 2,000ft ahead.

An estimated fourteen MiG-17s, four J.6s and four MiG-21s had scrambled to intercept, arriving just after the attackers pulled off the target. Two Phantoms had been hit by ground fire and were out of the fight; the remainder stayed to engage while the attack aircraft ran for home.

Having dropped their cluster bombs on the ground defences, Cunningham and his wingman Brian Grant came under attack. It was the biggest multi-bogey dogfight of the war, and the confusion ruled out the use of Sparrows. Within two minutes Cunningham despatched two MiG-17s with Sidewinders. On his way out, he encountered a solitary MiG-17:

> I attempted to meet this MiG head-on just as I had the A-4s from Top Gun, and disregarded his guns . . . Other MiGs had turned in the horizontal, or just ran, so we pitched into the vertical as he passed abeam. We found ourselves in the vertical with the MiG-17, which turned into a rolling high-speed scissors, evolving to a slow-speed rolling scissors. The -17 was gaining the advantage, so I disengaged out his six o'clock when he had his nose in the extreme . . .

The heavier but more powerful Phantom handily outclimbed the MiG, but all this did was to put it out front where it could be shot at! Twice more the Phantom and MiG entered an ascending scissors; on the second occasion Cunningham chopped his throttle. The Phantom slowed:

> . . . as soon as I saw relative motion I re-selected afterburner and locked into his seven o'clock position but within minimum range. The -17 driver rolled over attempting to follow us visually as we scissored to the outside of his turn. When he attempted to reverse, his nose fell through, and he moved further out in front . . . He went for the deck, and we fired an AIM-9 which only caused minimum damage to his aircraft. Then a small fire developed, so we followed him down until he impacted the ground.

The excitement was not yet over. After yet another inconclusive brush with MiG-17s, Cunningham's Phantom was hit by a SAM-2. He and Driscoll ejected over the sea, were rescued by helicopter and returned to the USS *Constellation* to be fêted as the first American aces of the war.

The MiG-17 pilot was at first identified as Colonel Nguyen Toon or Tomb, credited with 13 victories, but it appears that no such person existed. North Vietnamese sources name Cunningham's victim as Nguyen Hang.

After the war, Cunningham spent a tour as a Top Gun instructor, another as a planner, then was the executive officer of an F-14 Tomcat squadron. He then commanded a USN adversary squadron before retiring from the Navy in January 1987.

North Vietnamese Aces

American records show total losses in air combat as 90, plus two 'probables', which includes six losses to the People's Republic of China. This cannot, however, be regarded as totally accurate; for example, the cause of loss of more than 60 US carrier aircraft remains either unknown or uncertain. Some of these may well have fallen to MiGs. There is also an uncertainty factor in the USAF records.

The following NVAF ace list, supplied by Dr Istvan Toperczer, totals 105. If the historical proportion of 40 per cent of victories falling to five per cent of aces holds good, this gives an approximate total of claims of 260 – somewhere between two and three to one, which is par for the course. To muddy the waters still further, we must remember that the USAF lost a considerable number of reconnaissance drones over Vietnam, and that the NVAF allowed these as victories.

Score	Name	Remarks
9	Nguyen Van Coc	MiG-21, 1967–69; inc. 2 drones
8	Mai Van Cuong	MiG-21, 1966–68
8	Pham Than Ngan	MiG-21
8	Nguyen Hong Ni	MiG-21, 1966–68
7	Nguyen Van Bay	MiG-17, 1966–67
7	Dang Ngoc Ngu	MiG-21, 1966–69
6	Le Than Dao	J.6/MiG-21, 1971–72
6	Vu Ngoc Dinh	MiG-21, 1966–70
6	Nguyen Ngoc Do	MiG-21, 1967–68
6	Nguyen Duc Soat	J.6/MiG-21, 1969–72; inc. 1 drone
6	Nguyen Tien Sam	MiG-21, 1972
6	Nguyen Nhat Chieu	MiG-21, 1965–67
6	Le Hai	MiG-17, 1967–72
6	Luu Hai Chao	MiG-17, 1966–68
5	Nguyen Van Nghia	MiG-21, 1972
5	Nguyen Phi Hung	n/a

Nguyen Duc Soat Soat's first claim was for an A-7 Corsair on 23 May 1972. The USN lost a Corsair from VA-93 on this date, although it is recorded as probably falling to a SAM. Further claims were Phantoms on 24 and 27 June, 26 August and 12 October. Whilst absolute certainty is impossible, the USAF lost a total of six Phantoms on these dates. Soat's sixth victory claim was for a reconnaissance drone.

6. DICHOTOMY

The air war over North Vietnam was very much a David-versus-Goliath strug-gle. Had the full might of the USAF and USN been deployed from the outset, it could have been concluded very quickly. But Goliath fought with one hand tied behind his back. In part this was due to political constraints, but another factor was the superb communications between the battle zone and Washing-ton. This encouraged both the politicians and the top brass to meddle at a tactical level, often overruling the unit commanders on the spot. As President Johnson is quoted as saying, 'They can't even hit an outhouse [given his usual vocabulary the word "outhouse" is suspect] without my say-so!' Mean-while David kept his distance and lobbed in a barrage of hurtful stones.

How hurtful can be judged by the loss figures. The USAF alone lost 1,259 jet aircraft to all causes between 1965 and 1973, 354 Phantoms and 332 Thunderchiefs among them. Jet losses over the same period for the USN and USMC were 467 and 177 respectively. Of course, not all these losses occurred over North Vietnam. But when one considers the minuscule num-bers of NVAF air combat victories during the conflict, barely 1 per cent of total losses, it becomes obvious that air combat was a relative sideshow.

While the effectiveness of the North Vietnam air defences, an integrated system of AAA, SAMs and fighters, is often greatly overstated, there can be little doubt that it was formidable. At this point the United States, the most technologically advanced and richest nation on earth, went off at a tangent. In the face of daunting losses, its forces had successfully planted bombs accurately on small targets. No matter that they were often the least impor-tant targets: the raiders had defeated an integrated modern defence system to hit them.

The obvious way forward was to concentrate on defence-suppression, which they did. But was it AAA, the biggest killer of all? Or SAMs, poten-tially the greatest threat of the future? No! Instead, the USAF and USN concentrated on air combat.

Several factors contributed to this decision. The kill/loss ratios achieved in Korea had not been remotely approached, and this was against a Third World country, much of the equipment of which was outdated. The Russians were widely regarded as the 'First Team', and the meagre air combat results in Vietnam posed questions as to how the Americans would fare if and when they were encountered.

By this time, an East-West confrontation was widely expected to occur in the form of a conventional war in Europe. In this scenario, the United States and its NATO allies would be heavily outnumbered. The lessons of history, that air forces were most easily destroyed on the ground, underlined in 1967 by the Israeli pre-emptive strike, were largely ignored. Once again the siren song of the Richthofen syndrome reared its ugly head. A still-classified post-war study of all air combat over Vietnam was actually code-named 'Red Baron'. The conclusion was that the enemy had to be subdued in the air. The only question was how? Whereas the controversy had once been performance versus manoeuvrability, it now became quality versus quantity.

The requirement was now for an ace in every cockpit; in an outnumbered scenario, pilots had to not only survive but succeed, against heavy odds. The first step was to provide a fighter far superior to that of the opposition. Given that the US was generally reckoned to have a technological lead over the USSR of between ten and fifteen years, this was a reasonable aim. The second was to provide the superior fighter with an equally superior pilot. This was a far harder proposition.

Fighters: The Next Generation

Without doubt the greatest fighter of its era was the McDonnell Douglas F-4 Phantom. A huge, ugly, twin-engine two-seater, it was once described as a triumph of thrust over aerodynamics. Originally designed as a fleet air defence interceptor, it proved amenable to other tasks and became a workhorse in the service of many nations, including Israel.

In Vietnam it became the primary air superiority fighter of the USAF and USN. What it lacked in agility, which was plenty, it compensated for by sheer performance and capability. In fact, it was less a fighter than a weapons system, needing a second crewman to operate the radar and other avionics. Whereas most of its contemporaries carried two air-to-air missiles, the Phantom carried eight – four medium-range SARH Sparrows and four heat-seeking Sidewinders.

For the USAF and USN, the next step was to produce better fighters across the board. Using the Phantom as a yardstick, this meant longer-ranged and more capable radars, better warning systems and secure communications, greater performance and the agility to defeat the Russian boy-racer fighters in close combat. For the US Navy this took the form of the Grumman F-14 Tomcat, a twin-engine, two-seat fleet air defence fighter with variable-sweep wings which gave it superior agility at the lower end of the speed range. The ultimate long-range killer, it could carry six AIM-54 Phoenix missiles which could be ripple-fired at six separate closing targets from up to 110nm away. An alternative AAM load was four AIM-7 Sparrows and four AIM-9 Sidewinders, but these had to be launched individually.

The USAF's choice fell on a twin-engine single-seater, the superb and hugely powerful McDonnell Douglas F-15 Eagle. The F-15 easily outperformed its naval counterpart, with a maximum speed exceeding Mach 2.5, and was more agile in the transonic and supersonic regimes. The normal weapons load was four Sparrows and four Sidewinders. Both types mounted a 20mm M61 Vulcan cannon.

One thing introduced at about this time was the multi-mode radar. This covered various functions – range-while-search, track-while-scan, single-target track and many others, including navigation modes. This had the disadvantage that the pilot's head was too often buried in the cockpit, rather than keeping a look-out. Of course, with a back-seater to handle all the magic, life in the F-14 was much easier.

To reduce the workload on the single-seat F-15, a system called HOTAS (Hands on Throttle and Stick) was introduced. This put every switch needed in air combat, including radar modes, on either the throttle levers or the control column. Although it demanded a high degree of manual dexterity, described at first as 'playing the piccolo', Eagle drivers soon learned how to get the best out of the system.

Both the F-14 and F-15 were large, heavy and extremely expensive. Whilst they filled the 'quality' part of the equation admirably, costs were so high that they were unaffordable in sufficient numbers. In air combat, numbers create confusion, and confusion degrades technology very quickly indeed. However capable a fighter was, it could be overwhelmed by sheer numbers, as a pack of wolves pull down an elk. This was the projected scenario in the event of a full-scale conventional war in Europe. A compromise solution was sought in the 'hi-lo' mix – a few 'high-tech' fighters backed by many austere, and therefore much more affordable, fighters.

The austere lightweight fighter concept was far from new. Germany experimented with the Heinkel He 162 *Volksjäger* in 1945. Britain developed the Folland Gnat, which fought with India against Pakistan in 1965 without, it must be admitted, outstanding results. The USA produced the Northrop F-5A Freedom Fighter to provide aligned nations with a nominal supersonic capability. But to take on hordes of MiGs over Europe something far better was wanted.

Traditionally, stability made aircraft easy and safe to fly. From the fighter viewpoint this was a mixed blessing: when rapid manoeuvre was needed, stability had to be overcome, making for less than instant control response. However, by this time computers had become very clever. The answer was to design an unstable fighter and process its control inputs through the black boxes. Thus in normal flight the fighter would feel stable, but when hard manoeuvre commands were received the electrons would feed the control surfaces with as much as they were capable of handling, given altitude, speed etc. Heavy and complex hydraulic systems were abandoned in favour of electrical circuitry. This became known as fly-by-wire, one of the benefits of which was carefree handling. Lost control became a thing of the past.

This resulted in the General Dynamics (now Lockheed Martin) F-16 Fighting Falcon, although no one who flies it refers to it as anything other than the Viper, or maybe the Electric Jet. A small airframe wrapped around a large engine gave it outstanding climb and acceleration, although, with Vietnam combat experience in mind, Mach 2 top speed was not a requirement.

The initial armament consisted of a 20mm M61 Vulcan cannon and two AIM-9 Sidewinders on the wing-tips, backed by a simple ranging radar. This was austere all right, but the flaw in the concept is that, in the eyes of a fighter pilot, 'austere' is perceived as 'inferior'. This does nothing for morale. After many vicissitudes, the number of AAMs was increased and a multi-mode radar was fitted. The F-16 became an extremely agile and capable multi-role middleweight, with the slogan 'Float like a butterfly, sting like a battleship!'

Meanwhile the US Navy needed not only a replacement for the Corsair attack aircraft; a fighter that could supplement the Tomcat would be more than welcome. Their choice fell on the Northrop F-17, the rival of the F-16 in the Light Weight Fighter Competition. Reworked for carrier operations by McDonnell Douglas, it became the F/A-18 Hornet, almost equally capable in the attack or fighter roles. Fitted with a multi-mode radar, the Hornet carried two Sparrow and two Sidewinder missiles in addition to a 20mm M61 Vulcan cannon. It was the first fighter to have a 'glass cockpit', wherein the dials were replaced by display screens. Added to HOTAS, in its day it was the nearest thing to man/machine symbiosis.

Red Star

Meanwhile the opposition had not sat still. The next Soviet tactical fighter to enter service was a far cry from the agile but limited MiG-21. The MiG-23 was a large and heavy single-engined single-seater, with a variable-sweep wing. Its radar was the pulse-doppler Saphir-23-SH, which had a useful range and a rather shorter look-down capability, and provided guidance for two R-23R medium range AAMs. Other armament consisted of a twin-barrel 23mm GSh-23L cannon and two heat-seeking R-23T AAMs, or four R-13M AAMs. A single Khatchaturov R-23-300 turbojet rated at 27,558lb static thrust with afterburning gave what has been described as 'jack-rabbit' acceleration, but in manoeuvrability the MiG-23 was deficient. This being the case, the correct tactics were to make high-speed slashing attacks. First flown on 10 June 1967, it entered large-scale service in the early 1970s. The MiG-23 has seen aerial action in two conflicts, with the Syrian Air Force over the Beka'a in 1982 and with the Iraqi Air Force in the Gulf War of 1991. In neither did it make any impression.

The emergence during the early 1970s of the American F-15, F-16 and F/A-18 forced the USSR to rethink. The answer was a pair of extremely agile fighters, the MiG-29 and the Sukhoi Su-27. Since these first appeared in the West they have undergone a series of upgrades, the most important of which have been a 'glass cockpit' and fly-by-wire. At the time of writing (mid-April 1999), the MiG-29 has been in action with three air forces – Iraq since 1991 and Yugoslavia and Eritrea in 1999. Despite its formidable reputation, it has yet to score, while suffering losses in all three theatres. By contrast, the Su-27 opened its account on 25 February 1999, flying for Ethiopia against Eritrea, and shot down a second aircraft on the following day; ironically, both victims were MiG-29s.

BVR versus Close Combat

Beyond-visual-range (BVR) combat is to a great degree a matter of systems usage, and as such can largely be practised on simulators. But in the real world, with closing speeds of a nautical mile every four seconds, it is difficult to stand off at medium range. In a numerically small encounter it may be possible to pick off one's opponents at a distance, but in a multi-bogey scenario it is close to impossible.

Positive identification is another problem. A couple of 'own goals' early in the Vietnam War resulted in the requirement to identify targets visually, which virtually ensured that the fight would close to knife range. In the final year of the war, 'Combat Tree', the MiG IFF interrogator, solved many a problem, but it was not foolproof: misidentification by 'Combat Tree' is known to have caused the loss of one American Phantom. In any future conflict there was no guarantee that a device of this nature could be made totally reliable.

Returning to the multi-bogey scenario, it is generally possible for ground radar or AWACS to keep track of who is who in the early stages. But directly the opposing aircraft reach the merge, uncertainty and confusion sets in. Identification can then only be visual. What really counts is a pilot's recognition ability, combined with how well he can manoeuvre his fighter in any given situation. He must know and be confident in standard manoeuvres and counter-manoeuvres. Air combat can never be reduced to the level of chess, but certain moves give better percentage probabilities than others. He must equally know the strengths and weaknesses of his own machine *vis-à-vis* those of his opponent. For example, there is little point in trying to out-turn or scissor with a better-turning co-speed opponent.

The USAF attacked the problem of producing better pilots from two angles – selection and training. Selection was largely ignored in the 1960s, when the policy of the universal pilot was pursued. Thus Bill Lafever, having sometimes flown as the back-seater to Robin Olds, on at least one occasion found himself sitting behind what he described as a 'SAC retread', a former tanker driver. It is hardly surprising that this man found himself out of his depth in the big league over Hanoi.

After the war, the Defense Advanced Research Projects Agency sponsored a comprehensive feasibility study to predict fighter pilot effectiveness. Only two factors appeared truly relevant – motivation, and the ability to keep track of events in a highly dynamic situation, otherwise known as situational awareness (SA). In a few highly gifted pilots this seemed innate, but to a lesser degree it could be acquired by experience. Training seemed the most practical answer.

As air combat is such a potentially lethal occupation, the greatest need is for realistic training. Of course, the most realistic training is that provided by the enemy, but this is uneconomic and frequently counterproductive –

i.e. the wrong side wins! The object is therefore to get as close to reality as possible without using live weapons.

The Ace Makers

As genuine MiGs were unobtainable, at least in sufficient numbers, the US adversary programmes were forced to use their nearest available equivalents. Top Gun started by using the A-4 Skyhawk to simulate MiG-17s. In terms of performance this was not a bad match, although the A-4 was far faster in the rolling plane than the Russian fighter. The MiG-21, which was of course a far more lethal threat, posed greater difficulties. The choice fell on the T-38 Talon supersonic trainer, then the F-5E Tiger II. The latter was not of course Mach 2-capable, but despite the brochure figures doubts existed whether the MiG-21 could achieve this speed without running itself out of fuel. In any case, experience had shown that only the lower end of the supersonic speed range was usable in air combat, so the lack of Mach 2 capability hardly mattered.

The Tiger II was about the right size, it turned well and like its Soviet counterpart it had a fast rate of roll. When the USAF launched the Aggressor programme in 1972, it used T-38s and F-5Es. Three things were taught, Basic Fighter Manoeuvring (BFM), Air Combat Manoeuvring (ACM) and Dissimilar Air Combat Training (DACT), the adversary programme.

How valuable was this? In 1970, the only authorised ACT in the USAF consisted of what has been described as 'canned basic ACM perch setups', with everyone in the same type of aircraft and sharing a common radio frequency. This boiled down to a contest of flying skill and experience, and it was far from realistic. The underlying failing was the emphasis on flight safety. Aggressor pilot Lloyd 'Boots' Boothby had a lot to say on the subject: 'How do you train for the most dangerous job in the world by being totally safe?' And 'Some commanders use flying safety to keep their jobs at the expense of losing the next battle!' And 'I never saw a strafe panel in Hanoi!'

He had a point. A fighter pilot is not a good insurance risk. Realistic training is inherently dangerous. As one Aggressor pilot commented to the writer, 'Even in training, I sometimes get into situations where I think I am going to die!' But this of course adds to realism. Training is a sterile environment: after the fight, the pilots go home to their families and a cold beer or two. But just occasionally it does not work out. In August 1978 my friend Bill Jenkins misjudged and augered into the North Sea off Denmark. He was never found.

Aggressor pilots were intensively trained before they joined their squadrons. They learned Soviet tactics, they learned to fly their aircraft to the limit and they learned to use vertical manoeuvring at least as much as horizontal. While this hardly needs stating, the tendency to launch into hard horizontal turns was often too tempting for the inexperienced. As an Aggressor instructor pilot once reported, 'The difference between Captain S——and a telephone pole is that the telephone pole knows how to use the vertical!'

For the first ten years or so, the main task for the Aggressors was to teach Phantom crews how best to tackle the Russian lightweights. In all, four Aggressor squadrons were formed, the 64th and 65th at Nellis AFB in Nevada, the 26th in the Philippines and the 527th at Alconbury in England. Detachments from the latter deployed all over Western Europe, and on one occasion even to pre-Ayatollah Iran, providing DACT to aligned nations.

Typically the Aggressors, and their US Navy Top Gun counterparts, flew over 250 air combat training sorties a year, usually of about 45 minutes each. Like the Soviets, they operated under close ground control, often on specially instrumented ranges, which allowed the actions to be replayed on debriefing, when they were analysed and mistakes corrected. (Ground controllers were familiarly known as 'Dregs'.) The course they taught was a steep learning curve for their friendly opponents. Naturally, winning over their own side was not the object of the exercise. As the pilots of the frontline squadrons grew in experience they gradually improved, and towards the end of the course they were expected to start winning. At this sort of intensity the Aggressors got very sharp indeed, and in the event of hostilities in Europe the 527th were assigned to assist the Norwegians, who flew the F-5A.

In war, as in life, nothing ever stays still. As the 1970s drew to a close the MiG-23 entered large-scale service. This posed more difficult problems for the F-5E to simulate. The acceleration of the Russian fighter could not, of course, be duplicated, but the rest was largely overcome by limiting turn capability to a close approximation of that of the Soviet fighter. Tactics remained largely unchanged.

Even when the new F-15s arrived in force, DACT with the Aggressors proved valuable. The Eagle was a very large aeroplane, and could be seen from much greater distances than the tiny F-5E, giving the latter an advantage in visual combat. Like the MiG-21, the F-5E was very snappy in the roll, much more so in fact than the F-15, which set fresh manoeuvre problems for the Eagle drivers. To quote 'Dregs' George 'Jet' Trainor and Robert Bowker,

> . . . trying to figure out how to kill an F-15. I mean, this airplane was a quantum leap in aerial warfare. It was an autonomously lethal face-ripper that spelled the end of job security for a Dreg. Anyway, Rooster and A.T. figured that Eagles like to go up, so you just wait for them to come down rather than trading speed for altitude and an ass-whipping. A.T. was fond of yelling 'You got him tree'd Rooster! Go git him boy! He's got to come down sometime! Then we strap him on and **** him 'til he's bingo!

The use of 'we' in the final sentence indicates the degree of involvement between drivers and Dregs.

The writer remembers an Aggressor training film which showed an F-15 trying desperately to follow an F-5E in a vertical ascending scissors. Although the former had a far superior rate of climb, the F-5E was rolling fast enough to stay out of the gun sight. Almost inevitably the result was an overshoot. But the main value of the Aggressor programme to the Eagle drivers was its ability to provide few-versus-many training scenarios.

Aggressor pilots were carefully selected and generally very experienced. As a minimum they were on their second fighter tour, although not all could match Tom Lesan, who flew a full tour of F-105 missions over Vietnam, gunning down a MiG-17 in the process, followed this by a tour in F-106s on continental air defence and then flew U-2Rs for the CIA. In wars past, the top-scoring Aggressor was John Madden, credited with two MiG-19s and a MiG-21 over North Vietnam in 1972. While there can be no aces in peacetime, the Aggressors can be regarded as ace-makers.

The 'Silver Bullet' Solution

According to tradition, it takes a silver bullet to slay a werewolf. The air combat equivalent is advanced technology – to detect first, to fire first and unerringly to bring down the enemy before he even realises that he is under attack.

In theory, BVR missiles fulfilled this function, but the historical record fails to bear this out. Insofar as can be established, 632 attempts were made to launch Sparrows in Vietnam, the October War of 1973, and the Beka'a action of 1982. They gained just 73 victories, or 11 per cent. Further research showed that *only four of these* were true BVR victories; the rest were all gained from within visual distance, which was hardly the object of the exercise.

One indisputable disadvantage of the SARH missile was that the launching fighter had to continuously illuminate the target during the time of flight.

If during this time it was forced to manoeuvre to evade attack, the radar broke lock and the Sparrow went ballistic. What was needed was a 'fire-and-forget' weapon. This already existed in the form of heat-seekers, but not only were these short-range weapons, they could be baulked by cloud or other climatic conditions. The next step was to create a 'launch-and-leave' radar homer for medium-range work.

This also existed, in the form of the AIM-54 Phoenix, which initially used inertial guidance, updated by the parent fighter in mid-course then switched to active radar for terminal homing. But Phoenix was far too large and expensive for use with tactical fighters. Something smaller and more affordable was needed.

A suggestion widely mooted was an anti-radiation weapon which could home on fighter radars. These had been moderately effective against ground and SAM guidance radars, and the idea was that as soon as a fighter radar started to emit, it could be hunted down by a simple and cheap anti-radiation missile. Trials with a hypothetical AAM showed tremendous advantages, and, had it worked, it would have revolutionised air combat.

I quote: 'You can conquer the world with the weapon you haven't got!' And so it proved. While it was easy enough to detect a fighter radar, there was nothing to indicate range. Add to this factors such as mode changes, frequency agility, channel hop and the fact that when ground or airborne radar cover was available fighters spent much of their time in standby, accurate targeting assumed monstrous proportions. In any case, there was no way in which an anti-radiation AAM could have been simple and cheap. Trials began in 1974, but were abandoned soon afterwards.

Small Wars

Several small-scale conflicts and a similar number of aerial clashes took place during the two decades between 1975 and 1995. At the bottom end of the scale, USN Tomcats downed two Libyan Su-22s over the Gulf of Sidra in August 1981, both with Sidewinders, then followed this up in January 1989 by shooting down two Libyan MiG-23Gs, one with a Sparrow (at the third attempt) and the other with a Sidewinder.

During operations in Afghanistan from 1979, Afghan and Russian aircraft sometimes got too near to the border and were intercepted by Pakistani F-16s. Over the years, a handful of Antonov transports, Su-25s and MiG-23s fell to the defenders. It is, however, possible that an F-16 fell to a MiG-23 during these operations in April 1987, as one was lost at this time.

The British operated the Sea Harrier in the South Atlantic in 1982. A firmly subsonic STOVL carrier fighter, it was opposed by the Mach 2 Mirage III and Dagger (the Israeli Neshr) and by the Skyhawk. Although theoretically outclassed by the Mirages, and potentially less manoeuvrable than the Skyhawks, the Sea Harrier accounted for 23 Argentine aircraft for no losses. Nineteen kills were scored with the AIM-9L Sidewinder.

Two factors must be remembered here. First, it was winter in the South Atlantic, and the fact that most combat took place at low level in poor visibility reduced the effective reach of the Sidewinder to barely one-third of the brochure figure. Several accounts refer to the missile falling short of its target at low level. The other factor was that the STOVL ability of the Sea Harrier enabled it to operate in conditions where any other carrier jet would have been grounded.

Prior to sailing to the South Atlantic, the Sea Harriers trained intensively with the USAF 527th Aggressor Squadron at Alconbury, against which they claimed a considerable kill/loss ratio. This did, however, include a number of 'canned' victories, which Fleet Air Arm commander 'Sharkey' Ward allowed to stand. Reported by the aviation press, it did nothing to improve Argentinian morale. But as faintly disgruntled Aggressor Pete Brennan told me at the time, 'The Sea Harrier was good, but not that good!'

Although much has been made of the ability of the Sea Harrier to vector its thrust, producing unorthodox manoeuvres, this attribute was not used in combat. There were no aces in the South Atlantic. 'Sharkey' Ward claimed a Pucará, a Dagger and a Hercules; David 'Mogs' Morgan claimed two Skyhawks (at first misidentified as Mirages) and a Puma helicopter, which he forced to fly into the ground. 'Mogs' also destroyed another Puma on the ground, and shared in the destruction of a third.

The combat début of the F-15 took place on 27 June 1979, when a mixed force of Israeli Eagles and Kfirs met Syrian MiG-21s over Lebanon, shooting down five. Further clashes followed, and on 13 March 1981 an F-15 shot down a MiG-25 – the first time that one of these had been defeated. It was not the last.

The Beka'a action in June 1982 has already been alluded to in the previous chapter. The generally accepted score was 84 to nil in favour of the Israelis, all except one the victim of the new F-15s and F-16s. Jamming was intensively used, reducing the situational awareness of the Syrian pilots to little more than what they could see 'out of the window'. The Israelis had the additional advantage of Hawkeye AEW aircraft, which, high and back

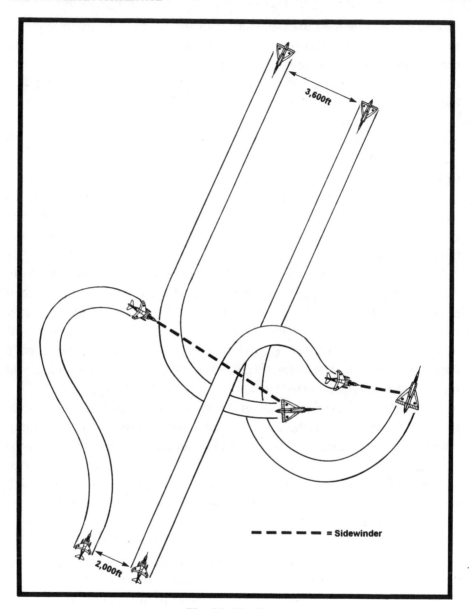

Fig. 22. The Hook
*Widely used in Vietnam, the hook was also used by the Fleet Air Arm
in the South Atlantic in 1982. In the first decisive combat of that conflict,
two Sea Harriers encountered two Argentinian Mirage IIIs. Radar contact
was made at 17nm and visual contact at 8nm. The lead Sea Harrier failed to
acquire a target and flew through; his wingman turned away, then curved
in behind the Mirages, sending one down with a Sidewinder.
The lead Sea Harrier broke hard and, from astern,
inflicted mortal damage on the other Mirage.*

from the battle area, monitored every Syrian move. Thus forewarned, the Israelis lurked in the radar shadows cast by the terrain, then hurtled out to pounce on their unsuspecting prey, mainly MiG-21s and MiG-23s. Once again the vast majority of victories were scored with heat-seekers – Sidewinders and home-brewed Pythons.

The First Gulf War

Iran and Iraq fought a long-drawn out war between 1980 and 1988. In terms of sheer quality, Iran should have had an edge. Its tactical fighter force consisted of F-5s, Phantoms and the mighty Tomcat. In practice the revolution which ousted the Shah and subsequent events had caused US assistance to be withdrawn. The F-14's extremely complex radar and its Phoenix AAMs could not be maintained, and the aircraft took little part in the air war, while the Phantoms were only kept flying with assistance from Israel.

Iraq operated the French Mirage F.1E and the Russian MiG-21 and MiG-23 in the fighter role. Though aerial encounters were fairly frequent, they were usually inconclusive. Both sides were poorly trained, which was not helped by purges for failure, or for doubtful political reliability. Few details have emerged, but it is known that an Iraqi, Ahmed Salah, claimed two victories. Early in the war he claimed a Cobra helicopter while flying a MiG-21; then in 1987 he accounted for a Phantom off Kharg Island while flying a Mirage F.1. Salah survived by defecting. He claimed also that one Mirage F.1 squadron was composed almost entirely of Jordanian pilots.

In one more incident of note in the area, an Iranian Phantom violated Saudi Arabian air space on 5 June 1984. It was shot down by a Saudi F-15 for the first air combat victory by that country.

The Second Gulf War

The Iraqi occupation of Kuwait in 1990, with its attendant threat to Saudi Arabia, looked like a bid to dominate the world's oil supplies. Certainly a large proportion of the world reacted; from the giant United States to the pygmy Afghan rebels, who sent a token force. Ignoring ship-based helicopters, the international Coalition air forces which gathered to free Kuwait was composed of American, British, Canadian, French, Italian and Saudi units, plus those Kuwaiti elements which had escaped to the south.

On paper, the Iraqi Air Force was formidable. Hundreds of tactical aircraft, of which the best was the modern and extremely agile MiG-29, were ranged over dozens of huge airfields, the very size of which made them difficult to knock out. On the ground the aircraft were protected by hard-ened shelters.

The Coalition's build-up was slow but inexorable. When in January 1991 hostilities commenced, great holes were blown in the Iraqi radar cover. Those communications not initially destroyed were jammed, and the air defence system quickly collapsed. Only token resistance was offered, and those Iraqi fighters which did take to the air were quickly hunted down.

The mainly American fighter force, backed by tankers, dedicated jam-ming aircraft and AWACS, took advantage of their ability to operate at night, something in which the Iraqis lacked experience. Only 41 aerial victories were scored, including seven helicopters – 38 by F-15s and, surprisingly, 24 with Sparrows. A Saudi F-15 pilot, Ayedh Salah al-Shamrani, knocked down two Mirage F.1s in a single sortie, an American fighter controller in an E-3 AWACS having directed him into a perfect Sidewinder launch position. Two Hornets on a bombing raid justified their multi-role title by switching to air-to-air mode and sending down two MiG-21s before reverting to their origi-nal mission.

Even in 1991, radar had its limitations. Eagle driver Benjamin Powell takes up the story:

> Until we [he and his element leader, Jay Denney] got within 20 miles of them, we thought the [Iraqi] formation had one or two planes in it. But then the formation split apart and we could distinguish three individual aircraft on our radar scopes.

The two F-15Cs cut the corner and bent their throttles against the stops. At 30,000ft they were showing about Mach 1.2, but then the targets de-scended from 3,000ft to about 50ft. As the range closed, they both took BVR Sparrow shots, using the look-down pulse-doppler mode. Both missed.

Soon they reached visual distance, and Powell identified the Iraqis as three MiG-23s. He and Denney dived steeply to about 6,000ft and Powell locked on to the left-hand contact. Only when about 2½ miles astern did he see that it was not one aircraft but two – a Mirage F.1 in very close formation with a MiG-23. His radar had failed to discriminate between them:

> . . . as I was about to fire my second missile I saw Jay shoot an AIM-9 Sidewinder heat-seeking missile at his target. The missile made a straight beeline and blew up the Flogger; it just exploded in a fireball.
>
> Two seconds after that I fired my own missiles, radar-guided AIM-7 Spar-rows. Both the Mirage and the Flogger were hit. The Flogger took a direct hit and just exploded in a fireball. The other missile detonated about 5–6ft off the Mirage's wing-tip and that set off a secondary explosion.

236

Main Fighters in Combat, 1980–98

Type	Dassault Mirage F.1	Mikoyan MiG-23MF	Mikoyan MiG-29	Boeing F-15C	Lockheed Martin F-16C
Span	27ft 7in	Variable	37ft 3¼in	42ft 7¾in	31ft 0in
Length	50ft 0in	51ft 7½in	48ft 9½in	63ft 9in	49ft 3in
Height	14ft 9in	14ft 4in	15ft 6¼in	18ft 5½in	16ft 7in
Wing area	269 sq ft	402 sq ft	409 sq ft	608 sq ft	300 sq ft
Take-off wt	25,350lb	34,715lb	33,590lb	44,500lb	26,536lb
Power	1 × SNECMA Atar 9K 50, 15,870lb	1 × Khachaturov R-23, 27,558lb	2 × Klimov RD-33, 18,298lb	2 × F100-PW-220, 23,450lb	1 × F100-PW-100, 23,450lb
Wing ldg	94lb/sq ft	86lb/sq .ft	82lb/sq ft	73lb/sq ft	88lb/sq ft
Thrust ldg	0.63lb/lb	0.79lb/lb	1.09lb/lb	1.05lb/lb	0.88lb/lb
Vmax	Mach 2.20	Mach 2.35	Mach 2.3	Mach 2.5+	Mach 2.0
Climb rate	41,930ft/min	n/a	50,000ft/min	50,000ft/min	50,000ft/min
Ceiling	65,000ft	60,680ft	55,760ft	65,000ft	50,000ft
Armament	2 × 30mm DEFA, 2 × Super 530, 2 × R550	1 × 23mm GSh-23L, 2 × R-23R, 2 × R-23T	1 × 30mm GSh-301, 6 × R-60T, 2 × R-73	1 × 20mm M61, 4 × AIM-7, 4 × AIM-9	1 × 20mm M61, 4 × AIM-9, Python or Shafrir
Combat with	Iraq	Iraq, Syria	Iraq, Eritrea, Yugoslavia,	Israel, Saudi Arabia, USA	Israel, USA, Pakistan

Meanwhile Denney had accounted for the third MiG-23 with a Sidewinder.

Powell and Denney were just two of half a dozen pilots to get two victories during the war. There were, however, a few skirmishes after the end of hostilities which allowed two F-15C drivers to bring their scores to three.

Of their adversaries, the MiG-29s lost five of their number; Mirage F.1s nine and MiG-23s eight, all in air combat. Losses on the ground were far heavier. After barely a week the Iraqi flyers started to defect to Iran, although why they thought they would be welcome there is hard to understand.

After the war, the Coalition established 'no-fly zones' over northern and southern Iraq. Infringements have resulted in a few further Iraqi losses.

Bosnia

The break-up of the former Yugoslavia has resulted in some bitter ground fighting. NATO has intervened to provide air power, based in Italy, but, to date, the only serious aerial clash took place on 28 February 1994. A patrolling AWACS detected a flight of six Serbian Jastreb armed trainers and warned them off. The warning was ignored, and the controller sent for the cavalry, in the form of a two-ship F-16 patrol.

Further warnings were ignored, and the F-16 leader shot down a Jastreb with an AIM-120 AMRAAM. He followed this up with two Sidewinders, both of which connected, making his tally three for the mission. Meanwhile his wingman launched a Sidewinder, but this missed.

Two more F-16s joined the fray, the leader of which gained a visual and shot down a fourth Jastreb with a Sidewinder. The two survivors escaped over the border.

After several years during which the Balkan skies were relatively quiet, fighting flared in the Serbian province of Kosovo. Launched on 24 March 1999, NATO air operations were briefly opposed by the Yugoslavian Air Force. The only combat losses reported at the time of writing are three MiG-29s, one of which fell to a Dutch F-16.

EPILOGUE

Fighting in the air was born of necessity less than a hundred years ago. While nations seek to settle their differences forcibly, the need will remain for the foreseeable future. Two questions remain. What form it will take? And what is the future of the fighter ace? From our position at the end of the twentieth century, we can see trends. They may continue, or unforeseen circumstances may well reverse them. Only one thing is certain: on the rare occasions when the pundits of air power have been proved right, it has generally been many years later, when the technology to achieve the desired end has finally become available. Therefore we can do little more than trace the trends and the reversals, and attempt to project them into the future. Pull up a sandbag, sit comfortably, and we'll take a look.

Starting from first principles, a fighter aircraft was, and still is, a platform which is capable of bringing weapons to bear on the enemy. Back in the 'stick and string' days of the Great War, the machine gun was, by default, the only viable fighter weapon. Consequently, the race was on to produce fighting aircraft which combined high performance and manoeuvrability. As we have seen, this was inevitably a compromise, and it thus fell to the pilots to make the best use of their mounts.

As in all fields of human endeavour, some were better than others. Thus was born the fighter ace, whose deeds depended on his flying ability, his marksmanship and a strange, difficult-to-define quality called situational awareness, which enabled the gifted few to keep track of fast-moving events around them. Chance was also a factor. The difference between life and death could often be measured in inches. As Napoleon invariably asked before appointing a new Marshal of France, 'Is he lucky?' And Napoleon, we must admit, knew a thing or two about warfare.

There were times during the Great War when fighters of both alliances were fitted with bombs and sent off to 'have at' the unfortunate pongos, but, in the main, their task was to gain air superiority over the Front, to allow

239

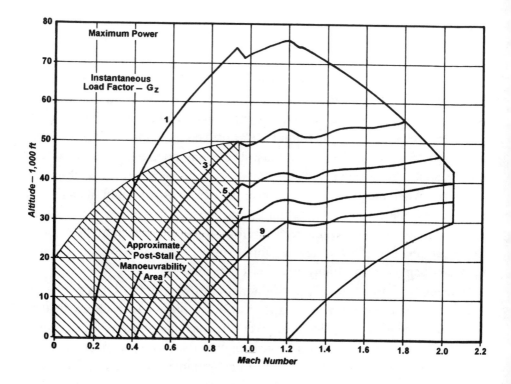

Fig. 23. Post-Stall Manoeuvrability
This diagram shows lift-limited instantaneous manoeuvrability for
a conventional fighter. It can be seen that as g-loading increases,
an ever-larger section of the envelope becomes unusable.
Thrust-vectoring allows controlled flight below the conventional
stall speed, making much of this area usable.

their artillery spotters and reconnaissance flyers to carry out their tasks unmolested while denying similar facilities to the enemy. An abundance of targets resulted in literally hundreds of pilots becoming aces, the top scorers among them counting their victories in dozens.

The gun, albeit improved, remained the supreme fighter weapon throughout World War II. Whereas Great War operations had been almost entirely tactical, strategic campaigns now took place, notably the Battle of Britain and the daylight and night air assault on Germany.

The leading German aces handily outscored their Western and Russian opponents, with victories measured in hundreds rather than dozens. This has led some commentators to conclude that the Germans were naturally better fighter pilots. A brief glance at the ace lists of the Great War quickly dispels this illusion, which was perhaps nurtured by the 'Richthofen Syndrome'. The fact is that the *Jagdflieger* had far more opportunities than their Western counterparts.

There is, however, one interesting point which became obvious in this conflict. A superior fighter did not necessarily ensure victory. In the Great War, some fighters were certainly better than others, but the difference between them was fairly marginal. Between 1939 and 1945, performance and agility margins were often rather wider. This served to highlight pilot ability as the crucial advantage. Often, the superior pilot in the inferior fighter won the contest.

Another break in the trend became evident in this conflict. Situational awareness has been stressed as a primary attribute of the fighter ace, but, at night, with little or nothing visible 'out of the window', SA was virtually non-existent. This was redressed by airborne radar – the first step towards electronic SA. As with pilots, a handful of radar operators proved to be exceptionally gifted, both at interpreting their displays and directing the interception.

Korea was in many ways an aberration. The majority of sorties were flown in support of the ground forces, although the need for air superiority pushed fighter-versus-fighter combat well into the stratosphere. As usual, scores were related to opportunities, although a handful of aces did extremely well. The difficulty here was a combination of high speed and lack of turning ability in the attenuated air at very high altitudes, which put dynamic judgement of speed and distance at a premium. Few really mastered it.

From this point onwards technology started to take over. Whereas the difference between maximum and cruising speeds had hitherto been

241

perhaps 20 per cent at most, supersonic capability opened this out to more than 100 per cent. At the same time homing missiles increased effective weapon ranges to several miles. Surprise had always been the dominant factor in air combat; now closing speeds from astern of the order of a mile or more every four seconds, coupled with missile launch ranges at or beyond the limits of visibility, made surprise far easier to achieve.

Looking 'out of the window' was no longer enough: electronic detection and warning systems became essential, backed by ground or airborne radar and control. Fighters became far more complex and less affordable. Numerical strengths dwindled, which in turn resulted in fewer victory opportunities. Only the Israelis have managed to score on a regular basis, and this only in a series of short conflicts in mainly visual conditions against less well-equipped and trained opponents. Even so, more than fifteen years have passed since the last fighter ace was crowned, while the air fighting in the Gulf War of 1991 was largely a victory for technology rather than for individuals.

At the time of writing, the future is uncertain. BVR combat is widely regarded as the way ahead, the theory being that opponents should be picked off before they are able to launch their own weapons. But until such time that it is combat-proven, it remains theoretical. Although BVR weapons have been around for decades, it is significant that only a handful of victories have ever been truly BVR. One of the main problems has traditionally been positive identification of a target as hostile. While the two sides remain well separated this is fairly easy, but the slightest confusion makes it increasingly difficult.

BVR missiles use radar homing, and are therefore potentially vulnerable to electronic countermeasures. Stealth technology also poses problems, in that it significantly reduces detection and homing ranges. A head-on encounter between opposing stealthy fighters at supersonic cruising speeds will give little time to get a BVR missile away before they approach visual range.

Heat-homers are used for visual-range combat, and the modern breed is a formidable weapon indeed. They can be launched from any aspect; imaging infra-red seekers make them difficult to decoy and, with the advent of helmet-mounted sights, they can be launched from high off-boresight angles. This opens up the field of fire to the point where it is very difficult for an opponent to stay out of it, and in a multi-bogey combat it becomes virtually impossible. The point must, however, be made that while modern missiles

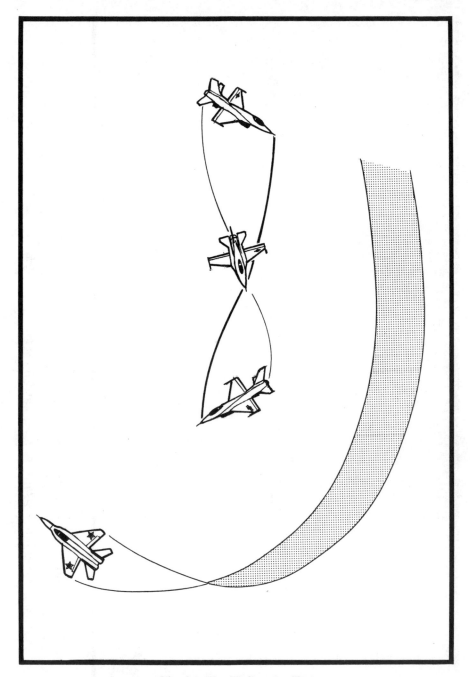

Fig. 24. The Helicopter Turn

Thrust vectoring allows 'impossible' manoeuvres to be made. The helicopter turn, seen here, enables the fighter to stay within the radius of turn of the conventional fighter while keeping its nose on the target at all times.

243

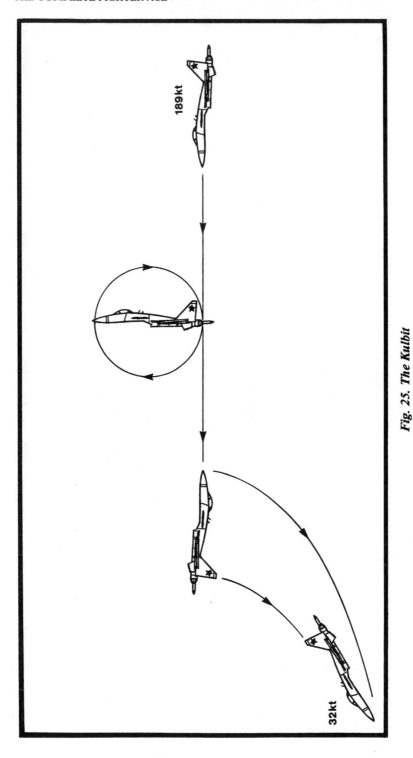

189kt

32kt

Fig. 25. The Kulbit

First demonstrated at Farnborough in 1996 by Eugeny Frolov in the Su-37, the kulbit, or somersault, allows the fighter to flip over on to its back, stabilise long enough to get a missile or two away at targets directly astern, then drop the nose through and fly out in the original direction under full control.

are far more capable than their predecessors, they are not yet ten feet tall. The infallible missile is still well in the future.

As we saw in a previous chapter, the first generation of AAMs made hard turning essential for evasion. This was underlined by the difference between maximum and cruising speeds of the Mach 2 generation of fighters, which made the bounce from astern far quicker and deadlier than it had previously been. When the Lockheed F-16 entered service in January 1979 it set radically new standards of fighter manoeuvrability. In the world of military aviation, it became the one to beat. Even after twenty years it was difficult for fighter designers to improve on it by a significant margin while using conventional aerodynamics.

The breakthrough came with thrust vectoring. This had been used by the BAe Harrier for many years as a means of short or vertical takeoff and landing. It could also be used in forward flight to nibble off a few degrees of angle to obtain a gun firing solution, or to produce unorthodox manoeuvres, although the latter, in the Harrier, were a trifle imprecise.

Given the advances in computer power, thrust-vectoring nozzles could be tied into the flight control system of a conventional fighter to allow it to fly in regimes where previously it could not have ventured. Called post-stall manoeuvring, this opened up a whole new area of the flight envelope, while allowing 'impossible' manoeuvres to be performed. This gives the pilot enhanced survivability in combat. It allows him to stay on the inside of a hard turn by any conventional fighter in the world and outside the angle of its off-boresight missiles, while keeping his nose on the target. On the offensive it gives superb 'pointability', the ability quickly to bring the nose (and thus the weaponry) to bear on the target. Even with helmet-mounted sights this is still of value, as it gives the missile a heart-of-the-envelope shot. Then, has anyone seen Eugeny Frolov pull the Su-37 through 180 degrees in a couple of seconds, then stabilise inverted? Or seen him hang in the air while pointing vertically upwards?

The latest and greatest from the United States is the Lockheed F-22A Raptor. This fighter is conventionally agile, with thrust vectoring as a bonus, is extremely stealthy and can cruise at high supersonic speeds on dry thrust alone. This sort of performance makes it very difficult to attack from astern; it crimps in missile envelopes considerably.

What of the future? Stealth, obviously. Supercruise, almost certainly. Thrust vectoring likewise. Ace pilots? In the long term this is doubtful. One trend likely to continue is for short and sharp conflicts, with the odds against any individual being in the right place at the right time to score five victories. Another trend is for ever better technology in the form of 'smarter' weapons systems. Unmanned aerial vehicles have been used for reconnaissance missions for many years, and the next step is an unmanned attack aircraft project. The logical progression is an unmanned fighter, either completely programmed for air combat or remotely piloted.

The idea is far from new. The American F-106 Delta Dart and the Russian MiG-25 Foxbat were semi-automatic interceptors, partly controlled from the ground, with the pilot as a systems manager, responsible for take-off, fuel monitoring, weapons release and landing. Technology is now rapidly approaching the stage where full automation is possible. It would also have one tremendous advantage. At present, manoeuvres are basically limited by the accelerations the pilot can stand and still function. With no pilot, fighters can be made far more agile!

Summary

The twentieth century was the era of the fighter ace, an era which seems to be passing, if it has not already done so. Which brings us to the final point. Who was the greatest of them all?

By the simplest measure, the victory tally, Erich Hartmann is the supreme champion with 352. This will never be approached. Few modern air forces have this many aircraft to lose, let alone to a single pilot. But is a high score enough? Hartmann fought almost entirely against the Russians, where kills were relatively easy. This brings us to the next point: how can we assess the relative difficulties of fighting on various fronts, in different time periods and even in different wars. The short answer is that the task is impossible!

The most famous fighter pilot of all time was Manfred von Richthofen, the 'Red Baron', with a mere 80 victories, all against the British. But was he really the 'compleat' fighter pilot – an outstanding leader, tactician, marksman, and fighter? There was one greater who, had he lived, would almost certainly outscored the *Rittmeister*. This was the man who became Richthofen's mentor; Oswald Boelcke, the 'father of air fighting'. When air fighting was in its infancy he developed tactics from scratch. He trained his men carefully and was an inspirational leader. At the time of his death following a mid-air collision with one of his own men, he was the ranking ace of the war with 40 victories.

Of the aces of World War II, the choice is simply too wide. Germans Adolf Galland perhaps, or Heinz Baer, the top-scoring German jet ace and one of only two pilots to score well on all fronts? For the Allies, Dick Bong against the Japanese, or 'Johnnie' Johnson against the *Luftwaffe*? 'Sailor Malan' or the indomitable Douglas Bader? Don Blakeslee, one of the great fighter leaders of the war? Who can say!

The transition from propeller-driven fighters to jets was a difficult one. Many World War II aces flew in Korea, but few achieved spectacular results. How much more difficult, then, to fight in the missile-armed but gunless Phantom over Vietnam two decades after becoming an ace against the *Luftwaffe* over Europe?

The record shows that victories over North Vietnam were hard to come by, but World War II ace Robin Olds accounted for four MiGs to remain the top scorer in the theatre until the final year of the war. Given the difference between conflicts more than two decades apart, this was a remarkable achievement. He also became a byword for inspiring leadership. By most standards his score was modest, yet he deserves to be ranked among the greatest.

BIBLIOGRAPHY

Belyakov, R. A., and Marmain, Jacques. *MiG: Fifty Years of Secret Aircraft Design*. Airlife, Shrewsbury, 1994.

Bowen, Ezra, *et al. Knights of the Air*. Time-Life Books, Alexandria, Va, USA, 1980.

Boyd, Alexander. *The Soviet Air Force since 1918*. Macdonald & Jane's, London, 1977.

Brown, David. *Carrier Fighters*. Macdonald & Jane's, London, 1975.

Caldwell, Donald L. *JG 26: Top Guns of the Luftwaffe*. Orion Books, New York, 1991.

Camelio, Paul, and Shores, Christopher. *Armée de l'Air*. Squadron/Signal Publications, Michigan, 1976.

Campbell, Christopher. *Aces and Aircraft of World War I*. Blandford Press, Poole, Dorset, 1981

Christienne, Charles, and Lissarrague, Pierre. *A History of French Military Aviation*. Smithsonian, Washington DC, 1986.

Cunningham, Bob, *et al. Tumult in the Clouds*. General Dynamics, Fort Worth, Tx, 1990.

Davis, Larry. *MiG Alley*. Squadron/Signal Publications, Warren, Michigan, 1978.

Dudgeon, James M. *"Mick"*. Robert Hale, London, 1981.

Engle, Eloise, and Paananen, Lauri. *The Winter War*. Sidgwick & Jackson, London, 1973.

Francillon, René J. *Tonkin Gulf Yacht Club*. Conway Maritime Press, London, 1988.

Fricker, John. *Battle for Pakistan*. Ian Allan, London, 1979.

Futrell, R. Frank, *et al. Aces & Aerial Victories*. Office of Air Force History, USA, 1976.

Gibbons, Floyd. *The Red Knight of Germany*. Cassell, London, 1930.

Goette, John. *Japan Fights for Asia*. Harcourt, New York, 1943.

Gordon, Yefim, and Rigmant, Vladimir. *MiG-15*. Motorbooks International, Osceola, Wisconsin, 1993.

Gray, Peter, and Thetford, Owen. *German Aircraft of the First World War*. Putnam, London, 1962.

Green, William. *Famous Fighters of the Second World War*. Macdonald & Jane's, London, 1962.

Halperin, Merav, and Lapidot, Aharon. *G-Suit*. Sphere Books, London, 1990.

Jackson, Robert. *The Red Falcons*, Clifton Books, London, 1970.

Kiernan, R. H. *Captain Albert Ball, V.C.* John Hamilton, London, 1939.

Larrazabal, Jesus Salas. *Air War over Spain*. Ian Allan, London, 1974.

Lerma, Duke of. *Combat over Spain*. Neville Spearman, London, 1968

Lloyd, John. Aircraft of World War I. Ian Allan, London, 1957.

McCudden, James. *Flying Fury*. John Hamilton, London, 1930.

McKee, Alexander. *The Friendless Sky: The Story of Air Combat in World War I*. Souvenir, London, 1962.

Mersky, Peter B. *Israeli Fighter Aces*. Specialty Press, Minnesota, 1997.

Morris, Alan. *Bloody April*. Jarrolds, London, 1967.

Nemecek, Vaclav. *Soviet Aircraft from 1918*. Key Publishing, Stamford, 1986.

Okumiya, Masatake, and Horikoshi, Jiro, with Caidin, Martin. *Zero!* Dutton, New York, 1956.

Richthofen, Manfred von. *The Red Air Fighter*. Aeroplane and General Publishing Co., London, 1918. Reprinted by Greenhill Books, London, 1990.

Roberts, John. The Fighter Pilot's Handbook. Arms & Armour Press, London, 1992.

Robertson, Bruce, (ed.). Air Aces of the 1914–1918 War. Harleyford, Letchworth, 1959.

Sakai, Saburo, with Caidin, Martin. *Samurai*. Dutton, New York, 1957.

Sekigawa, Eiichiro. *Japanese Military Aviation*. Ian Allan, London, 1974.

Shores, Christopher. *Air Aces*. Bison Books, Greenwich, Ct, USA, 1983.

————. *Fighter Aces*. Hamlyn, London, 1975.

————. *Regia Aeronautica*. Squadron/Signal Publications, Michigan, 1976.

————. *Spanish Civil War Air Forces*. Osprey, London, 1977.

Shores, Christopher, and Williams, Clive. *Aces High*. Grub Street, London, 1994.

Sims, Edward. *Fighter Tactics and Strategy 1914–1970*. Cassell, London, 1972.

Smith, J. R., and Kay, Anthony. *German Aircraft of the Second World War*. Putnam, London, 1972.

Smith, Peter C. *The Battle of Midway*. New English Library, London, 1976.

Spick, Mike. *All-Weather Warriors*. Arms & Armour Press, London, 1994.

————. *Jet Fighter Performance, Korea to Vietnam*. Ian Allan, London, 1986.

————. *Fighter Pilot Tactics*. Patrick Stephens, Cambridge, 1983.

————. *The Ace Factor*. Airlife, Shrewsbury, 1988.

————. *Allied Fighter Aces*. Greenhill Books, London, 1997.

————. *Fighters at War*. Greenhill Books, London, 1997.

————. *Luftwaffe Fighter Aces*. Greenhill Books, London, 1996.

Swanborough, Gordon, and Bowers, Peter M. *United States Navy Aircraft since 1911*. Putnam, London, 1976.

Thetford, Owen. *Aircraft of the Royal Air Force since 1918*. Putnam, London, 1957.

Udet, Ernst, (ed. Ulanoff, Stanley M.). *Ace of the Iron Cross*. Newnes, London, 1937. Reprinted by Doubleday, New York, 1970.

"Vigilant". *French War Birds*. John Hamilton, London, 1937.

Werner, Johannes. *Knight of Germany: Oswald Boelcke*. John Hamilton, London, 1933.

Winton, John. *Air Power at Sea*. Sidgwick & Jackson, London, 1976.

Magazine sources used include various issues of *Air Forces Monthly*, *Air International*, *Air Enthusiast*, *RAF Flying Review*, *Fighter Weapons Review* and *Retired Officer*.

INDEX